AN ANZAC ZIONI

This book is dedicated to
Sonia,
my own Aussie Zionist

AN ANZAC ZIONIST HERO

The Life of Lieutenant-Colonel Eliazar Margolin

RODNEY GOUTTMAN

VALLENTINE MITCHELL
LONDON • PORTLAND, OR

First published in 2006 in Great Britain by
VALLENTINE MITCHELL
Suite 314, Premier House, 112–114 Station Road, Edgware, Middlesex HA8 7BJ
and in the United States of America by
VALLENTINE MITCHELL
c/o ISBS, 920 NE 58th Avenue, Suite 300, Portland, OR 97213 3786
Portland, Oregon, 97213-3644

Website http://www.vmbooks.com

British Library Cataloguing in Publication Data:

A catalogue record for this book has been applied for

ISBN 0 85303 646 2 (cloth)
ISBN 0 85383 647 0 (paper)

Library of Congress Cataloging-in-Publication Data:

A catalog record for this book has been applied for

Typeset in 11/13pt Sabon by Vitaset, Paddock Wood, Kent

Printed in Great Britain by
MPG Books Ltd, Bodmin, Cornwall

Contents

List of Plates   vii
Acknowledgements   viii
Prologue   ix

Episode One
  1. A Case of Invisibility   3
  2. Rehovot 1892   13
  3. Eliazar's First Aliyah   19
  4. In Limbo Down Under   27
  5. Behind the News   34
  6. A True-Blue Anzac   41
  7. The Jewsiliers   53
  8. The Origin of an Idea   62

Episode Two
  9. Realpolitik   69
10. The New Battalion   76
11. The AIF–Jewish Connection   86

Episode Three
12. Military Zionophobia   99
13. The First Judeans   106
14. Civilian Rule   115
15. May Day Mayhem   121
16. A Distasteful Affair   132
17. Return to Sender   140
18. Homeward Bound   151
19. Hawaja Nazar   155
20. Postscript   159

Glossary   161
Notes   163
Bibliography   177
Index   185

Plates

1. Lieutenant E. L. Margolin in the uniform of the citizens' militia in Australia prior to his enlistment in 1914.
2. Enemy map showing Allied forces in the Palestine campaign.
3. The insignia of the Jewish Legion.
4. Margolin leading the 39th Battalion Royal Fusiliers through Ben Shemen.
5. Lieutenant-Colonel Margolin consulting a map of Wadi Keith on the way to Jericho.
6. Eliazar Margolin on his beloved horse.
7. Flag of the First Judeans.
8. Laying the foundation stone of the Hebrew University of Jerusalem, 1919. Margolin second from right in military uniform.
9. Eliazar and Hilda Margolin on the steps of their Nedland home.
10. The memorial service for Margolin in Tel Aviv, 1944.
11. Margolin's reburial in the presence of former Legionnaires, Rehovot Cemetery, January 1950.
12. Margolin's swords and medals.
13. Hilda Margolin at the Weizmann Institute, Rehovot, January 1959. Left to right: Jacob Pat, Hilda Margolin, Chaim Weizmann, Yitzhak Ben-Zvi.
14. Hilda Margolin at a ceremony honouring her husband, Jerusalem, 1950. Left to right: Yitzhak Ben-Zvi, Hilda Margolin, David Ben-Gurion, Jacob Pat.
15. Eliazar Margolin's grave, between those of his parents, Rehovot Cemetery, Israel.
16. Colonel Margolin Street, Rehovot.

Acknowledgements

A number of people in the wings helped bring this book to life. Prime among them are my wife Anne, and then Erica Place, who sought to guide me along the path of clarity and syntactic correctness. At no time did I make their task easy. Special thanks to Nurit Kapara for her incisive translations of the relevant Hebrew material, and to Ruth England, who allowed me a glimpse of the married life of Eliazar Margolin and her Aunt Hilda. To Sian Mills and her team at Vallentine Mitchell, my indebtedness for their grand efforts on my behalf.

Prologue

Shrines to the 'Unknown Soldier' are found across the world. They are not just eulogies to the ultimate sacrifice and expressions of national gratitude, but are haunting reminders of a past intended to inspire future generations. They stand mute, evocative of a history that, with the passage of time, has increasingly been infused with mystique, mythology and legend. The universalized nature of individual self-sacrifice is poignantly expressed by the anonymity of the entombed. The absence of a name focuses attention on the noble ideal.

Of those who put their lives on the line for this ideal, however, many did return. In the lists that adorn war memorials, they are named, although most are now forgotten. Some returned soldiers actively sought anonymity, willing to have their individual bravery either not remembered or submerged in mass commemorative ceremonies, and relived only privately or in social gatherings with digger mates.

Lieutenant-Colonel Eliazar Lazar Margolin DSO[1] was never one to court publicity. On the contrary, he shied away from it. He was often to be found in the forefront of ceremonies to remember his comrades-in-arms who never returned from the First World War, or subsequently died because of it. He attended without fanfare. He worked tirelessly to serve his mates who did return, but beyond certain circles in Perth, western Australia, he was an unknown rather than a forgotten figure. His name is prominent in the records of the 16th Division of the Australian Imperial Force (AIF) with which he served for much of the Great War. His name, however, barely appears in major military histories of that war, and is – distressingly – mostly absent from the Australian Jewish historical literature, even though Margolin was, in this conflict, one of Australia's most decorated Jewish soldiers. Where he is mentioned at all, it is usually only in passing.

What distinguishes Eliazar Margolin from others is his direct participation in the foundation stories that have since attained the status of national legends in two completely different nations, many thousands of kilometres apart. He played his part in Australia's most celebrated and pervasive ANZAC legend, which began on the shores of Gallipoli. After serving in that disastrous campaign, he went on to the butchery of the Western Front. He was the commander of the last group of Allied forces to vacate Gallipoli. After the war, he was involved in caring for his digger mates and their shattered families.

Although he is hardly known in Australia, Eliazar Margolin has been formally recognized in Israel and his name is venerated as a hero of that nation's pre-State days, celebrated in two distinct periods in the development of the modern Jewish community of Palestine known as the *Yishuv*. The first phase was when, as a pioneer farmer, he helped found and defend the settlement of Rehovot. The second was as the Russian-born Australian commander of the 39th Battalion of the Royal British Fusiliers, one of the three battalions of the Jewish Legion, which was to serve in Palestine in the Middle East campaign during the First World War. When the Jewish Legion was demobilized, the remnants of these three units joined to form the First Judeans in Palestine under Margolin's command, until he was forced by the British authorities to leave the *Yishuv* because of an infamous episode – in their view – associated with a week of Arab anti-Jewish mayhem that began on May Day 1921. This incident caused Margolin's reluctant return to Australia; it also became an excuse for the British to renege from the pro-Zionist clauses of its own Balfour Declaration of 1917.

As an officer in both the Australian and British armies, Eliazar Margolin saw action in Asia Minor, Western Europe and the Middle East. While involved with the latter campaign, he was also selected – albeit briefly – to be the first Jewish military governor in the Holy Land in some eighteen hundred years.

This Russian-born proto-Zionist pioneer and naturalized Australian was unique in death, as he had been in life. Twice he was buried with full military honours, first in Perth, Australia, and then in Rehovot, Israel. In Perth he was fulsomely praised by his digger mates and politicians, but this was trumped in Israel, where he was eulogized by many, including two former soldiers in the Jewish Legion, David Ben-Gurion and Yitzhak Ben-Zvi, both later prime ministers of the Jewish State.

On 28 January 1918, a note appeared in Sydney's edition of the *Jewish Herald*, entreating all men of military age to fill the growing

gaps in AIF ranks caused specifically by the carnage on the Western
Front. Its argument was based on that quintessential Australian
word, 'cobber':

> Its significance means more to an Australian than any higher form of
> eulogy. The word was taken overseas in October 1914 by the twenty
> thousand Australia's first contingent, and as 'cobbers' they charged
> up the rugged slopes of Gallipoli to add another word to their
> vocabulary – the word Anzac. As 'Anzacs' means one big army corps
> of 'cobbers', so it is related to the latter term. 'Cobber' is the brief
> expression used to signify the spirit of mateship. Australia has sent
> three hundred and eighty thousand of her gallant men to fight for the
> emancipation from the thraldom of Kaiserism, and in doing so look
> to eligible men left to reinforce their 'Anzac cobbers' ...

The essential trait of 'Anzac cobbers' was mateship.

There was little doubt that Eliazar Margolin was an 'Anzac cobber'
who entirely personified the concept's noble traits. Ironically a Jewish
etymology is suggested for the word 'cobber': it is said to come from
the Hebrew word *haver*, meaning friend, or in Australian parlance,
mate. The word is thought to have been introduced to the Australian
vernacular by Yiddish-speaking Jews who joined the culturally poly-
glot society of the Australian gold fields of the 1850s. Whether
or not it had a Jewish origin, there is no doubt that one Jew who
exemplified 'mateship' was Eliazar Margolin, in his many roles:
Zionist pioneer, soldier on the battlefields of the Great War, defender
of the *Yishuv*, or post-war carer under the aegis of the Returned
Soldiers' League, Legacy and the Red Cross Society.

It must be admitted that this story of Eliazar Margolin is necessarily incomplete. There is a tragic dearth of personal details about
his life: there are no private reminiscences, memoirs, letters, speeches
or any material that might provide intimate access to his feelings,
attitudes, values, motivations, loves, hates and aspirations. The
observations of people who knew him at various stages of his life
have consequently had to compensate for this lack, despite the fact
that gaps exist even here. Moreover, problems of 'contamination' as
a result of subjectivity, creative memory and self-interest have also
had to be taken into account. In addition, the author has had to
make sense of the flawed data before him in an attempt to do justice
to the life of Eliazar Margolin. This narrative crosses many other
biographies and national histories, but these are not investigated in

any depth. Rather, they serve to provide an essential backdrop to the Margolin saga.

Eliazar Margolin's story – previously untold – occupies a unique place in the annals of Australian, Israeli and Australian Jewish history. It is the story of a person, born in Russia, who became an Australian by adoption, an Anzac by chance and a Zionist by inclination. Ultimately, the Margolin story is about the fulfilment of a dream which, unfortunately for him, was realized only after his death.

Episode One

1

A Case of Invisibility

Diplomatic protocol and taste demanded that when Australia's first ambassador to the State of Israel, O. C. Fuhrman, presented his diplomatic credentials to his Israeli hosts in Jerusalem in January 1950,[1] he emphasized those elements that linked the two nations. Undoubtedly for Fuhrman – a known Judeophobe – such positive statements could not have come easily.[2] He would have been expected to mention Australia's then Minister for External Affairs, Dr Herbert Vere Evatt, whose efforts in the United Nations were instrumental in having that body's acceptance of the possibility of a Jewish state in Palestine followed by its admission as a member of that august institution.[3]

He might well have recalled, but did not, the botanical connection between the two countries. In the last years of the 1870s and into the 1880s, eucalyptus trees and other native bushes had been planted by the earliest settlers of the *Yishuv* – the Jewish community of Palestine – to bind the soil, extract its murderous salt and provide wind breaks.[4] Then, of course, in 1921, Mrs L. Slutzkin, with the help of Mr Cronin of the Botanic Gardens in Melbourne, selected other Australian plants deemed suitable for the climate and soil, to beautify the grave of her son and those of other Australian soldiers of the First World War buried in the Commonwealth Cemetery on Mount Scopus in Jerusalem.[5]

Fuhrman did mention, however, two Australian soldiers of the Great War. The first was Lieutenant-General Sir John Monash, whom he called 'one of the British Empire's most distinguished soldiers'. The inclusion of the general in this context seems on the surface somewhat out of place. As he did not serve in Palestine, his personal ties with the *Yishuv* were tenuous at best, and could be regarded only in the most general terms as a consequence of the status he attained as both an Australian and Jewish soldier in the First World

War. It is true, however, that he was coaxed into becoming the titular head of the Australian Zionist Federation in 1927.[6]

The second of the two soldiers was Lieutenant-Colonel Eliazar Margolin. What may have concentrated Fuhrman's mind at this time was the knowledge that, a short time later, he was to be Australia's representative at the reinterment of Margolin's ashes in the Israeli town of Rehovot.[7] Given his personal attitudes, it could not have been a ceremony he would have wished to attend, if only because Margolin's desire to be buried in a Jewish state would have confirmed Furhman's views about Jewish ingratitude.[8] Fuhrman had served in the AIF in the Great War, as had Margolin, both in Gallipoli and on the Western Front.[9]

While Margolin's name rang positive bells in Israel, in Australia, with the exception only of the Perth Jewish community, it would have been unknown. On 22 August 1919, Melbourne's *Jewish Herald* belatedly recorded that Lieutenant-Colonel Eliazar Margolin, DSO, had been appointed Military Governor of Ramle in Palestine, an area in which, it noted, he had lived in his early adulthood. Such a momentous event – an Australian Jew selected for such a major post in Palestine, even if temporary – might have been expected to be received with excited acclaim by Australian Jewry. Alas, this was not to be.

Margolin was the first Jew to be made a military governor in the Holy Land since the days of the Bar Kokhba insurrection against the Roman forces, almost eighteen hundred years previously. That revolt closed the period in the Zionist historical understanding called 'Antiquity', which, as Yael Zerubavel points out, began with God's promise in the Bible to give Israel to the seed of Abraham.[10] It also began the long and perilous period of Jewish exile from the 'Promised Land' that the proto-Zionist settlement of Palestine in the 1880s sought to bring to an end. Of course, Jews had lived in the Holy Land during the years of the Dispersion (except when they were driven out, as they were by the Crusaders), returning, and – before the establishment of the modern proto-Zionist establishment – living in confessional enclaves aided by charity from Jewish communities in the Diaspora.

Australian Jews should have been proud that one of their number, who had taken part in that historic awakening, should now be granted this post in the land of Zion, the focus of their constant prayers. News of Margolin's appointment, however, did not evoke acclaim, but was received with indifference. This disregard made nonsense of a note that appeared in Sydney's *Hebrew Standard* on 22 September 1922, which read: 'Lieutenant-Colonel Margolin, who was in command of the Australian Jewish Battalion in Palestine, and whose fine war record is well known, is on a visit to Sydney.'

Few would have known or cared about his 'fine war record'. Some may have heard of him because he had been defamed in the Australian Parliament the year before.[11] Some may have read of him in the *British Jewry Book of Honour*, published in 1922 to record and celebrate the deeds of Jewish soldiers in the Great War,[12] but for most Jews on Australia's eastern seaboard, the words in the *Hebrew Standard* were just journalistic hyperbole. Throughout the war years and with very few exceptions beyond, Margolin's name was absent from the Jewish press; if Australian Jewry was not willing to celebrate one of its own heroes, they could hardly expect others to do so.

Several reasons – some general, some specific – may be proffered for mainstream Australian Jewry's neglect of Eliazar Margolin. The first goes to the heart of Jewish social discourse on Jewish–Gentile interaction in Australia. In historical terms, this has been couched in terms of what might be called 'the great man or person approach'. It is important to note, however, that this approach relates not only to this interface in the past, but has also continued to the present day. In the military sphere, the field is dominated almost completely by the towering figure of one man: Lieutenant-General Sir John Monash. Most other Australian Jewish warriors have consequently been neglected. Although his iconic status is richly deserved, the massive concentration on Monash's story has left little space for others such as Lieutenant-Colonel Eliazar Margolin. The reasons for this approach lie deep within the psyche of the Jewish Diaspora, and have become almost a social/genetic reaction to life in exile.

When Margolin arrived in Australia at the dawn of the twentieth century, Australian Jewry was a collection of variously sized – but mainly extremely small – enclaves, insecure and religiously attenuating, stretched across the length and breadth of a vast continent.[13] Then and even since, the Jewish population was desperate to demonstrate its national *bona fides*, and prove that the citizenship accorded it was deserved. The communities lacked cohesion, and their national political structure was to emerge only many years later, when the Executive Council of Australian Jewry was formed towards the end of the Second World War.[14] Even then, it was another handful of years before all the communities were included.[15] In essence, each

community was an isolated small boat, bobbing on an uncharted
sea.

Australian Jews did indeed contribute to national culture in
colonial times – and certainly have done so since – to a far greater
extent than their numbers warrant. Nevertheless, the need felt by
Jews to justify their presence has been a constant, manifesting itself
in their consistent stress on the many cases in which their brethren
have scaled the heights of Australia's various elites. It is as if they
felt obliged to express their thanks for this opportunity, something
frequently denied them in other lands.

Such a situation raises at least two fundamental questions. The
first is: why was this insurance policy needed during Margolin's time,
and afterwards, in the liberal democracy that is Australia?[16] The
obvious answer, of course, is that the Jewish communities needed
reassurance. Jewish history had impressed on them the simple truth
that even where Jews had sojourned for hundreds of years, and
in some places had even attempted to assimilate into the host culture, this had not protected them against bigotry, assault, murder
and dispersion. Such experiences had left an indelible mark on the
Jewish psyche. The consequence of this for Jewish communities,
even in Australia, was a perceived need in their public discourse
to concentrate on those among them who had reached patrician
rank. Those like Margolin, apparently more proletarian figures, were
ignored.

Of course all this begs the second question: did Australian Jews
then and later really have anything to fear? Academic Inga
Clendinnen has somewhat erroneously written in her award-winning
book, *Reading the Holocaust*, that anti-Semitism in Australia has
only ever been 'the pathology of the periphery'.[17] Even a cursory
study of the history of Australian Jewry would show that for many
years anti-Semitism has been present, in both the Left and mainstream Right, in Australia.[18] It is true that in either case, it was not
a dominating feature, nor did it in any way bear comparison with
the divisive and bitter Protestant–Catholic divide.[19] The small Jewish
population posed no threat to any person or group; nevertheless,
anti-Semitism did exist socially, culturally, occupationally and
linguistically, while it also affected government policy, especially in
the area of immigration.[20]

Traditional Christian anti-Semitism was also given a fillip, in the
emerging Labor consciousness of the later decades of the nineteenth
century, by some leading poets and writers, who saw Jews as a

canker on the body politic.[21] Under the rubric of the 'White Australia
Policy', anti-Semitism was arguably influential in rendering mainstream parties across the political spectrum quite willing to reject
Jewish refugees from the burgeoning influence of Nazism in the
1930s.[22] There was no dissent from the Jewish clauses in the immigration documentation specifically designed to exclude Jews from
Eastern Europe.[23] Although these clauses were undoubtedly unconsti-
tutional, they remained on the books until the early 1950s, when
there was an attempt to use them once more to exclude Jews of
Middle Eastern origin.[24] Indeed, anti-Semitism in the immediate
post-Second World War years curbed the extent to which, following
the Holocaust, Jewish displaced persons were permitted entry into
Australia.[25] That is not to say, especially before the terrible years of
the Holocaust, that there was not support in Australia's Anglo-Jewish
community for these policies of exclusion.[26] Ever since the 1880s,
when rumours had reached colonial Australia of masses of Jews
looking towards the Antipodes as a place of refuge from the pogroms
in Russia, there had been some support for a policy to keep out
'foreign Jews'.[27] This stemmed from a deeply held fear that these
people, with their 'foreign' – meaning non-British – ways, might stoke
the fires of latent anti-Semitism.

Some commentators have suggested that the high social esteem in
which both Monash – whose own early career suffered because he
was a Jew[28] – and Sir Isaac Isaacs, the nation's first locally born
Governor-General, were held had made anti-Semitism unfashionable
in Australia.[29] It was none the less fashionable enough to prevent
all but a few 'foreign Jews' immigrating into Australia before the
Holocaust and to sharply curtail the post-Holocaust Jewish intake.
Of course, prior to both these instances, it is arguable that anti-
Semitism was the significant factor in the ignorant lambasting of
Margolin's reputation that occurred in the Australian Senate in May
1921 over the quality of his leadership in the 16th Battalion AIF. If
any factor made the overt expression of anti-Semitism considered
anti-social and politically gauche, it was the Holocaust.

It must be said that Clendinnen's claim regarding the negligible
presence of anti-Semitism in Australia has attracted a fair amount of
popular Jewish support.[30] Ignorance on the part of some Jews, and
wishful thinking or rationalization on the part of others aside, however, this assertion comes from the definition of anti-Semitism only
in empirical terms. When acts defined as anti-Semitic are tallied in
Australia, and compared against the benchmark of modern European

history, which reached its apogee with the Holocaust, they pale into insignificance. Even when the damage caused to Jewish institutions in Sydney and Melbourne during the Gulf War in 1991[31] is taken into account, compared with the European experience, Australia has been a veritable paradise.

The empirical aspect, however, is only one dimension of the problem. The other is the social psychological side, which has also been alluded to.[32] It not only affected the mindset of Australian Jews about the significance of the First World War in general, but also provided a reason for the lack of interest in Margolin in particular. Anti-Semitism, real, imagined or feared, has often seriously affected the public attitudes and behaviour of Jews individually and as a distinctive group. Nevertheless, this phenomenon is rarely discussed, and seldom the subject of research. It is encapsulated in the Jewish preoccupation with 'What will the *goyim* (Gentiles) think?' This has always been an influence in Jewish decision-making in the public domain, and no less so concerning public utterance about the Great War and Jewish military performance in that tragic long engagement. Jewish leaders took great pains to say nothing that might detract from the picture of Australian Jews as the most loyal subjects of king, country and the British Empire. It was a view Margolin shared, and which governed his military practice. His service, from Gallipoli to the Western Front, and later in Palestine, albeit under the colours of Great Britain, would reinforce that image. One incident in which he was intimately involved, however, that of putting down the Arab anti-Jewish riots in the Palestinian port city of Jaffa, might well have been considered a mite traitorous by Australian Jewish leaders, and consequently have the potential to arouse passions of Judeophobia. To protect against this, silence about Margolin might well have been considered the best defence.

Another aspect of Jewish unease and insecurity caused intra-communal tensions between the entrenched Australian Anglo-Jews and the 'foreign Jews' in their midst.[33] Margolin was one of these 'foreigners'. This schism was as much a feature in the thin and scattered Jewish community of Western Australia as in the other communities. It was one thing for the entrenched Anglos to dispatch moneys overseas to alleviate the undoubtedly monumental distress and oppression of their brethren in Europe, especially in the East,[34] but it was another to suffer the presence of such people on home soil. As he was a 'foreign' Jew, the Anglo establishment would have felt some ambivalence towards Margolin, and would have been unlikely to acclaim his heroism with the enthusiasm they might have demonstrated for a person sharing their own background.

Even within the 'foreign' Jew classification, however, Margolin was in many ways an isolate. Much of his early time in Western Australia was spent away from the major concentration of Jews in Perth, and it is unlikely that he socialized with many Jews, either Anglo or foreign. The latter contingent came either directly from Eastern Europe or via Palestine,[35] and arrived in Western Australia from around the beginning of the twentieth century through to the First World War. What Margolin shared with other immigrants from Palestine was a belief that they would be able to make enough money in a short time to allow them to return quickly to the Holy Land. Three elements tended to cut him off, even from his fellow *émigrés* from Palestine, however: language difference, non-religiosity and his own idiosyncratic version of Zionism.

Naturally, as many of the foreigners spoke little or no English on arrival, they mainly conversed with each other in Yiddish. This was also true for those from Palestine, where Hebrew had yet to gain linguistic ascendancy in the *Yishuv*. Not only were most of the *émigrés* Yiddish speakers, they were enthusiastic about Yiddish culture. Margolin's mother tongue was Russian, however, not Yiddish, of which he had picked up only a smattering, by osmosis, in Palestine.

Religiosity for Margolin was also a problem. One of the clashes between the 'Anglos' and the 'foreigners' was over the practice of Judaism itself. Two interpretations of Orthodoxy were in conflict. The entrenched adherents of Anglo-Orthodoxy looked askance upon the newcomers' European Orthodoxy.[36] These immigrants practised their faith more intensely, and with a greater observance of ritual and traditional interpretation of Jewish law and lore. Margolin was neither a son of the former nor a follower of the latter. There is some conjecture over the religiosity expected of him in his parents' home in his teenage years in Russia. What is clear, however, is that while he never rejected Judaism as such, and came to understand the role Orthodox Judaism – as it became known in the European Enlightenment – had played in maintaining the Jewish group during the long years of the Dispersion, it remained a problem for him throughout his life. This said, while a commander of Jewish soldiers, his camp had a thoroughly Jewish ambience. On occasions in the field he even led religious services.

His spiritual being was not God-centred. If at core it was meta-

physical, this was of a most physical nature. It was anchored in the
land of *Eretz Israel* (the Land of Israel), and associated with its
Jewish community. It was not a metaphysical relationship in the
abstract or ideological sense in any way, however, but emerged out
of his actual experience of the settling and regeneration of the land.
This labour, for him, was spiritually transcendent.

The third and final matter that separated Margolin from many of
his 'foreign' *confrères* was his version of Zionism. While he was later
to join with others in the Western Australian Zionist Association,
his metaphysics was of a different brand. By definition, Zionism was
traditionally acquired in the Diaspora, but his commitment to *Eretz
Israel* had been acquired *in situ*.

Western Australian Jewry was the principal home of Zionism in
Australia in the first decade of the twentieth century.[37] It was led by
Reverend David Isaac Freedman, the rabbi of the Anglo-Orthodox's
Perth Hebrew Congregation, the centre of Anglo-Orthodoxy in
Western Australia.[38] His attitude to foreign Jews was negative, though
later this was reported to have softened. Paradoxically, most of
those who classed themselves as Zionists were 'foreigners', not from
Palestine as one might have expected, but from Eastern Europe.
They had usually been involved with Zionist organizations and
education in their places of origin. Not surprisingly, there was little
sympathy, let alone support, for Zionism, from the Anglo establishment in the various Australian Jewish communities across Australia,
including Western Australia. Zionism, after all, asserted that the only
place where Jewish life was truly possible was in *Eretz Israel*. Not
only did the Anglo establishment in the communities disagree with
this position, they considered it disloyal, and showing a great lack
of appreciation of, and hostility towards, Australia, a nation that
had afforded Jews complete social and political freedom. It was
believed that if Zionism were to take hold it could place their social
position at risk.[39] Although in fact Margolin's Zionism was not the
same as others', in the eyes of the Anglo establishment they were
all tarred with the same brush.

One reason for Margolin's reputation not spreading beyond the
borders of Western Australia was the enormous size of the continent,
the great distances between the major centres of population and the
difficulties of communication these caused. Australian history pro-
fessor Geoffrey Blainey has coined the phrase the 'tyranny of
distance' to describe these problems. Had Margolin lived on the
eastern seaboard, especially in Sydney or Melbourne where the

majority of Australian people and indeed Jews lived, his deeds would most probably have attracted greater attention. Apart from the casual visit, all that was known of the smaller Jewish communities came from brief jottings in Sydney's and Melbourne's Jewish communal press. No mention was made of Margolin during the war, and only a few perfunctory references were made to him after it.

One major means by which the communal press gained its information about the war was via recycled letters from family or close friends. This was not an avenue open to Margolin, due in part to his not being comfortable with the two major communal tongues, English and Yiddish. Moreover, he lacked the necessary family or friends back home in Western Australia with whom he might have corresponded.

Leaving the above obstacles for a moment, one reason for the lack of research into the lives of men like Eliazar Margolin has been that the major concern of the Australian Jewish community has not been with its own national history. With a few notable exceptions, interest in this area after the Second World War has been swamped with what might be called Holocaust memory. This is hardly surprising, given the extremely high percentage of survivors of that atrocity among Australian Jews. Whether for therapeutic reasons or from a desire to pass their testimony on to future generations (given that their mortality is increasing its toll), or indeed to authenticate the historical record, these victims have had a pressing need to tell the story of what really happened to them. As a consequence, there has been a lack of interest in the history of the local community that sheltered and supported them. Possibly, as a consequence of this large 'foreign' component, there has also been a 'cringe factor' at play. With the long and complex European Jewish history as the comparison, there has been a tendency falsely to dismiss Australian Jewish history as both colourless and lacking in substance.

Margolin himself never courted attention, feeling that his actions spoke for him. After his arrival in Australia, he suffered in silence from a self-induced malady of dual loyalties, though never the kind with which Judeophobes have charged the Jews in many lands throughout history. His loyalty to Australia, and his dedication to the care of his former comrades, particularly their families damaged by war, was absolute. This, on the other hand, in no way dented his spiritual loyalty to *Eretz Israel*, which remained unwavering. His physical home was Australia, but his metaphysical abode was always in the *Yishuv*. No doubt it was a duality from which he suffered greatly emotionally, and it must have made social life difficult for him. It was the very private pain of a very private man.

In a Greek drama, Eliazar Margolin would have been a tragic figure. Whenever the glittering prize of dwelling permanently in *Eretz Israel* seemed within his grasp, the fates denied it to him. Ironically, his heart's desire was achieved only after his death. Indeed, he was the very embodiment of the exiled Jew, forced to wander the world in spiritual angst, ever longing to return to the Promised Land. This physical trek took him through three distinct empires: Russian, Ottoman and British.

2

Rehovot 1892

According to his Australian naturalization certificate, Eliazar Lazar Margolin was born on 5 February 1875 in Bielgorod or, as it is often spelled, Belgorod, in the Koviskoy (or Kovisk) Department of Russia.[1] In Russian, Belgorod means 'white city'. Jewish sources referred to it as Weissenburg or Ir Lavan, a name referring to the reflection of the chalk hills in the nearby Dniester River. It was the centre of the Belgorod-Dnestrovski region, formerly known as Akkerman, adjacent to the Ukrainian border on the south-eastern edge of Bessarabia, on the periphery of the Pale of Settlement, where the majority of Jews under the Russian tsars had been forced to live in the nineteenth century. Bessarabia was annexed by Russia in 1812, and incorporated into Romania under the Treaty of Paris of 1856. Three years after Eliazar was born, however, it reverted to Russia, and very soon after, the Pale of Settlement was swept by murderous pogroms and expulsions. Its Jewish population sought refuge not just overseas, but also in other parts of Russia. An immediate consequence was the burgeoning of Belgorod's Jewish population from 2,422 in 1864 to 5,613 by 1897.[2]

How long the Margolin family had lived in Belgorod is not known, but it seems they were not among the newcomers. Eliazar's father, Joseph, was a merchant. His mother, Liata Frieda, née Cartlin, cared for the family at home. In the occupational system that existed in Russia, Jews of the Pales of Settlement at the time were required to register with the authorities in one of three categories: merchant, businessman or peasant. Although many Jews of Belgorod were in the grain industry, others were scattered across the artisan class.[3] One account of Eliazar Margolin, no doubted sourced to Moshe Smilansky, a Margolin family friend in Palestine, relates that Joseph Margolin supplied food to Cossack regiments.[4]

Those commentators who have mentioned Eliazar Margolin have

taken note of brief biographies that have relied uncritically on the
memories of *Yishuv* writer Moshe Smilansky, who immortalized
Eliazar in his well-known short story, 'Hawaja Nazar'.[5] Because of
the dearth of information about Eliazar's life before his arrival in
Palestine, and indeed his departure from there, the Smilansky record
was also examined. It reveals that there are at least two important
issues that this source does not address: the degree of religiosity of
the Margolin parents in Russia, and the reasons for – let alone details
of – their decision to decamp to Palestine or *Eretz Israel*, as it was
called by pioneer settlers of the new *Yishuv*.

Smilansky says that although Eliazar's parents were religious, their
son, on arrival in Palestine, was so ignorant about Judaism that he
was virtually a Gentile. This poor education is said to have been
the product of adolescent rebellion against the wishes of his father,
who had employed a Jewish teacher to teach him the ways of
Judaism.[6] While adolescent rebellion is a plausible reason for such
ignorance, if the household had at least been minimally observant,
one may have concluded that Eliazar should have picked up at least
rudimentary knowledge of Judaism and its festivals. Smilansky calls
Joseph Margolin religious, and at one stage even calls him 'Rabbi
Mordechai Margolin'. That this was intended as irreverence or
sarcasm is a possibility, especially as Smilansky says that Eliazar was
nurtured in the 'goyish' environment of the eastern Ukraine. There
the young man acquired a love both of the natural Russian environment – its wide-open plains and the Rivers Don and Volga – and
of Russian literature, especially the works of Pushkin and Lermontov.
He was also reputed to have been greatly inspired by the apparently
free spirit of the horse-riding Cossacks.[7]

During Eliazar's four-year attendance at his local gymnasium, his
admiration for Russian culture deepened. Assimilated or assimilating
Jewish families in Belgorod, when affluent enough, often sent their
children to Russian-speaking schools rather than the traditional Jewish
religious system of *cheder* and *yeshiva*. The language of Eliazar's
home was Russian, not the Yiddish of the Pale of Settlement. As
Smilansky notes, Eliazar acquired a smattering of Yiddish only
after his arrival in *Eretz Israel*.[8] Knowledge of Eliazar's upbringing
in Belgorod might have been clarified to some degree by his older
siblings. These details, however, are not available. They may have
helped slay the ghost of wilful teenage recalcitrance as a reason for
their brother's lack of Jewish education.[9]

Zionism, notes Smilansky, was not the motivation behind the

Margolins' emigration to Palestine. Rather, he says, the reason was purely economic pragmatism. They were said to have decided on moving from Belgorod to Palestine because they were attracted by the lure of available arable land there that could be purchased for farming. The story goes that Eliazar's parents used guilt to goad him into accompanying them to a distant and culturally foreign land. He could not resist the cry of his parents: 'Will you abandon us in our old age?'[10] As his brother had been completely blind from birth, and his sister was unmarried, his labour was essential for the future economic sustenance of his family; even more so, since his father was a merchant and had never been a tiller of the soil.

Jews in the Pales of Settlement, suffering vicious pogroms in the early 1880s during the reign of Tsar Alexander III,[11] were faced with a number of possible options. They could remain in place somewhere within its borders, quiescent and in misery, either accepting their fate or awaiting divine intervention; or, they could remain in the Russian Empire and join a cosmopolitan revolutionary movement – socialist, communist, anarchist – seeking the overthrow of the tsar's regime, hoping to replace it with a just, all-inclusive society. Some pursued this end via a specifically Jewish socialist proletarian movement, the Bund. Another option was to leave Russia and join these movements abroad in the hope of returning to revolutionize their homeland. Emigration to the West was also open to them, with the hope of refuge and fortune, particularly in Great Britain and the United States of America. Rumours also spread in the early 1880s that Australia was a possible destination.[12] Another possible move was migration to the Jews' ancient homeland in Palestine, where for many centuries Jews had maintained a presence, principally in the confessional cities of Hebron, Jerusalem, Safed and Tiberias. This essentially religious settlement, known as the old *Yishuv*, was sustained by Jewish charity from the Diaspora known as the *Haluka*. The first reference to the *Haluka* in the Australian colonies appeared in the late 1850s in the archives of Sydney's York Street Synagogue.[13] The reality was that only a small minority of Eastern Europe's persecuted Jews took the Palestine route.

The initial establishment of the new *Yishuv*, or modern settlement of Jews in their ancient homeland, was a secular affair. This happened even though much of the early ideational groundwork had been laid by two religious thinkers, Rabbi Yehuda Hai and Rabbi Zwi Hirsch Kalisher.[14] Return to Zion, meaning to Jerusalem, and therefore to the Holy Land, had been a passion of the religious imagination, expressed in religious ritual, throughout the attenuated Jewish Exile. Although the renewed movement of return followed a secular ethos, often socialist in spirit, religious settlers later became actively engaged in the productive settlement of the land outside the Zionist movement, even if in concert with it.[15] Many members of the most engaged proto-Zionist cultural organization in Eastern Europe, the *Hovevei Zion*, or Lovers of Zion, came from traditional households. The movement was sparked into life by the murder, assault and dispossession caused by the vicious pogroms of the 1880s, and especially the infamous May Laws of 1882, which denied Jews in the cities the right to return to the countryside.[16] Bereft of the protection of officials in rural areas, Jews flooded into the cities, where their material existence was extremely tenuous. Organizationally, the *Hovevei Zion* propagated no single ideology, but promoted a general vision of a productive Jewish society in *Eretz Israel* free of the political dictates of others. Its message was to return, settle and make *Eretz Israel* productive.[17] Some members became enamoured of the ideas of Leon Pinsker, as expressed in his work *Autoemancipation*.[18]

Only a relatively small quantum of Jews emigrated to Palestine to help initiate the early period of settlement between 1880 and 1904, known in Zionist parlance as the First *Aliyah*. This attempt at creating a utopian Hebrew peasant society was not particularly successful. Its early pioneers were mainly young intellectuals, ill equipped to meet a confronting and uncompromisingly harsh physical and human environment. It left many of them, known collectively as the *Bilu* (an acronym for *Bet Ya'akov Lekhu ve-Nelkhah* or 'the House of Jacob let us arise and go') ill, exhausted, defeated and disillusioned. A number turned their backs on *Eretz Israel* and returned to Europe. The settlement that did succeed was aided by the French Jewish entrepreneur and philanthropist, Baron Edmund de Rothschild. Dreams of a co-operative Jewish rural utopia, however, collapsed, and ventures such as Rishon Le-Zion, Petah Tikva, Rosh Pina and Zichron Ya'akov became private colonies profoundly influenced by Rothschild and his employees.[19] He expected these settlements, based primarily upon viticulture, to become commercially self-sufficient. Dependence on Rothschild, however, meant that their fortunes were tied to the vagaries of the international wine trade.

Smilansky mentions that the Margolins had not been encouraged to immigrate to Palestine by pro-Zionist ideals. As there is no suggestion they were either members or even fellow travellers of *Hovevei*

Zion, one must ask the question why they chose Palestine when others, even those with a Zionist background, did not. And why was Rehovot their preferred place of settlement? Undoubtedly, the expulsion of Jews from Moscow in 1891[20] provided the final confirmation for some Jews that their existence under the tsar could not be anything but extremely precarious, and this encouraged them to leave for Palestine. The Margolins may well have belonged to this group, given that they arrived in Rehovot in 1892 to join the estimated 50,000 Russian Jews who had already reached Palestine by 1890.

In 1884, Asher Hirsch Ginsberg, or *Ahad Ha'Am* (One of the People), was elected to the central committee of *Hovevei Zion*. He was to become known as the father of Cultural Zionism. Three years after settling in the Black Sea port of Odessa in southern Russia, he formed a group named *B'nei Moshe* (Children of Moses).[21] Comprising many *Hovevei Zion* notables, it attempted to improve the dissemination of Hebrew literature and learning, and to further Jewish settlement of Palestine. In 1890 the branch in Warsaw formed a society, *Menuha V'Nahalah*, to buy land in *Eretz Israel* to establish settlements there. They were to be democratically organized and reliant neither on the influence nor the finances of Baron Edmund de Rothschild.[22]

Land for this purpose was purchased from a Christian Arab by Yehoshua Hankin of Rishon Le-Zion[23] at the request of Aharon Eisenberg of *Menuha V'Nahalah*. Situated fifteen miles south-east of the port city of Jaffa and forty miles north-west of Jerusalem, it was in the vicinity of Doron, a Jewish settlement of the Mishnaic period of Jewish history, in the fourth century of the Common Era. On the suggestion of Israel Belkin, another of the *Menuha V'Nahalah* group, it was called Rehovot. He took the name from the twenty-sixth chapter of the Book of Genesis, Toledoth, verse 22, which tells of the well in the Valley of Gerar from which Abraham, the Father of the Jewish People, was able to replenish his herds and supply of water *en route* to Be'ersheva. The Hebrew Bible recounts, 'And he [Abraham] removed from thence, and digged another well: and for that they strove not. And he called the name of it Rehoboth; and he said, "For now the Lord has made room for us, and we shall be fruitful in the land."'[24]

The word used in the Hebrew text is 'Rehoboth', translated as 'broad places', describing the expansive physical environment that attracted its latterday purchasers. The first general meeting to set the establishment of the settlement in motion occurred during the Palestine autumn in 1891. In the first years, the land was prepared for agriculture and the planting of vineyards. Initially some 6,000 dunams were set aside for members of the society. Other portions were bought by individuals such as Joseph Margolin.

3

Eliazar's First Aliyah

The Belgorod-Dnestrovski region was influenced by the social and cultural ethos radiating from the Black Sea port city of Odessa. In 1871 this city was the scene of a terrible pogrom. By the 1880s, it had become not only a centre for Zionism, but also the point of embarkation for Russian Jews seeking out Palestine.[1] It is conjectural whether or not the eddies of Zionism emanating from Odessa affected the Jews of Belgorod, including the Margolin family, who sailed from Odessa in 1892.

En route to Palestine their ship passed through the Dardanelles. Had Eliazar, then only sixteen years old, been blessed with prescience, he might have marvelled over the fact that, some twenty years later, he would return to this same place, during wartime, as a soldier of a nation whose name he had probably never heard of at that stage. As it was, his family was to settle in a land in the claw of the Ottoman Empire whose motherland, Turkey, he would be destined to fight against on two separate occasions, once in Asia Minor and then in the Middle East. That very year, 1892, was the moment chosen by Constantinople to place restrictions on land sales and building permits to Jews in Palestine in an attempt to forestall any increase in Jewish immigration. Esther Benbassa states that pressures for this were both internal and external. Internally, there was the desire to avoid having to cope with yet another nationality within the empire. Externally, the same tsarist Russia, whose horrific treatment of its Jews had forced the mass Jewish egress from its own lands, now demanded that Turkish authorities abort the immigration to Palestine on the grounds that it might threaten the status quo in the Holy Places. Pan-Islamic and Arab pressure was also being exerted on Turkey to achieve the same ends.[2] All these attempts to exclude Jews from Palestine failed.

The economic foundation of the 1880s settlements in Palestine was agriculture. Ran Aaronsohn states that they were neither collective nor co-operatively organized, but were comprised of individual property owners, as had been the case in European villages.[3] After an initial short period in which the pioneers co-operated in preparing the land for agriculture, individual farmers were on their own. Unfortunately for many, basic agricultural ignorance, a harsh climate and marauding Bedouin caused failure and unremitting debt.

By the late 1890s, Aaronsohn notes that the settlement of Rehovot covered 10,658 Turkish dunams. Of these 4,405 were planted with vineyards, 795 cultivated mainly with almond and citrus trees, and the rest was pasture or remained virginal.[4] Under Baron Edmund de Rothschild's influence, viticulture dominated the settlers' production. While there was no love lost between the baron and *Hovevei Zion*, sheer economic necessity locked independent settlements like Rehovot into the wine industry. Rothschild's notions of private enterprise ran contrary to the cultural ambitions of many pioneers. *Hovevei Zion* in Russia feared that the settlements would be totally at the economic mercy of wine markets in Europe. It also considered that the settlements' extensive employment of Arab workers would detract from the envisaged Jewish society, as well as resulting in limited time for learning and speaking Hebrew due to the need to supervise these workers. Grapes, even from the independents, were bought at subsidized prices by Rothschild's Rishon Le-Zion winery, crushed, then shipped to competitive European and Mediterranean markets. Throughout the period the Margolins farmed in Rehovot, the settlement's economy depended on the baron's continuing financial direct hand in the *Yishuv*'s viticulture;[5] this, however, was to last only until 1900. The loss of this aid had an extremely deleterious effect upon Eliazar's life.

The botanical link between colonial Australia and the Jewish community in Palestine was forged when Australian eucalyptus trees were brought to Palestine in 1878. They were planted and nurtured in the newly-established agricultural college of Mikve Israel near Tel Aviv.[6] These 'Jewish trees',[7] as the Arabs called them, were then grown along the coastal plain, in settlements such as Petah Tikva and Hadera, at first to help drain mosquito-infested swamps, and then in towns of the Galilee. Casuarina and strains of acacias from Australia were also used to border avenues and as windbreaks.[8] It was probably the first time many of the pioneers had ever heard of Australia, a place to which some among them, including Eliazar Margolin, would soon relocate.

Although the Western world, including colonial Australia, was severely hit by economic depression in the first half of the 1890s, the *Yishuv*, with the help of Rothschild's money and organization, was able to weather the storm. In contrary fashion, it experienced an upswing in building and agriculture.[9] Not only Jewish immigrants, but also many thousands of Arab labourers gained employment.[10] Paradoxically, the presence of Arab workers did not prevent settlements being attacked by marauding Bedouin and pilfering Arab villagers. The settlements were forced to form self-defence teams to guard their farms.

From the moment Eliazar set foot in Rehovot in 1892, he was the family's prime breadwinner, responsible for supporting his ageing parents, unmarried sister and blind brother.[11] Given that Moshe Smilansky was a lodger in the Margolin house, he was in an excellent position to observe his idiosyncrasies. Eliazar was always presented as a hero in Smilansky's romantic style, his protégé whom he mentors in matters Jewish and Zionist. This newcomer to the fledgling settlement of Rehovot is described as a 'tall and high headed, strong handed' youth of sixteen years of age who in *Eretz Israel* learns that Hebrew is not only a means for entering the religious texts, but also a tongue for daily living and the conduit of a new national literature. *In situ*, as Smilansky tells it, he quickly replaces his former allegiance for Russia with a love for the Jewish people and its pioneers.

There is no doubt that Eliazar acquired the Hebrew language and general Jewish cultural knowledge in Palestine, but at what level of fluency and depth? What is certain is that he fell in love with *Eretz Israel*, a sentiment that remained with him throughout his life. Concentration on the family's economic sustenance, extensive recreational touring of the Palestinian countryside and his defence of Rehovot must have left him little time for formal learning. All commentators agree with Smilansky that Eliazar was a person of few words. This no doubt reflected his unassuming character, but no one seemed to ask if it might also have been the outcome of not being confident in the spoken word.

In one respect the Smilansky account is contradictory. We are told that Eliazar also had a rebellious side, which manifested itself in his engaging in rigorous debate in Rehovot, often between the older and younger members of the settlement. We are not informed of the substance of these rigorous discussions, but they could not have been a place for the reticent and the inarticulate.

With his father of little help due to age, ill-health and an ignorance of farming, Eliazar spent much of his time absorbed in the family's vineyard and almond grove, and in supplementing the coffers with outwork on neighbours' farms. His father seems to have been some-what of a financial liability, piling up debts. For a short time Eliazar also taught mathematics on the side. Capital was required both to purchase farmland in Rehovot and to develop it. In the practical life of farming, no matter where, there is always a time gap between the planting of grape vines and almond trees and their bearing fruit. In this prolonged interval, the Margolin family of five had to be fed and clothed. Eliazar's labour on other farms, however financially helpful, could not cover everything. In his florid style, Smilansky says of him: 'he soon became famous as a vine pruner and a famous rider and many wanted him to work for them. He also wielded mattock and spade in hand as an artist and he loved the plough, and ploughing after the first rain was like a joy for him.'[12]

Contrary to the original *Hovevei Zion* belief in a society of Jewish farmers, the settlements employed many Arab workers. Eliazar's reputation was built not just on his own capacities as a farmer, but also on his ability to organize the Arab workers on his neighbours' holdings. He familiarized himself with their language and ways, and this knowledge of both was to assist him in his later escapades. An Arab guard taught him to be a superb shot with a rifle, while a Bedouin friend tutored him in horsemanship, for which he became renowned. His skills in both won him such respect from the Arabs they called him affectionately *Hawaja Nazar*.[13] The title *Hawaja* means 'a man, by the prophet of Moses' and was reserved by the Bedouin only for those they held in the greatest esteem. *Nazar* was simply a play on Margolin's own middle name, Lazar.

Despite *Hovevei Zion*'s ideological reservations over dealing with Baron Rothschild, independent farmers such as Eliazar had to take their grapes to his lordship's wine press at Rishon Le-Zion, where the produce was crushed and sold. Smilansky tells the story of a fateful meeting there between Eliazar and the son of a Be'ersheva Bedouin sheikh, called Hassan. The latter had come to inspect his father's camels, which were being used to drive the wine press. A fight broke out between the farmers and the Bedouin camel drivers. Other farmers and the camel drivers fled the scene. Only Hassan was left to fight against his opponents. Eliazar, who just happened upon the fray, joined Hassan to drive off his attackers. The two became very close friends, often riding in the countryside together, and Eliazer would spend weeks in his friend's father's 'Bedouin tents in the Negev'. His peripatetic trips criss-crossing Palestine on horseback gave him a profound appreciation of its physicality. He is said to have been disappointed that the Jordan River compared poorly with the great rivers of Russia, though he found some consolation in the tidal lake, the Kinneret, and peace of mind in the open spaces of the Negev desert.[14]

One aspect of communal service in which he excelled was as a defender of Rehovot and its environs. For not only were farmers plagued with a foreign soil and climate, they had to suffer harassment from local Arabs and – especially at night – assault and pilfering from marauding Bedouin. To combat this, various settlements formed self-defence groups to protect their lives and property. In the settlement's early years, the workers of Rehovot formed an organization, *Ha'asarot*, to improve the material situation of the settlement and organize its defence. It was a body that would certainly have attracted the young Eliazar. Though the settlers sought to have good relations with the nearby Arab villages, in the summer of 1891 Arabs from Zarnugah attacked them over grazing. The *Satariah* tribe repeated this several times, claiming it owned the land on which the settlement stood.

In hindsight, the different settlements' attempts at self-defence were the first murmurings of the movement of Jewish self-defence in Palestine that evolved into the *Shomer*, *Haganah* and, in 1948, the Israel Defence Force. Given his previously mentioned skills it was hardly surprising that Eliazar volunteered to help defend Rehovot. His efforts did not go unrewarded, for he was chosen by fellow farmers to lead the honour guard that met and escorted the father of Political Zionism, Theodor Herzl, when he ventured to Palestine in 1898 to meet another visitor, the German Kaiser Wilhelm II, near the agricultural college of Mikveh Israel.[15] The German monarch was in Palestine as a gesture to the Turks, whose friendship he had been successfully courting and which was ultimately proven by their partnership in the First World War.[16] Herzl wanted to take advantage of this friendship, hoping that the monarch would convince Constantinople of the merits of an autonomous Jewish homeland in Palestine. He was forced to confront the difficult reality of the *Yishuv* face to face for the first time. On the other hand, he was very favourably – indeed, emotionally – impressed by the guard of honour of young pioneers that welcomed him in Rehovot. As Herzl recorded in his diary:

We drove on. A cavalcade came galloping towards us from the settlement of Rehovot: about twenty young fellows who put on a kind of fantasia, lustily singing Hebrew songs and swarming about our carriage. Wolffsohn, Schnirer, Bodenheimer had tears in our eyes when we saw those fleet, daring horsemen into whom our young trouser-salesmen can be transformed. Hedad they cried, and dashed away cross-country on their little Arab horses. They reminded me of the Far-West cowboys of the American plains who I once saw in Paris.[17]

No one contributed to this more than Eliazar, resplendent in Arab *abaya* and *kaffiye*, riding a fine mare borrowed from his Bedouin friend. According to Smilansky, the baron and Eliazar were said to have shaken hands. Baron de Rothschild, who shortly was to become the latter's financial nemesis, was said to be greatly impressed with Eliazar.[18]

Little can be gleaned about Eliazar's personal life in Rehovot. On summer nights his vineyard and home became a place of singing and merrymaking. He had a pleasantly strong bass voice which resonated in the folksongs of Russia and the *Yishuv*, which he loved to sing, and apparently he was an active thespian in local productions. Even the mention of his name was said to send pioneer and Bedouin girls' hearts aflutter. In Smilansky's words, 'his generous warm heart knew to return warm heartbeat for warm heartbeat … and his eyes to return lightning glances for lightning glances'.[19]

We do not know, however, of any long-term relationships or even a momentary favourite. Possibly the blending of family obligations with ever present penury prevented such a development.

Not even Eliazar's reputation could keep the debt collectors from the door. His utter contempt for the mainly absent governing Turks with their taxes, corruption, administrative neglect of Palestine and disdain for both Jew and Arab alike, was matched by a contempt for Rothschild's officials and moneylenders. He saw the latter particularly as bloodsuckers engaged in activities that true Jews should be spurning.[20] In 1901, his parents died only a week apart, first his mother, then his father. They were buried in adjacent plots in the small Rehovot cemetery. Though he had been the de facto family breadwinner, this position now became, as it were, official. It fell to him, in his mid-twenties, to care for his brother and sister, despite an insurmountable debt to moneylenders.

The problems of his domestic situation were exacerbated by the *Yishuv*'s plunge into economic recession, if not depression. By 1900,

Baron Edmund de Rothschild was no longer directly financially interested in the settlements.[21] The local wine industry, upon which they all depended, could not compete with traditional growers from France and Italy on the European market. When Eliazar realized that the price he had previously received for his grapes from the baron had been subsidized, and that, in effect, he had been receiving welfare in disguise, he felt dehumanized, deflated and extremely angry.[22]

He felt there was only one way to pay off his crippling debt, and it devastated him. This was to liquidate the family farm with its vineyard and almond trees. Once the debt had been repaid, he placed the remaining money into a trust fund for his siblings. He ensured that his sister found a home with a suitable family, and organized residence for his brother at the Blind Institute in Rishon Le-Zion. He then planned to travel to far-off and little-known Australia just long enough to earn the money that would allow him to return to *Eretz Israel* to live comfortably and permanently.

What he had heard of Australia and why this was his preferred destination remain open to conjecture. Four possibilities might be suggested. Australia had been spoken of as a place of refuge for Russian Jews escaping the pogroms of the 1880s. In addition, knowledge of the gold finds in Coolgardie, Western Australia, in 1892, had spread across the world.[23] Earlier gold rushes in the Australian colonies of New South Wales and Victoria had similarly drawn Jews from abroad.[24] And then there was the eucalyptus connection with the settlements, which must have been accompanied by some knowledge of Australia, albeit extremely limited. Finally, there was a claim that Eliazar had been attracted to the Antipodes by the possibility of buying vast quantities of cheap land.

At the time of his leaving Palestine after his parents' deaths, the Boer War was in full swing in South Africa. While in Egypt, *en route* to Australia, it is said that Eliazar attempted to enlist in the British force dispatched to that theatre.[25] Assuming this to be true, it may be that Eliazar thought his experience in the defence of Rehovot might have helped his advocacy, but he was neither a British citizen – a requirement for enlistment – nor could he speak a word of English, the language of command. We are told that he was rejected. There is also a suggestion that he refused to accept this, and that he paid his own fare to England to convince the authorities there that he was a worthy recruit. Such a story, however, appears to be apocryphal.

The log of the SS *Weimer*, sailing from Bremen to Australia, notes that an Eliazar Margolin, listed among its passengers, joined the voyage, along with a handful of other Jews from Palestine, at Port Said in Egypt. Further, it advises that he arrived at the Western Australian port of Fremantle in April 1902.[26]

4

In Limbo Down Under

There is no clear account of what happened to Eliazar Margolin after he arrived in Australia this first time. A number of short biographies describe him going to Sydney to find work as a navvy and wharf labourer, and then to open a none too successful medical supply factory.[1] They relate that his previous experience in intensive agriculture in Palestine was irrelevant in the extensive acre farming in Australia. Even had he wanted to learn new methods, however, it would have taken him too long if he desired to make his fortune quickly. In addition, he had no commercial experience and, moreover, was also hampered by his lack of English. Because of this impatience to make his fortune, we are told, he left Sydney for the mining areas of Western Australia, where he opened a bottle factory in the coal-mining town of Collie.

The problem with this scenario is that there is no evidence of his ever sailing on to Sydney after his ship had docked in Fremantle, Western Australia. Indeed, the manifest of the SS *Weimer* seems to indicate that after joining the ship in Port Said he disembarked in Fremantle, his declared destination.[2] This of itself does not mean he did not take passage on another ship to Sydney. The work attributed to him, in and around Sydney, was of the physical kind being undertaken by those unskilled in the English language. Many Jewish immigrants to Australia who were not English speakers did indeed enter the commercial world, but usually first as hawkers across the Australian hinterland. The wholesale medical supply business he was reported to have established in Sydney suggests the need for a technical language and business acumen that Eliazar just did not possess.

Eliazar's application for Australian naturalization on 5 July 1904 intimates that he did not travel on to Sydney.[3] Indeed, 1904 was the first time non-British persons could apply for Australian nationality, a consequence of the Nationalization Act passed by the Australian Parliament in 1903. Eliazar's papers were witnessed by William Griffith, a Justice of the Peace in Lawlers, where he was then living.[4] If this document is to be believed, Eliazar did not leave Western Australia from the date of his arrival in Fremantle on 10 April 1902. It states that for the first five months he lived in Perth, then spent eleven months in Coolgardie, three months in Kalgoorlie and the final three months in Lawlers. In other words, he spent much time around the Western Australian gold fields, though by this time the rush had long passed its peak. Nevertheless, the mining districts of Western Australia would have been a natural lure for someone needing to make a quick fortune. One account has him working as a 'navvy and a teamster', before 'drifting into business'.[5] It could be that Eliazar falsified the documents in order to strengthen his residential claims for naturalization. An unbroken residence in Western Australia would have indicated that his wish to stay in Australia was not flighty but serious. Nothing in Eliazar's prior history, nor his subsequent behaviour, however, suggests that he was the kind of person to practise such a deception.

The origin of this confusion may be attributed to two sources. The first of these is Abe Troy's A. G. Korsunski Memorial Lecture on Colonel Eliazar Margolin, delivered in Perth on Sunday, 19 September 1982.[6] This lecture is quoted in all contemporary profiles of Eliazar Margolin, including the one in *The Australian Biographical Dictionary*,[7] which in turn influenced a similar account in *The New Encyclopedia of Zionism and Israel*.[8] Troy admitted in his lecture that his acquaintance with Eliazar dated only from the late 1920s. At no point does he mention if the early biographical details came from the subject himself, though this is highly unlikely because he includes the glaring error that Eliazar had once been appointed Governor of Jerusalem.[9] If Margolin had indeed been his source, perhaps Troy misunderstood what he had been told. It is more likely, however, that his principal reference was an Israeli author, Yehoash Biber, who Troy believed must have served in the Jewish Legion under Colonel Margolin.[10]

On the other hand, there is Moshe Smilansky's account, which describes his friend's early years in Australia as being very hard. Smilansky says Eliazar hated trade and wanted to be a farmer, but that, failing in this, he turned to that dreaded occupation.[11] It is ironic that this son of a trader was forced ultimately to follow in his dead father's footsteps. Whether Eliazar first travelled to Sydney, as Abe Troy claims, or remained in Western Australia, his labours failed to bring him enough money to return to Palestine as quickly as he had wished.

He did, however, open a bottle factory in the Western Australian town of Collie. In April 1969, the town's newspaper, the *Collie Mail*, reported that members of the local historical society had found a collection of old bottles in a riverbed. One of these bottles bore the brand 'P.M.R.', said to be the insignia of Margolin's factory, which had stood on the present site of the Co-Op Produce Department. The first time Eliazar's name appeared on the Western Australian electoral roll was in 1912, in the subdivision of Collie. Somewhat puzzling is that the occupation given in his naturalization papers in 1904 is that of a greengrocer, whereas the 1912 electoral roll listed him as a merchant of Johnson Street in Collie.

Smilansky says that in correspondence with his friends in Palestine Eliazar had begun to talk about returning to *Eretz Israel* when suddenly the First World War broke out.[12] If this is true, it is not certain whether or not these plans represented a hope born of frustration or if he had in fact accumulated enough money to consider such a move possible. Undoubtedly, his application for Australian citizenship had stemmed from a realization that his stay in Australia would be much longer than he had previously thought. His calculations were also influenced by the fact that the *Yishuv* still faced an uncertain future.

In Australian Jewish communal demography, the tendency has been to count every Jew present in its bailiwick without asking permission. Doubt surrounds Eliazar's willingness at this time to consider himself a member of the Western Australian Jewish community. He was far more emotionally connected to the *Yishuv* than to his local community. It was one thing to develop a loyalty to the land of his present domicile, quite another to join the collective of Jews in yet another foreign environment. His ambivalence about Judaism would also have made him waver in this regard. He was only one of a number of *émigrés* from Palestine who had come to Western Australia around the beginning of the twentieth century to escape the dire economic circumstances that prevailed in the *Yishuv*. They joined those who had come directly from Eastern Europe, fleeing the pogroms and general anti-Jewish oppression. Others continued to arrive from Great Britain to bolster the already 'Anglo'-dominated community.[13] The foreign *émigré* component – from wherever they came – were Yiddish-speaking in the main, and willing consumers of Jewish culture. Eliazar Margolin was neither of these things.

In the year before Eliazar Margolin's arrival in Fremantle, Australia's first Commonwealth Census of 1901 calculated that there were 1,259 Jews in Western Australia. In the 1911 Census that number rose to 1,790.[14] As Mossenson establishes, this increase included immigrants direct from tsarist Russia, who, for whatever reason, were not permitted to enter the United States of America, or saw Australia as their first land of refuge and opportunity.[15] Some, no doubt, were lured by news of gold discoveries. For those who left Palestine because of penury, Turkish oppression or a combination of both, a third-class steamer ticket from Port Said costing no more than ten pounds was an affordable attraction. On arrival, they either stayed in Fremantle, moved to Western Australia's capital city, Perth, or to the beckoning provincial towns of the already declining gold fields in the east.[16]

As already noted, both language and religiosity tended to form a gulf between Eliazar and many of the other émigrés, even those from Palestine. He was not fluent in Yiddish, and those from the Holy Land were not necessarily fluent in Hebrew as a spoken tongue. Before their departure, Hebrew had not yet become established in the Yishuv. While it increasingly gained ascendancy among the pioneer community in Palestine, it became an officially recognized language there only under the British in 1921. Although he was never one to deny his religious affiliation, it would not have been surprising if relations Eliazar had formed with other Jews on the gold fields would have been, at best, of the mildly social kind. Synagogues had been established at Coolgardie and Kalgoorlie, where, according to Eliazar's naturalization papers, he had been living. It is unlikely, however, that he ever attended their services. When Eliazar arrived on the gold fields, their decline had already contributed to the contraction of these two satellite pockets of Western Australian Jewry.[17]

One area in which Eliazar might have conceivably found some soulmates was through a common interest in Zionism. In the first decade of the twentieth century, most commentators agree that the heart of Australian Zionism could be located within Western Australian Jewry.[18] The extent of this should not be exaggerated, since the espousal of pro-Zionist sentiment among any of the 'Anglo'-dominated communities was barely a whisper, and an ephemeral one at that. Put simply, if Zionism had not sparked the majority of those smarting under the jackboot of tsarist Russia to rush to Palestine, it was hardly likely to have inspired Australian residents not suffering such oppression. Support for any ideology or general sentiment that suggested the true calling of the Jew lay in Palestine was seen by Anglo-Australian Jews as tantamount to disloyalty to the land that had given them succour.

When practical Zionism took root in Palestine in the 1880s and 1890s – that is, when the Margolin family beat its path to *Eretz Israel* – the grand battle in Australia, both ideological and material, was concentrated in the conflict between labour and capital, from which emerged the Australian Labor Movement,[19] and an evolving Australian nationalism.[20] It was also a period that saw a growing erosion of commitment to Judaism in colonial Jewry. In such communities, the vision of Zionism held little sway. Australia was itself a pioneering society, though not one driven by any sense of metaphysics. From an ideational perspective, Zionism competed with the love of Australia for the bodies of Jews, if not for their souls. It was a vastly unbalanced competition, however, if competition at all. There were few prepared to surrender their freedom for an unknown future under the Turks. Certainly, few would have been attracted, as many of them, in relative terms, had hardly established themselves in their new land. The hope that they would be, however, was not new. Alan Crown has cited a diary note of Moses Montefiore in the 1850s, expressing the wish that those bound for Australia drawn by the gold rushes in New South Wales and Victoria, would redirect themselves to Palestine.[21]

The ink on the decision of the Australian colonies to federate into a single nation had barely dried when Eliazar Margolin disembarked at Fremantle. Prominent colonial Jews such as Victoria's Isaac Isaacs[22] and South Australia's Vlaiban Louis Solomon[23] had been in the vanguard of this movement. A Zionist cultural group had just been formed in Perth under the leadership of Reverend David Isaac Freedman of the Perth Hebrew Congregation, ironically a bulwark of Anglo-Orthodoxy. Zionism, however, did not draw the degree of support from those who had left Palestine that might have been expected. That came from the *émigrés* from tsarist lands who had experienced Zionist organization or education there. A number of those coming directly from Palestine, such as Margolin, hoped that Australia would be an instant financial Eldorado that would allow them a speedy return to Palestine. They were, consequently, less interested in the intellectual aspects of Zionism and more concerned with material self-advancement.

In the wake of the infamous Kishenev pogrom of 1903, Australia came to be considered as a possible alternative destination for the persecuted Jews of Eastern Europe, as had been rumoured in the 1880s. British author-playwright and former Zionist, Israel Zangwill, now prominent in the Jewish Territorial Organization, had promoted a scheme for a colony either in Queensland or the Kimberley region of northern Australia, which would accommodate five hundred to one thousand families. Despite some support, including that of the Reverend Freedman, the scheme was decisively rejected by Australia's prime minister, Alfred Deakin.[24] Nevertheless, its promotion by persons such as Freedman undermined the minuscule and brittle enthusiasm for Zionism.[25]

It is clear that the commercialism involved in the bottle factory in Collie would never satisfy Eliazar Margolin's soul, let alone his finances. He hankered for the excitement of the life he had led in his local defence team. Providence came to his aid. Upon Federation in 1901, consideration was given to how Australia could best defend itself against an external aggressor. Prior to 1901, each colony had its own defence forces. The great fear of the time was that the nation might well be swamped by an Asian aggressor from the north. It had long been expected that the British navy would always be there to help defend Australia in time of crisis.[26] Hitherto, troops from the Australian colonies had served under the flag of the British, in the Sudan and Boer Wars.[27] In December 1910, Field Marshal Lord Kitchener – of Khartoum fame – was invited by the Australian government to assess the state of the nation's armed forces, and suggest improvements. He was to advise a grossly ambitious scheme for a standing army of 84,000 in eighty-four battalions, half to defend cities and ports, the rest as a land-based rapid deployment force. Another suggestion was for an officer training institution, implemented at Duntroon in 1911 as the Royal Australian Military College.[28] Not only was the Kitchener plan financially over-ambitious, but it failed to meet the nation's current need. Compulsory military service was eventually introduced in 1911. An estimated 155,000 young men registered. Initially, 92,000 underwent training, augmented by 20,000 per year until the outbreak of the First World War in 1914.[29]

These circumstances provided Eliazar Margolin with the opportunity to participate. One aspect of the military expansion was the formation of local citizen militias composed of part-time volunteers. In 1911, with the rank of second lieutenant, he helped form the

Collie Company of the Western Australian Infantry Regiment.[30] By the time the Great War erupted, in August 1914, he was in charge of the army's area office in Collie and captain of his local volunteer unit. The story goes that he saw that war with Germany was imminent and prepared himself and others for this cataclysmic event.

His attachment to the military life resulted in Eliazar being among the first enlistees when Australia entered the First World War. In fact, when Great Britain declared war on Germany, Australia was legally automatically at war. This aside, as shown at the Imperial Conference in London in 1911, there had been much enthusiasm on Australia's behalf to help Great Britain defend its imperial interests.[31] Under the existing Defence Act of 1903, no one in Australia could be conscripted for overseas military service.[32] This ensured that any force dispatched abroad would be composed of volunteers. Compulsory pre-war military training now provided a ready source of volunteer citizen officers and men. Eliazar Margolin was among the first of these to enlist.

According to Jeffrey Grey, some 79 per cent of those who enlisted in the Australian Imperial Force (AIF) in 1914 were aged between eighteen and twenty-nine years. Some 20 per cent were in their thirties, and the remaining 1 per cent either under-age or over-age.[33] Although approaching his fortieth year, Eliazar's application was accepted without question, a testimony to his experience, mental approach and physical fitness. Of the initial recruited intake in 1914, only 21 per cent were born outside Australia, most of them in the British Isles.[34] Eliazar was not only one of the few 'foreigners', but after twelve years in the country, he left for war in its volunteer army as a naturalized citizen and officer.

5

Behind the News

Army enlistment records show that Eliazar Lazar Margolin was thirty-nine years and six months old when he applied for a commission in the AIF on 19 September 1914. His education is given as six years' attendance at a gymnasium in Russia. Previous military service is listed as three years in the 86th Western Australia Infantry Regiment (WAIR). The records add that he was naturalized in 1904. Further information tendered includes the fact that he was a merchant by occupation, unmarried, and specified his sister Esther in Palestine as his next of kin.[1] Smilansky recalls that when Eliazar had arrived in Rehovot at the age of sixteen, he was a tall, strong lad. Army statistics show him in his maturity, as a man five feet ten inches tall, weighing thirteen and a half stone, with a chest size of forty-one to forty-four inches, and a visual acuity score of 'six-six'.[2]

On 1 October 1914, he applied for a commission in the 16th Battalion AIF and, a few months later, on 16 December, he was elevated to the rank of captain.[3] When war broke out, the newly established Royal Duntroon Military College was graduating only its first intake of officers. Necessity dictated that many of the AIF's officer class be drawn from the citizen forces. Jeffrey Grey's studies have shown these men to have been of mixed ability, but no more so than the existing professional corps.[4]

Eliazar Margolin proved himself to be one of the better leaders. He was appointed to the B Company of the 4th Brigade 16th Battalion AIF, which mainly comprised men from South Australia and Western Australia, and was commanded by Colonel John Monash. The 16th had its birth at Blackboy Hill, Western Australia, on 16 September 1914. Initially, the Brigade's 'B' Company had a Major Abrahall at its helm, but he soon left to serve in the British Army, and was replaced by Captain Eliazar Margolin. Following strenuous training, the 'B' Company moved to Broadmeadows in Victoria for fine-tuning and organizational matters. On 22 December 1914, it sailed for overseas duty on the Troopship A40 *Ceramic* (18,500 tons). Though the 4th Brigade was not in the first convoy of Australian troops to leave, it soon caught up with its brothers in Egypt.[5]

Despite the fact that, since the last quarter of the nineteenth century, Australian-born residents for the first time comprised the majority of the population, when 'the war to end all wars' was declared, the local population, both Jew and Gentile, was still referring to Great Britain as 'home'. To defend Great Britain or its imperial interests was seen by a great majority of the population as equivalent to defending Australia's interests. Australia was a unique culture, but one with strong links to British culture and literature despite a handful of local triumphs.[6] Even most of the foreign news read at the time by Australians came from, or was routed through, London.[7] Consequently, it reflected a British world view.

Australians were led to believe that national survival was dependent on their young men offering themselves on the battlefield.[8] Only a minority dissented. This grand vision aside, there were, according to Joan Beaumont,[9] a number of private reasons why Australians signed up, and they ranged from loyalty to Great Britain and the empire, popular pseudo-scientific beliefs about a biological struggle between the English and other racial types, to the very personal. These personal reasons stretched from a wish to make money to a desire for adventure, or for an escape from familial relationships. Australian troops were known as 'six-bob-a-day soldiers'; they earned much more than a day labourer did. Some leaders of the non-Roman Catholic churches, to which the majority of Australians of the day adhered – at least nominally – first rationalized the war as a God-given chance to bring Australian civilization to the notice of the world through the suffering and baptism of fire that were often the precursors to nationhood.[10] Australia's legitimacy needed to be proved on the battlefield, a trial that had not occurred when it federated into a single nation in 1901. These church leaders felt that this constitutional binding lacked, as it were, this military – and hence spiritual – dimension. Anglicans and Protestants of various kinds comprised 79 per cent of the early enlistment. Though enlistment for Roman Catholics, the majority of whom were of Irish ancestry, became more problematic later, their 20 per cent component of the early intake was certainly in proportion to their numbers in the population.[11] The figures show a 1 per cent non-Christian recruitment; in this category were Australia's Jews.

Historians agree that few religious or cultural groups could match the passion of Australian Jewry for king, country and empire. Patriotism and loyalty laced the official statements of its Anglo-dominated leadership, which still looked to its mother Jewry in Great Britain for its attitudinal cues with respect to matters affecting the Jews internationally. As there was no single democratically elected political voice or organization to express its opinion, public statements were usually those of leading Jewish personalities, including rabbis from the dominant Anglo-Orthodox synagogues in each of the communities, or editorials in the communal press which, in some cases, were a funnel for those very same views. As for enlistment in the AIF, there is no reason to believe that Jews were not at least equally susceptible as their non-Jewish neighbours to the range of motivations for joining up. There was an extra Jewish dimension to the question, however, which added to the pressure to enlist.

To suggest that the high level of exhortation with which Jewish leaders spoke in this matter was due simply to self-interest would be disingenuous and highly offensive. Their statements mirrored the current emotions in their communities and reflected strongly held convictions.[12] Nevertheless, the hyperbolic nature of their statements was also driven by a deep and abiding sense of Jewish insecurity. In the matter of enlistment, Jews felt the need to be more loyal than other citizens. This loyalty was the talisman to protect them against the evil eye of anti-Semitism. Enlistment thus became the public measure of Jewish Australians' worthiness of the citizenship so freely accorded them.

Hilary Rubinstein has shown that by 1915, at least some '600 Jews were in uniform'.[13] *The British Jewry Book of Honour*, published in 1922, cites Lieutenant Harold Boas's figures, which state that a recorded 2,000 Australian Jews served in the First AIF, although this statistic was an understatement because some Jewish soldiers, for their own reasons, did not disclose their religious affiliation. Jews constituted around 0.3 per cent of the Australian population, but comprised at least 0.45 per cent of the soldiers sent to the Great War.[14] Suzanne Rutland argues that these figures were even more remarkable because of lower birth rates; Australian Jews had a smaller number, proportionately, of those of military age. Her explanation of the proportionally greater Jewish rush to the colours is the traditional one: gratitude that Australia was a safe haven for their people.[15] It was, however, more than just a case of gratitude, as the rhetoric of Jewish leaders demonstrated. These spokesmen echoed the profound fears of their English counterparts over traditional medieval anti-Semitic canards circulating that Jews were the eternal shirkers, and that their natural make-up made them utterly ineffectual as soldiers. A common and heavily emphasized thread running through the public utterances of Australian Jewish leaders was that these excoriations should be disproved by Jewish enlistment and superior military performance.[16]

If the level of anti-Semitism was so low in Australia at the time, as commentators have suggested, why did some Jewish soldiers refuse to disclose their religion to the authorities? Of course, they may have already opted out of the faith or have been in the process of doing so. It is also possible that racialist sentiment was common in the armed services, though the generally held view is that there was very little anti-Semitism in the trenches. This is hardly surprising, for where human survival depended on the behaviour of digger comrades, religious affiliation counted for little. If the issue had arisen, it would have been only on religious holy days, during the burial of a comrade, or in seeking out a chaplain for personal counselling. The reality was that because of a dearth of chaplains in the field, many of them were forced to minister to persons of a faith or denomination different from their own.

Writing after the Armistice, the senior Jewish chaplain to the British forces, the Reverend Michael Adler, spoke of the friendly treatment of Jews in the British military, a category in which he doubtlessly included Dominion forces[17] on the Western Front. Such comments were supported by Jewish Anglophile chaplains to the AIF, Rev. David Isaac Freedman of the Perth Hebrew Congregation,[18] and Rev. Jacob Danglow of the St Kilda Hebrew Congregation.[19] Such positive comments, however, were not accurate with respect to the treatment of the Jewish battalions with whom Eliazar Margolin served in Palestine. British historian David Cesarani has commented that in England, 'background anti-Semitism of pre-war years was evidenced in the treatment of volunteers from the earliest days of the war'.[20] Indeed, an editorial in the Melbourne edition of the *Jewish Herald* on 30 July 1915 stated that in the British Army, a fear of anti-Semitism encouraged a significant number of Jews either to refuse or be reluctant to disclose their religious affiliation. The purpose of the editorial was to suggest that the situation was better in the AIF, but without corroborating evidence. The newspaper declared:

We have no doubt that if a complete roll call were available of Jews in the Australian Expeditionary Force it would be found relative to the population. Their numbers would compare favourably with those of other sectors of the citizens. It would be most desirable to draw up an exhaustive list as possible of our co-religionist soldiers ... the list in the United Kingdom is not complete. This appears to be mainly from the fact that many Jewish recruits there have, on enlisting, changed their names, and concealed their religious affiliation. We are inclined to believe, indeed, that the unfortunate policy adopted by these misguided young men proceeds not from their race and faith as from apprehension of encountering prejudice and consequential ill-treatment, on the part of their comrades. But in this they are greatly mistaken, for all accounts show that in the Australian army the relations between Jewish and Christian soldiers are most invariably of the most friendly character, and particularly when the former have had the moral courage not to avoid their origins and creed unreservedly. Concealment usually leads to more difficulty ...

The question is, if Jewish recruits in the AIF found anything to worry about with respect to anti-Semitism? Obviously, some thought there was a problem.

The great issue that divided Australians during the war was that of conscription.[21] By law, Australian army recruits for overseas service had to be volunteers. Initially it was believed that the war would soon be over. Beginning with Gallipoli, however, and then on the Western Front, campaigns cannibalized men at an ever increasing rate, which could not be met by volunteers. The debate over conscription was pitted by class politics and later by bitter Roman Catholic opposition, because of the excesses of British rule in Ireland.[22] The official Jewish position in the political debate was in one sense totally irrelevant, since it considered it the sacred duty of Jews to serve, and indeed, to volunteer to serve. It was not merely a question of simply filling in the gaps left by the dead or wounded. In a most grandiloquent manner, the *Jewish Herald* of 7 July 1915 put the case of Jewish leaders:

The Jews of the British Empire, from the humblest to the highest, despite or rather because of their desire for peace, are rallying ... in response to their country's call to arms. The patriotism of the Jew towards the land of his birth or adoption has been sufficiently proven again and again. But the British Jew, in addition to his keen sense of civic responsibility at this time of grave national crisis, realises full well that the most vital principles of civilisation are at stake ... basic principles of Judaism – liberty, justice, and honour – which made for England's greatest – are being vividly assailed. Prussian arrogance and the baneful spirit of militarism are threatening to wrest and reverse the vital wheel of human progress. For the Jew who tasted the full fruits of liberty beneath the British flag it is an unshackled conviction that ruthless enemies of this civilisation must be restricted and overcome, at whatever costs.

The pressing appeal for men and women will not fall on deaf ears. So far as the Jew of the British Empire is concerned, he will not be driven to the front by the whip of conscription. Already more Jews are fighting in the various theatres today than we engaged in the defence of Jerusalem against the Roman armies two thousand years ago. Many of them have won distinction on the battlefield and all of them have convincingly demonstrated their physical moral courage ... the Australian Jewish soldier will bear comparison with his comrades of the same front in other parts of the Empire, no doubt, for he is inspired with the same ardent loyalty to the King and Country that animates them. The sentiments of every Australian Jew are well voiced by a gifted sister of the faith with the words:

> Now we Jews, we English Jew, O Mother
> England
> Ask another boon of thee
> Let share with them the danger and the
> Glory,
> Where they best and bravest lead, there let us follow
> O'er the sea

If the proletarian Australian Jew were indeed so saturated with the above chauvinist sentiment for the empire, why was there a need for this clarion call to serve? Was it window dressing to attack the attention of the non-Jew? Or was it that these values were not as universally held as historians of Australian Jewry have led their readers to believe? Why would the extent of the carnage on the various killing fields have not caused as much anguish, fear and contemplation within the Jewish community as in the population at large? Indeed, why should the bravery of Jews as a collective be considered different to that of others? As the war lengthened, so the general scepticism about it deepened.

It becomes clear that the constant declamations of loyalty, whether through editorials or rabbis' sermons, were not simply to quarantine Australian Jews from any negative fallout from the conscription issue in particular, but also to fireproof them against traditional anti-Semitic accusations. In the context of escalating war fatigue and disillusionment over the apparent never-ending bloodbath, particularly on the Western Front, the *Jewish Herald* of 16 November 1917 returned to an old theme. It reaffirmed in a most chauvinistic manner that it was the duty of Australian Jews living in 'perhaps the most democratic country in the Empire' to fight for 'the subjugation of a nation whose acts and deeds, have befouled the very name of civilisation'. Again at stake was the honour of Australian Jews, determined by the performance of Jewish soldiers in the field.

The call in the larger Jewish communities to follow the patriotic path was echoed in the smaller ones, and these included Western Australia. There, as elsewhere, the 'Yiddishers' or 'foreigners' were at one with their Anglo brethren. According to the historian of that tiny community, David Mossenson, by 1915, at least forty had enlisted and four had made the supreme sacrifice. In the context of the whole war, 180 served overseas, with forty-seven killed and an unspecified number wounded.[23]

While Eliazar Margolin was no less drawn to defend king, country and empire, it is doubtful if the prevention of anti-Semitism as such was his only motivation to enlist. He was acutely aware of it, if only because of his family's experience in Russia. At this stage, however, this was not his driving force. It is extremely unlikely that the exhortations of Jewish leaders would have affected his thinking, given his tenuous contact with the Jewish community. There is little doubt that he believed that the British Empire had to be defended against Germany. It also provided him, however, with the opportunity to fill an emotional need for an ordered and purposeful life, which he had not satisfied to date in his civilian life in Australia.

6

A True-Blue Anzac

Captain Eliazar Margolin sailed from Melbourne for overseas duties in a convoy on the *Ceramic*, along with his 4th Brigade of the 16th Battalion AIF. On board the *Ceramic* were seventy-one officers and 1,263 men.[1] They thought their destination was England, and expected further training there, to prepare them to aid British forces in Belgium and France. It was not until the flotilla reached the mouth of the Suez Canal that orders were received to disembark in Egypt and help defend the international waterway against an aggressive Turkey, which had allied itself with Germany on 29 October.[2] The men were advised of the diversion only on 28 November. They received these orders with mixed emotions.[3]

The decision to divert to Egypt was conveyed to Australia's Defence Department in Melbourne by Lord Kitchener, the Secretary of State in the British War Cabinet, on 17 November. The reason given was that there was no longer any suitable space available in England for training, but more to the point, the Australians were now needed to help bolster the number of troops in Egypt required to help defend British interests along the Suez Canal should the Turks attack.[4] Such an assault was indeed to be repelled later, in February 1915, but without Australian help.[5] Throughout their training in Egypt, the men continued to see it only as an extended stopover *en route* to Europe. Denise Winter has written that 'training in Egypt and fighting the Turks on Gallipoli seemed inexplicable to most Australians in 1915'.[6]

The *Ceramic* reached Alexandria on 1 February 1915. From there, the 4th Brigade, including Eliazar's B Company, made the hundred-mile train trip of seven hours, finally arriving in Zeitrun in Cairo. This was followed by a two-hour march to their desert camp at Heliopolis. Training recommenced in a completely new and totally strange environment.[7]

Contemporaneously, events were occurring in Palestine which, in time, were to later affect Eliazar directly, in both general and specific ways. Turkish oppression of the *Yishuv* forced many Palestinian Jews to seek temporary refuge in Egypt. Fortuitously, this provided Eliazar with the opportunity to re-establish contact with persons from the settlements of the *Yishuv* he had left behind when he decided to move to Australia. Turkey's alliance with Germany resulted in gross hardships being inflicted on the *Yishuv*, especially after its advance on the Suez Canal had been repelled. Zionist institutions were closed, some Jews were taken to prison in Damascus, others conscripted into the Turkish army or worked to death in the granite pits of Tarsus.[8] As a consequence of the Turkish entry into the war, the British placed a naval embargo on goods flowing to and from Palestine. This included the produce of Jewish settlements. Even the *Haluka* or charity from Diasporan Jewry no longer reached the various religious enclaves throughout Palestine. Great starvation and destitution resulted, exacerbated by crippling Turkish taxes and expropriation of the settlements' property and produce. By March 1915 an estimated 10,000 Jewish exiles from Palestine had reached Egypt to be ensconced, penniless and bereft of all personal belongings, in refugee camps at Gabbari and Mafruza.[9]

Unruly as the social behaviour of the Australian troops under training became – as much from boredom as disrespect for the local Egyptians – one group to whom they did endear themselves were the Jewish inmates of these camps.[10] They did this through the children. One of the exiles here, Vladimir Jabotinsky, recalled that every morning a huge wagon driven by Australian soldiers training nearby arrived to take the children in the Gabbari refugee camp for joy rides. On some occasions, an Australian officer, Captain Eliazar Margolin, would visit and converse with its inmates in rudimentary Yiddish.[11] We do not know whether any of his former comrades from Rehovot or its environs, whom he had left thirteen years earlier, were among the camp members. The likelihood is that some were.

Whether or not former acquaintances were indeed present, Eliazar did share the internees' common experiences and their desire to return to *Eretz Israel* as soon as possible. He was, however, not to know that some of them would soon be comrades in battle at Gallipoli – that campaign had yet to appear on the Australians' radar screen – and he surely could not have had an inkling that he might serve with, and perhaps even command, some of these *Yishuvniks* in

Palestine. One person on whom Eliazar made an obvious impression was Jabotinsky, who, as will be related later, convinced this Australian to take command in the Jewish Legion, which was tasked to serve in Palestine. Jabotinsky claims that the Jewish Legion was born in the Gabbari camp.[12]

The Gallipoli campaign was to prove utterly inept in its execution, and dire in its consequences for the Allied cause. Its origins lay in the historic wish of tsarist Russia that its cargoes should pass freely through the Dardanelles from ports on the Black Sea to the markets of the Near East, Africa and the Mediterranean basin. This wish was tinged with the political goal of wresting Constantinople, once the capital of Eastern Christianity, from the Ottoman Muslims for the Russian Orthodox Church. To date, Turkey and Russia had already fought three wars, with Russia's success possibly stymied by the English and French in the Crimean War of 1854–65. Incidentally, that most bloody affair originated in an intra-Christian dispute between Orthodox and Catholic monks over which of them had precedence in the control of the Holy Places in Jerusalem and Nazareth. Russia thus chafed to replace the Turkish hegemony over the Dardanelles. Russian troop advances on Berlin also had the strategic potential to relieve the pressure on the Allied forces bogged down on the Western Front by necessitating the transfer of German troops from the west to the east. Moreover, Russia threatened the British and French that if they did not help secure the complete freedom of its shipping through the Dardanelles, it would withdraw from the war.[13]

Apart from its problems on the Western Front, Great Britain had to contend with a lesser, but still worrying, situation in South Africa. The Boers, led by Christian de Wet and Jo Beyers, had rebelled. Rumour spread that Australian and New Zealand troops destined for Europe might be diverted to South Africa to lend a hand. As it happened, the insurrection was snuffed out by Generals Botha and Smuts.[14] Had Eliazar found himself in South Africa it would have been somewhat ironic, given that he had, as noted, been rejected by the British Army from volunteering for the Boer War.

London was far from pleased by Turkey's attack on the Black Sea. This in turn emboldened it to roll across the Sinai Peninsula and threaten the Suez Canal, Britain's conduit into the Indian and Pacific Oceans. British apprehension was heightened when German strategist Liman von Sanders took charge of Turkish operations in the Near East, fuelling British fears of an invasion of Egypt. British warships were deployed to scour the Aegean Sea in order to prevent any arms reinforcements and supplies from reaching Syrian ports *en route* to the Sinai.

On 18 March 1915 the British Navy engaged in an abortive exercise, which had a number of interrelated objectives. The first was to remove Turkey from the war by penetrating the Sea of Marmora to threaten Constantinople. Such an action would win the allegiance of the Balkan states, thereby removing obstacles to a move against Austria-Hungary along the Danube.[15] Further, it would ensure that Russian goods could flow freely from its southern ports. Finally, it would enhance the protection of the Suez Canal to the Indian Ocean, and safeguard the route to Australasia.[16]

It is not the purpose of this narrative to describe the entire Gallipoli campaign in detail. Nor does it seek to explore the numerous explanations as to why such a débâcle has been elevated to the status of Australia's most enduring legend.[17] Nevertheless, well before the legend of Gallipoli took hold in Australia, on the first anniversary of the Gallipoli landing. Rabbi Frances Cohen of the Great Synagogue in Sydney declared from his pulpit that: 'there they bonded and stamped the name of Australia on the page of history in glowing colours ... like the Israelites of old on this day we now celebrate as Israelites, the people of Australia ... may be stimulated by this ANZAC Day more humbly to fear the Lord as the religious instruction of His Servants ...'[18]

An editorial in Sydney's *The Jewish Standard* on 28 April 1916 supported the Rabbi's sentiments: 'We Jews have every reason to share fully in the spirit of ANZAC commemoration for among the many who lie peacefully at rest in God's acre – Gallipoli, included several sons of the community whose lives have proved the extent of the sacrifice they were not only ready to make but have actually been called on to make ... young Australians in the defence of home and hearth ...'

Eliazar Lazar Margolin was not only present throughout this now celebrated defeat, but was one of the men personally involved in executing the withdrawal. On 11 April 1915, Eliazar's 4th Brigade decamped from Cairo by train to Alexandria. There they then sailed on the *Haida Paseha*, to the Greek island of Lemnos, the population of which was approximately 40,000. On Lemnos, the Australians joined fellow Allied forces for a brief training stint, readying themselves for an imminent assault on the Gallipoli Peninsula.[19] Writing at sea on 14 April 1915, almost as an aside, Monash notes that a probable result of this campaign would be the freeing of Jerusalem and Palestine from the Turks.[20]

The 4th Brigade left Lemnos harbour on the morning of 25 April, and approached the Gallipoli Peninsula late in the afternoon.[21] Although it did not sail with the first convoy of Australian troops, it soon saw action. Unfortunately, the vast military and naval build-up on the islands of Lemnos and Mudros had alerted the Turks to a probable invasion. As a consequence, the Turks fortified their defences on both sides of the straits in readiness for an attack that seemed imminent.

Allied forces, under the overall command of the British general, Sir Ian Hamilton, attempted to forge a path through the Dardanelles. Orders were for the attacking Australians and New Zealand troops, or Anzacs, as they soon became collectively known, to land on the west coast of the Gallipoli Peninsula, just north of Gaba Tepa. They met withering enemy fire even before they landed. First, the 16th Battalion's 3rd Brigade went into action, very soon followed by the 4th.[22]

Monash has recorded the terrible and terrifying scenes of the Australian landings on 25 April, in which many of his officers and men were slaughtered or severely wounded. During the first ten days of the carnage, the wounded were shipped back to Lemnos, Alexandria and Malta for treatment. Many died *en route*.[23] On 20 May 1915, just over three weeks after landing, Monash estimated that his own brigades took 2,300 casualties, with at least 300 dead.[24] As was common throughout this gory campaign, the enormous loss of officers necessitated the promotion of many men in the field. By 7 June only thirty-three of the 132 officers who had departed the Antipodes with Monash were left.[25] On 5 May 1915, Eliazar Margolin was promoted from captain to major, taking the place of Major E. K. Baker, who had been invalided back to Australia.[26]

The preparedness of the Turkish forces was not the only hazard facing the Allied forces. Their training in a desert clime in Egypt was completely inadequate to meet the hostile environment – both geomorphic and climatic – they were forced to endure throughout the campaign. To make matters worse, their supporting artillery was poor and often ill directed, and the sheer dimensions of the casualties completely overwhelmed medical logistics.[27] With death looming at every moment, Margolin was fortunate to survive. Of these survivors, many were wounded, but not badly enough to leave the line. Eliazar himself took a bullet wound in the upper arm on 2 May, but remained at his post.[28] At the battle for Quinn's Post, his life was miraculously saved by a notebook in his top pocket, which intercepted a bullet and prevented its deeper penetration.[29]

The records of C. E. W. Bean, Australia's official war correspondent at Gallipoli, specifically mention Eliazar Margolin on two occasions in respect of the abortive battle for Quinn's Post. The first is on 9–10 May, and the second on the twenty-ninth of that month.[30] Men not only suffered injury, they were debilitated by monumental battle fatigue and exhaustion. The campaign was a battle for hills surveying valleys. At the battle around Hill 60 on 27 August, Eliazar, along with three hundred men from the 16th Battalion, gave support to their brother the 15th, which was under unrelenting bombardment by Turkish guns. Their task was to hold the trenches, and provide covering fire for the assault on the enemy entrenched on the way to Sari Blair. By 28 August his men numbered only 185, with gunfire and the hellish physical conditions having driven them to complete exhaustion.[31]

As in other units, attrition in the 16th escalated as the physical conditions forced on the men left them utterly exhausted. Major Eliazar Margolin was appointed second-in-command to the leader of the 16th, Lieutenant-Colonel Pope.[32] He took command temporarily on 18 September 1915, when his leader, gravely ill, was transferred back to Egypt.[33] On 13 September, the men of the 4th Brigade, along with others, were permitted a month's rest leave on the island of Lemnos.[34] While there, on 21 September, the 4th Brigade was addressed at the Sapri Camp, Mudros West, by the divisional commander, Major-General Sir A. J. Godley:

> on the night of August 6, you executed a night march and night assault, which if possible, added still more to the reputation of the Brigade. Again in the assault upon Addel Rahman Blair, and in the capture of Kaiajik Aghala, this Brigade achieved a series of magnificent successes, and did all and more than could have been expected of it or any other brigade with such tasks set before it ... I am sorry to find you so reduced in numbers ... glad you have been afforded the opportunity to refit, and rest, and restore yourselves for the final effort ...[35]

Eliazar's leave took him back to Alexandria, in Egypt, where he enjoyed recreation with some of his fellow officers, including Monash.[36]

Allied forces had held their ground on the Aegean Sea at Anzac

Cove from May to August 1915, and at Souvla Bay until they were fully evacuated in December 1915. Elsewhere, however, the severely troubled Gallipoli campaign had utterly failed to deliver any benefit to the Allied cause. Eventually, after personal inspection in mid-November 1915, Lord Kitchener called for the front's evacuation. According to Jeffrey Grey, 26,111 Australians served in the Mediterranean Expeditionary Force, with '362 officers and 7,779 men killed in action, died of wounds or succumbed to disease'.[37] When the call to withdraw came, the 16th Battalion had been reduced to a mere 200 men. It boasted that for every casualty it took, it inflicted five on the Turks.[38]

The now celebrated evacuation of 40,000 men from the shores of Gallipoli was conducted over three days: 18, 19 and 20 December 1915. The last group, on the twentieth, comprising 815 men, was split into three groups or 'echelons'. They decamped from Gallipoli, two groups leaving at 6 p.m. and 10 p.m., with the third very early the next day at 2 a.m. Monash mentions in his letters that:

> The last 170, or 'the die-hards', have been chosen from the most gallant and capable men in the brigade. Even those will not leave the trenches in a bunch, but a few of the most daring men, who are good athletes, will remain in the front trenches and keep up the fire for another number of minutes, and then make the beach at the best possible speed. I am myself going to be in the first group of the last 170, as by that time the die will be cast, and I can do no good waiting for the last small handful ...[39]

What he fails to say is that he chose Eliazar Margolin as one of those 'die-hards', to supervise the third, and hence potentially the most endangered, of these echelons. Though later Monash was to call Eliazar his friend, Margolin's name appears in his records only in the context of honours won by the 4th Brigade,[40] and he portrays his own supervisory role of the grand evacuation in self-congratulatory tones.[41] Although Monash justly rose to the heights of command, commentators suggest he was rarely self-effacing. Orders for the evacuation were received by him on 8 December 1915.

The 'C' or third echelon was to comprise four officers and eighty-seven men. In contradistinction to the bloody campaign that preceded it, and the fear that the retreating men would be attacked, the casualty count for the whole evacuation was only two men. These two casualties were not caused by Turkish fire. Captain C. Longmore in his book, *Carry On: The Traditions of the A.I.F.*, described the situation:

> On the final night at dusk, the first of the three echelons into which the rearguard had been divided, left the beach. About 10 p.m. the second group moved, leaving the third echelon. A thin line from post to post, firing rifles and keeping up as far as possible the signs of normal activity. This last party consisted of officers and men chosen from those who had taken part in the Landing some eight months before. At about midnight this third echelon began to withdraw. Those furthest from the beach, first Lone Pine, Pope's Hill, Quinn's and Courtney's, were in succession abandoned, and shortly after 3 a.m. on December 20 Russell's top, the last sector, was evacuated. Down the beach, through the silent trenches, won and dug with blood and sweat – every last yard of them touching some bitter chord of memory – move the last ANZACS into the launches and lighters, and thence to the warships waiting out in the gloom. At 4 a.m. the last boatload pushed off and the Evacuation of the ANZACS was an accomplished and bloodless fact ...[42]

Jeffrey Grey has said that those Australian citizen officers who had volunteered for overseas duty were a mixed bag when it came to ability. On Gallipoli, Captain (then Major) Eliazar Lazar Margolin was to prove – under the most adverse conditions and circumstances – that he was extremely able. He himself would have recognized that, however brave and resourceful a soldier he might have been, survival at Gallipoli was a matter of luck. Nevertheless, his efforts were officially recognized by the authorities. He was awarded the Distinguished Service Order (DSO) promulgated in the *Commonwealth of Australia Gazette* No. 129 of 21 September 1916, and was again mentioned, this time in despatches No. 176 on 30 November, 'for distinguished and gallant service' in the same year.[43]

Those who had served by his side considered him a highly disciplined officer, generally taciturn, but quick to anger when something went wrong, or some injustice had occurred. One attribute shining through, however, was his constant concern for the welfare of his men, however difficult the circumstances. He spoke English with a heavy Russian accent, but his knowledge of Arabic, gained during his years in Palestine, was said to have proved an asset in the field.

One puzzling matter arising out of Eliazar's Gallipoli sojourn was whether at any time he had made contact with the Zion Mule Corps and its non-Jewish commander, Colonel Patterson DSO. This is of particular interest not only because among members of this corps were 500 *émigrés* from Ottoman Palestine via Egypt, but also because this corps was to form the nucleus of the Jewish Legion in which Eliazar would be a commander, as would Patterson. The Zion Mule Corps served with distinction as a logistic unit virtually throughout the Gallipoli campaign.[44] It was organized by Vladimir Jabotinsky and the Russian-born Yosef Trumpeldor, the latter not only a hero of the Russo-Japanese War of 1904, but a man who soon became a legend in Zionist history.[45] The corps was the first all-Jewish military unit to be organized since the time of the Bar Kokhba's revolt against the Romans in Palestine. Though it was initially hoped that its purpose would be to defend the *Yishuv*, because of great opposition in England, including that of the established leadership of its Jewish community, it was agreed that its destination would be Gallipoli, not as a combat but as a labour unit. In its British colours, like the Anzacs, it came to the theatre of war under the overall generalship of Sir Ian Hamilton, commander of British forces in the Mediterranean.

Patterson's own book, *With the Zionists in Gallipoli*, does not mention Eliazar Margolin, and there is no direct evidence that they ever met in that theatre. There is also a question mark over whether or not the paths of Eliazar and at least some members of the corps also crossed. As has been noted, during his initial training in Egypt before leaving for Gallipoli, Eliazar had visited the refugee camps from which men of the corps had been recruited. Whether or not they actually served together in the heat of battle, he could not have been ignorant of their presence on Gallipoli.

The Jewish chaplain to the Australian forces in Egypt was the Reverend David Isaac Freedman, the Rabbi of the Perth Hebrew Congregation. In a letter back to Australia from the Gallipoli campaign, he described the evacuation as 'a splendid achievement in the way it was carried out'. He also tells of Hebrew-speaking soldiers from the Zion Mule Corps attending his religious services on the Jewish Sabbath.[46] Eliazar is never mentioned at these services. It is unlikely he would have attended even had he had the opportunity to do so. Although Freedman had been the Rabbi of the Perth Hebrew Congregation when Eliazar arrived in Australia until the time he left for war, Eliazar, as has been said, was not drawn to attend religious services. At best Freedman might have known Margolin merely as a soldier of the Jewish faith, who might have required his religious attention at some time. Only once do Freedman's letters mention Eliazar, but not in a tone which exuded friendship or the sense of familiarity. In a letter sent back to Australia, he writes: 'I am pleased to find how well people speak of him (viz. Monash) and other Jewish officers ... Margolin too, is making good, and he enjoys the complete confidence of his men. On more than one occasion he has been given a post of honour, which was the post of the greatest danger.'[47]

What Freedman does mention is that the Australian soldiers in Egypt were unsettled by 'the new movement of the Australian army'. This was a reference to the reorganization of the force in Egypt following its Gallipoli experience. Eliazar was given a hand in this reorganization, refurbishment and necessary expansion.[48] With the departure of Colonel Pope, the new commander of the 16th Battalion was Lieutenant-Colonel E. A. Drake Brockman, soon elevated in rank to brigadier-general. When the restored 16th left Egypt for France to fight against the Germans there, Eliazar Margolin, now a senior major, went as second-in-charge to Drake Brockman.

As with the Gallipoli campaign, the plotting of battle lines on the carnivorous Western Front will be left to others who have done it more thoroughly. With fellow 'diggers of the renovated 16th Battalion', Eliazar fought all its bitter engagements until the Battle of Hamel. Bean notes his role in the 29–30 August 1916 attack on Mouquet Farm.[49] From June to September 1917 he temporarily left the 16th to command the 14th Battalion in Belgium with the field rank of lieutenant-colonel. His reputation among the soldiers was of one of being able to avoid bullets, as if death always ran away from him. Nevertheless, he was wounded on three occasions, but always refused to leave the battlefield.

In August 1917 he took leave in Paris, then returned to the 16th.[50] The early days of the Passchendael encounter saw him debilitated by a severe injury to a knee cartilage which forced him reluctantly to quit the front. On 23 September 1917, he left for London at his own expense to be cared for at a private hospital, where he knew he would receive the best treatment. His goal was a quick recovery and then an immediate return to the 16th Battalion in France. Unfortunately for him, the army authorities were of a different mind. The operation on his knee and the subsequent convalescence at the Australian Convalescent Home, Cobham, in Kent, went well, but Australian military headquarters in Great Britain stubbornly refused him – aged forty-two – permission to return to active duty.[51]

This decision was not acceptable to Eliazar. Under no circumstances was he prepared to vegetate, doing light duties behind an Australian military desk; it was simply not his style. What he passionately wanted was a posting that would utilize his assets as he saw them: those of an active soldier, who spoke Russian and knew the ways of the peoples of Palestine, both Jewish and Arab.[52] Such a place might well have been found for him with the Australian forces, then actively engaged in the Middle East campaign, but his military superiors were not convinced. The attitude of the general officer commanding the AIF stationed in England was one of great admiration for his military record, and sympathy for his desire for active duty. Nevertheless, on 12 December 1917 the AIF officially determined against his serving on any front. No family or occupation beckoned him to return to Australia. Rather, he felt himself wired for the military life, to which he had completely committed himself for the past three years.

A fortuitous meeting took place during his convalescence in hospital. Vladimir Jabotinsky, the Zionist nationalist activist and ex-member of the Zion Mule Corps, unexpectedly came to visit with a specific purpose: to convince Eliazar to take a commanding role in the nascent all-Jewish battalions, which later came to be known collectively as the Jewish Legion. He and Colonel Patterson were then attempting to form the first of these in England, to serve exclusively as a unit of the British Army in Palestine.

At first, as Jabotinsky has recalled, Eliazar hesitated joining an all-Jewish battalion because one would have 'to talk too much'.[53] More daunting than this tongue-in-cheek response, however, would have been his reluctance to leave his 16th Battalion and the bureaucratic hurdles involved in a transfer from the Australian to the British Army. Given their refusal to return him to active duty, the Australian military authorities might not sanction such a move. On the other hand, Jabotinsky's offer was the only one on the table that would prolong his active military career, and also facilitate his return to *Eretz Israel*. A bonus was that he, as an Australian – albeit in a British uniform – would once more be associated with the AIF, with the hope of defeating the German-influenced Turks, and thereby conclude unfinished business begun in Gallipoli. Of course, he would also play a role in lifting the hated Turkish boot from the neck of the *Yishuv*. Switching to the British Army would not have benefited him financially for the daily pay of an Australian soldier was far higher than that of his British counterpart.

Margolin's transfer from the AIF to the British Army was not a simple matter. During the war, secondment was not unusual, but not in Eliazar's case. If he wished to become a British officer, he had first to resign his commission in the AIF, which was adamantly unwilling to shoulder any future financial burden that Eliazar's service in another army might incur. His age and previous medical condition may have been telling. The authorities even balked at paying his return fare from London to Perth. Indeed, they declared that under Australia's War Pension Act, he was entitled only to money already owing him, and that came to a mere two hundred pounds.[54] All these matters notwithstanding, Eliazar took the plunge and resigned his commission in the AIF.

An all-Jewish unit known as the 38th Battalion of the British Royal Fusiliers had been formed under Colonel Patterson and had begun training. Very soon, another such corps was to follow suit, the 39th Battalion commanded by Eliazar Margolin with the confirmed rank of lieutenant-colonel.

7

The Jewsiliers

One might have thought that news of an Australian Jew leading an all-Jewish militia destined for *Eretz Israel*, and in British colours to boot, would have been received by the Jewish community down under with at least some curiosity, if not with great enthusiasm. This was not so. At least three factors militated against such a response. The first was the negative attitude of established Jewry in Great Britain to the all-Jewish battalions, nicknamed in some quarters as the 'Jewsiliers', a contraction of 'Jewish' and 'fusiliers'. There were significant differences in character and temperament between the 'motherland' English Jewry and its branch offices in Australia because of their unique histories and existential circumstances. Nevertheless, the antipodean communities generally followed the religious rulings of the Chief Rabbi of the British Empire in Great Britain, and the judgement of British Jewry's leaders of the mother Jewry head-quartered in London, regarding Jewish matters worldwide. Hence, the opposition of English Jewry to the Jewish Legion resonated in Jewish leadership circles in Australia. A priori, then, in these circles it is unlikely that Eliazar's new appointment would have been a cause to celebrate.

Much reportage in Australia's mainstream press of world events at the time was cycled through London, and thus became impregnated with British perceptions. Undoubtedly, an Australian leading an all-Jewish militia was, at best, of minor interest. Similarly, Australia's Jewish communal press relied heavily for its news of the Jewish world, including that of Great Britain, on British sources, particularly the *Jewish Chronicle*. This paper was aimed primarily at its local readership and Australian Jewish matters were of only peripheral interest. British eyes saw Eliazar Margolin as a soldier in the British Army rather than as an Australian, and thus not worthy of exceptional comment. As with the Jewish Legion, an often extensive time lag existed between the appearance of a report in the *Jewish Chronicle* and its resurfacing in some form in the Australian communal press.

Finally, one must query whether Australian Jews would have shown any interest at all in the formation of the Jewish Legion, which geographically – and even emotionally – hardly touched their lives. Their attention was firmly focused on the day-to-day concerns of the local war effort. Given that the Australian Light Horse was already in action in Palestine, the prospect of all-Jewish battalions serving there was hardly exciting news. There was also an absence of Zionist sentiment. These could have been contributing reasons for the silence of the Australian Jewish press over Eliazar's appointment. His name was omitted even in the *Jewish Herald*, whose own banner cried loudly that it was Australia's prime conduit of Zionist information.

A reader of the Jewish press, with Sydney's *Hebrew Standard* the exception, might have been given the impression that there was much energetic Zionist activity in Australia. Stringers from communities around Australia fed constant reports to the communal press in Sydney and Melbourne. There were articles exploring Zionism overseas, discussion of the different Zionist ideologies and copy on their principal spokesmen. Certainly, the dire circumstances of the *Yishuv* under the Turks was a frequently aired topic. Nevertheless, any suggestion that implied political Zionism in Australia was healthy and active would have been a product of smoke and mirrors. The fact was that the consciousness of the vast majority of Australian Jews was not touched by Zionism, except as religious sentiment. When it did attract some, action was more in terms of charity, of helping their unfortunate brethren suffering in *Eretz Israel*. As ideology, Zionism, of whatever kind, was not a movement with general appeal. Even in Western Australia, where Reverend Freedman led, arguably, the most active Zionist association in the nation prior to his leaving for an overseas stint as chaplain to the AIF, 'more stressing issues' tended to take precedence.[1]

Alan Crown provides two potent reasons for this lack of enthusiasm for Zionism. He notes that both before and following the First World War, Australian Jews feared being stigmatized as a people with dual loyalty. Support for Zionism might have been interpreted as evidence that the Jews' national affiliation lay elsewhere: in Palestine. Moreover, the German Jews' influence in the European Zionist movement made Zionism extremely problematic when Germany became the enemy of the British Empire.[2]

If anything were to prove the litmus test of the strength of Zionism in Australia, it was a certain letter, dated 2 November 1917, and signed by Arthur James Balfour, sent from the British Foreign Office to Lord Rothschild, better known as the Balfour Declaration. It signalled Great Britain's willingness to support the establishment of a Jewish homeland in Palestine under certain conditions.[3] On the face of it, such news should have been received with great rejoicing by Australian Jewry, but this was not the case. In explanation, at least three reasons can be offered. The revelation came in the midst of war, and therefore its impact was smaller than it might otherwise have been. Second, there was much ambivalence within the British Jewry leadership over the very establishment of a Jewish homeland. Third, the declaration, as such, was only a matter of intent, a goal for the future, when conditions might be fortuitous. As yet, British forces still had to redeem the Holy Land from the Turks. On the other hand, at least potentially, here was something that could turn hundreds of years of Jewish religious dreaming into a reality. That alone should have been worth celebrating. What is certain is that if the Balfour Declaration were not enough cause for rejoicing, the formation of a Jewish Legion for Palestine already in train, and helped and led by an Australian Jew, would not have been either.

At best, the declaration provided the circumstances that allowed for a slight lessening of the anti-Zionist feeling among the Anglo-Jewish leadership of Australia. For if the British government was now prepared to help establish an autonomous Jewish enclave in Palestine, these ideas did not appear as seditious as before. Nevertheless, defence mechanisms remained on total alert. A voice of Anglo-Jewry, Sydney's *Hebrew Standard*, was at pains to stress that the aims of Zionism envisioned by the Balfour Declaration would not in any way deleteriously affect the standing of other communities in Palestine, nor other Jewish communities in the Diaspora. On the contrary, it promoted justice for all. It cautioned that:

> On the face of it, the only confusion it offers is a sympathetic approval of this provision of facilities for a settlement of Jews on equal terms with others. The principal drawback to such accomplishment under the old regime was that it depended for its success on the continuous goodwill of the Turkish government. Settlement of the land for a greater part, is the ambition of the Jewish immigration to Palestine and he may be pardoned for hesitating to sink his savings in the soil without guarantees that he should be driven out by the ruling powers.

The salient factor of the new position is one of importance of which cannot be underestimated in this connection, is that the threat to the Jewish colony in Palestine would be guaranteed by the British Government. And since this discussion is hardly likely to have been reached without reference to the opinion of the Allies it is a fair assumption that the project will have their moral support; if not their indirect support as well.[4]

In a later edition, this same communal weekly was to declare that while the Balfour Declaration may well have surprised the Jewish masses worldwide, the British sponsorship of Zionist aspirations in Palestine 'had been intelligently anticipated by the leaders of Jewish organisations for some time'. Without stating its source, it alleged that two years earlier, the attitude of the British government had been unofficially known to Zionist leaders in London.[5]

A member of the Melbourne Jewish community, Hyman Bernard Raises, wrote to the Melbourne edition of the *Jewish Herald* on 22 February 1918, pondering the reasons for the lack of celebration of the Balfour Declaration in Melbourne. Although he referred specifically to Victoria's Jewry, he might as well have been speaking for all the Australian communities. He asked:

Why has not a meeting of Melbourne Jews been called to thank the British Government for its generous gift? Why are our leaders so unmoved by this good fortune that has come upon the Jewish nation? Why are our spiritual and communal leaders so silent upon this most important of questions? Are there outside organisations that compel them to say and act as they please? Or are they indifferent as to whether there be a Jewish State or not? ... I can understand why some materialistic men oppose the establishment of a Jewish State in Palestine, but why the great, intellectually important sections of Jewish people in Melbourne remain outside the ranks of Zionism is to me – and I am sure to many – a great puzzling mystery ...

The *Jewish Herald*, the self-proclaimed Zionists' friend, blamed the growing assimilation and secularization tendencies of the community, and claimed that, along with their Gentile friends, Australian Jews were caught: 'in the material advancement and commercial progress of a young and vigorous offshoot of Britain ... Jewish sentiment, the national pride of race, even the bloody story of Israel's centuries of martyrdom, find no stirring response in the breast of the average Australian ... [including] Jews ...'.[6] It added that assimilation had blunted specific Jewish sensibilities. No longer was there enough Jewish learning to appreciate the historic, and therefore momentous nature of the Balfour Declaration.[7] Not everyone, however, was devoid of such responsiveness. Journalist, author and later communal leader, Nathan Frederick Spielvogel, felt that the declaration was an epiphany, and expressed this in the poem he published in the *Jewish Herald* in 1918, entitled 'Zion Wakes':

For twenty bloodstained centuries,
We suffered scorn and blame.
The Cross, the Crescent cut our hearts,
Our soul, they could not tame.
Through twenty centuries of hate
We hoped. And hoped, our fate.

For twenty savage centuries,
Our name was but a jeer.
A bloody shamble was our home,
Our life – one long drawn fear.
Through twenty centuries of gall
We hoped. And hoped, our all.

For twenty callous centuries,
We wrote our scorner's songs.
We richened lands that harried us,
We righted others' wrongs,
Through twenty centuries of strife
We hoped. And hoped, our life.

For twenty stubborn centuries,
We held fast to our way.
For freedom and foes were even ours,
That foe is ours today.
For twenty centuries of wrong
We hoped. Oh God! How long!

Up Jewry! Up! The centuries
Of hope draw nigh their end –
The souls of myriad murdered Jews
The clarion, message send,
Let not the tyrant foe remain!
Then Zion lives again.[8]

The silence over Eliazar Margolin's prominent role was undoubtedly derived from British Jewry's attitude as relayed to Australia.
There was, however, another likely factor, though whether it was a
conscious act, or thoroughly inadvertent, is a moot point. It stemmed
from the Anglo–foreign divide that affected most local Jewish communities. A hint of it comes in a comment of Chaplain Rev. Freedman
speaking of a badly wounded Australian Jewish soldier he encountered
in France. This person, not named, belonged to a unit that was 'half
West Australian and the other half South Australian'. Originally, this
would certainly have described Eliazar's very own 16th Battalion's
4th. Freedman said: 'his face was grimy with shell smoke. His left
eye was filled with blood, and his right eye dimmed. He thought
that for him there would be no more fighting. I saw him a fortnight
later seemingly well recovered, and the main question he wanted
answered was when he would be permitted to get back to the front
line. He is a Russian Jew.'[9] The telling point here is the portrayal
of the soldier as a 'Russian Jew'. The question arises whether there
was a need to categorize him in this way, given that all Jewish recruits
had to be Australian citizens, even if by naturalization. There was
no difference in attitude towards the war between the foreign-born
and the dominant Anglo sections of the communities, and like Eliazar,
a number of the former had volunteered for overseas duty. It is possible that Freedman's emphasis was indeed to make this point, to
highlight a difference between the response in Australia in comparison with that in Great Britain. On the other hand, there did
exist social and religious friction between the two groups. Indeed,
Freedman himself, who was Rabbi of that bastion of Anglo-Jewry,
the Perth Hebrew Congregation, was hardly a favourite of the
'foreigners'. This was so despite the fact that they, especially those
direct from Eastern Europe – were the backbone of his Zionist
Association in Perth.[10]

Opposition to the Jewish Legion among the leaders of British
Jewry was influenced by a handful of connected matters. The first
was the unwillingness of East European Jewish *émigrés* in Great
Britain to enlist in the British Army. An acute sensitivity also existed
over the wisdom of having an exclusively Jewish battalion that might
recharge existing levels of anti-Semitism. There were concerns over
how an all-Jewish unit might affect the way Jews were treated in
other units. And foremost, it was feared, especially among the most
assimilated within British Jewry, that the existence of this special
separate unit might arouse antagonism which, in turn, might under-

mine their position in society. In places like London, Leeds and
Manchester, they felt extremely uneasy in the presence of *émigré*
Jews who dressed, spoke and prayed differently, and refused, for
genuine reasons, to enlist in the regular forces. This apparent shirking
of duty was particularly galling, especially at a time when the Allies
were faring so poorly on the Western Front, and replacements there
were sorely needed. This situation had its resonance in Australia.
The *Jewish Herald* explained:

> There are very few indeed, who would not admit to the role played
> by the Jews in the war as a distinctively honourable one. Still it would
> be foolish to flatter ourselves with the idea that our denomination,
> no more than others, is without its proportion of shirkers and
> invertebrates. It is true that no one would dream of charging any
> other group as a whole with the failings of a few among its number
> ... the reputation of the Jewish race in its entirety is habitually attacked
> by rumours of its quota of undesirables.[11]

Many of the *émigrés* in England refused to enlist while Russia
remained Great Britain's ally in the war. Why, they felt, should they
fight alongside a country from whose oppression they had so recently
escaped? The general point made by the *Jewish Herald* to its local
bailiwick was that those who enjoyed 'free citizenship of the British
Empire' should pay for that luxury, particularly at a time when that
self-same empire was fighting for its existence.[12]

Apprehension about the Jewish Legion was also caused by anxiety
over whether the motley crew of *émigré* Jews who would form it
would diminish the standing of Jewish soldiers in the eyes of Gentiles.
There was concern that no fuel should be provided to those anti-
Semites too ready to call Jews shirkers, war profiteers and genetically
disinclined to soldiering.[13] It was felt that no amount of argument
would lay these canards to rest. Their absurdities had to be demonstrated by actions.

In Australia, this desire was manifest in at least two ways. The
first was as a rationale for calling up every Jew of eligible age. Those
previously rejected by the army were cajoled to try again. It was
not the case that Jews *should* enlist, but that they *must* enlist, and
when they did, they should not conceal their religion from the
military authorities. With the second national plebiscite in 1917 over
conscription in mind, an editorial in the *Jewish Herald* asserted that
refusal to enlist was morally reprehensible.[14] If anti-Semitism existed

in the rank and file of the British Army, it was asserted that this was not the case in the Australian forces, where Jewish–Christian relations were said to be excellent. Obviously, there was a perceived problem in this regard, for some Jewish enlistees felt that disclosure of their religious identity might prove troublesome.

Chaplain Freedman saw the reason for this concealment, apart from simple ignorance, as a means of avoiding loneliness by adopting, if only nominally, the faith of the majority. A few indicated that they were adherents of the Church of England before being sent to Gallipoli, out of fear of how they might be treated as prisoners of war by the Islamic Turks should their Jewishness become known.[15] For the early Jewish enlistees such a claim was surely an excuse, for they did not know they were to be sent to Gallipoli before they left Australia's shores, although fear of the Turk might have taken root via rumours circulating in Australia of the mutilation of Jews in Palestine who had been taken prisoner by their Ottoman rulers.

It has to be said that no research into the degree of anti-Semitism in the ranks of the AIF has been undertaken. One knows, however, that the successes of John Monash on the Western Front did not exempt him from such prejudice.[16]

This concern that Jews perform at least as heroically as their non-Jewish brothers was undoubtedly the rationale for the post-war publication (in 1922) of the *British Jewry Book of Honour*. A consistent theme of its contributors, both Jewish and non-Jewish, was how well Jews in the collective British forces performed in battle defending king, country and empire. Praise that had been previously absent was also heaped on the Jewish Legion, including Margolin.[17] The fact that there were articles on the Jewish Legion by Vladimir Jabotinsky, and H. Wolfensohn on its Palestinian Battalion, illustrates the degree to which the old hostility towards the formation of distinct Jewish forces had abated by 1922. The implied message was that these Jewish soldiers, representing Jews throughout the British Empire, had proved that they were among its most worthy citizens. It was patently clear that the subtext of most of these writers was the hope that for once and for all times, anti-Semitic accusations of Jews being social parasites, economic bloodsuckers and cultural pariahs could be put to rest.[18] The Chief Rabbi of the British Empire, J. H. Hertz, speaking of his geographically dispersed religious constituency, claimed: 'The permanent record of the part played by Anglo-Jewry in the Great War will help the lovers of Truth in the warfare against the malicious slander that the Jew shrinks from sacrifice demanded of every loyal citizen in the hour of national danger.'[19]

That said, such optimism did not accompany the establishment of the all-Jewish battalions. From all accounts, Eliazar Margolin was always acutely aware of anti-Semitic smears. No doubt he had confronted them growing up in Russia. If only for this reason, he demanded that the crew he took charge of, which became the 39th British Royal Fusiliers, should perform to the highest standards of soldiering possible. He wanted their deeds to bring credit to the Jewish people.

8

The Origin of an Idea

In 1914, two young Zionist leaders, David Ben-Gurion and Yitzhak Ben-Zvi, each later to become prime minister of the State of Israel, attempted to convince the commander of the Ottoman forces in Palestine to raise a Jewish military contingent to help defend *Eretz Israel*. Some forty volunteers began training, but authorization was soon cancelled.[1] When Turkey entered the Great War on Germany's side, it viciously oppressed the *Yishuv*. It is estimated that 18,000 Jews were expelled, 12,000 to Egypt, the majority of whom ended up, as we already know, in the refugee camps of Gabbari and Mafruza.[2] Ironically, among those expelled were Ben-Gurion and Ben-Zvi. A few Jews sought Turkish citizenship in the mistaken hope that it would cocoon them from harm. Others were dragooned into the abominable conditions of the Turkish Army. Jewish schools, Zionist institutions and the Anglo-Palestine Bank were closed. Supplies were commandeered from the settlements, leaving their inhabitants to starve. Food kitchens were opened in Jaffa and Tel Aviv. One consequence was that 500 of the refugees in Egypt volunteered for the all-Jewish Zion Mule Corps, which served not in Palestine, as the men had wished, but on Gallipoli.[3]

Who was the actual proponent of the idea of a Jewish battalion within the British Army still remains an open question. One Israeli scholar, Mattityahu Mintz, has queried the commonly accepted view that it was Vladimir Jabotinsky. This is because such a claim rests squarely on Jabotinsky's own writings.[4] Mintz says that it was Pinchas Ruttenberg who also convinced Jabotinsky that Yosef Trumpeldor was doing the right thing, not only in mobilizing the Zion Mule Corps, but having it serve according to the demands of the war. Jabotinsky wanted the militia solely for Palestine. General Maxwell, however, the commander of the British forces in Egypt, was not convinced. He doubted the value of any Allied offensive in

Palestine, and questioned whether this proposed Jewish militia might easily assimilate into the British Army as a fighting force.[5] At first Jabotinsky rejected the notion that, instead of a fighting force, the Jewish group should serve as a mule corps service team somewhere on the Turkish front. With prescience, Trumpeldor held the view that the path from Gallipoli would ultimately lead to Palestine.[6]

With the Gallipoli fiasco over, the lobby to form an all-Jewish militia for Palestine was divided between Ruttenberg and Jabotinsky, with the former active in both Europe and the United States of America.[7] Jabotinsky soon became regarded by Ben-Gurion and Ben-Zvi as perhaps their greatest Zionist ideological competitor, but at least in one crucial matter he triumphed over them. They had initially wanted a Jewish army under the Turks while he was averse to it, favouring the British. Because of this, it is ironic that both Ben-Gurion and Ben-Zvi were destined to enlist in Eliazar Margolin's 39th Battalion of the British Royal Fusiliers while promoting the Zionist cause in the United States of America.

Whether or not Jabotinsky first conceived the notion of a Jewish Legion, as he might have claimed, the fact is that he enticed Eliazar Margolin to join it. Already, the first of the Jewish battalions, the 38th Battalion of the British Royal Fusiliers, had begun training under veteran Zion Mule Corps commander, Lieutenant-Colonel John Patterson. While Margolin and Patterson might not have met up in Gallipoli, they were now inevitably to be associated in the Jewish Legion in Palestine. It was a relationship that could be described only as frosty. They were men of different natures, background, culture, education and training, who saw their own role in Palestine in totally different terms. Possibly the only thing they might have had in common was that they were both commanders in the Jewish Legion.

Doubt has been cast upon Patterson's motivation for wanting to lead all-Jewish forces such as the Zion Mule Corps and, subsequently, the 38th Battalion of the British Royal Fusiliers.[8] It has generally been accepted that there was a goodly degree of philo-Semitism involved. He was well schooled in the detail of the Christian Bible since his youth. According to Patterson himself, his interest in Jewish customs and the Bible, along with its associated texts and religious practices, developed in the late nineteenth century while he was living in British East Africa.[9] He never disclosed, however, what initially sparked his curiosity in such matters. One might speculate that it was influenced by a Christian Protestant notion that he ought to help Jews return to the Holy Land as a necessary precondition for the Second Coming of the Christian Messiah. That said, when he took command of the Zion Mule Corps, he had no knowledge that in only a very few years a remnant of the corps would form the nucleus of the first of the Jewish battalions to serve in Palestine, and that he would take charge of them. In British East Africa, Patterson had been involved in infrastructural projects such as bridge building and railway construction. He also wrote two books, *The Maneater of Tsavo* and *In the Grip of the Nyika*. During South Africa's Boer War of 1899–1902, Patterson commanded a British battalion of the Imperial Yeomanry.

He himself suggests that the reason for his being chosen to lead the Zion Mule Corps was a matter of chance. He just happened to be in the right place at the right time – in Cairo – when General Maxwell asked him to take charge. Another interpretation of what actually happened suggests that it was the only post on offer for him.[10] Whatever the truth, it is unlikely that many other British officers would have willingly welcomed command of an untried all-Jewish crew. Patterson said:

> I felt deeply interested in the race, and I steadfastly accepted this offer ... I felt it extraordinary that I, who used, as a boy, to read about Job and the Captains of the people of Israel, should become a captain of a little group of that people myself. I realised that it was the first time in 2000 years that a Jewish military united existed and I was pleased to emphasise this remarkable historical event.[11]

Once the Gallipoli adventure with the Zion Mule Corps was over, he was reassigned to Ireland to command the Dublin Fusiliers.

The relationship between the first of the Jewish battalions under Patterson, and the second, led by Margolin, was rather cool.[12] Patterson was always at a loss to understand why, later, in Palestine, he and Eliazar Margolin did not become staunch friends. They were, however, men of different personality, temperament and ideological outlook. Both may have been Zionists, but their Zionisms were completely different. Patterson's version was religiously inspired, and was of neither a practical nor a political nature. He had no desire to live in or personally help the development of the *Yishuv*. That was for the Jews. Eliazar's perspective was terrestrially rooted, and was developed from experience working in the Holy Land itself. All this notwithstanding, Patterson's role has a special niche in *Yishuv* history, particularly in terms of the early developments of a Jewish defence force in Palestine.

The establishment of the Zion Mule Corps, and a few years later, the Jewish Legion, was met with great hostility not just from England's Jewish establishment, but also – initially – the Zionist movement. Singing the tune of the motherland, a *Hebrew Standard* editorial reminded readers that what was at stake for Australian Jews, whether local or foreign-born, was the dominance of the national over any sectarian interests. In Napoleon's terms, it affirmed that Anglo-Jews were 'Englishmen first – Jews after'.[13]

Episode Two

9

Realpolitik

It was certainly true that Jabotinsky's invitation provided Eliazar Margolin with perhaps the only opportunity to continue to utilize his talents in the way and in the place of his choosing. It was a particular confluence of historical, military, political and, arguably, meta - physical influences, however, that permitted the establishment of the Jewish Legion in the first instance. These created the same mindset that produced Arthur James Balfour's famous letter of 2 November 1917. Sent to Lionel Walter – the second Lord Rothschild – of the English Zionist Federation, it established Great Britain's parameters of support for a Jewish homeland in Palestine.[1] A major difference was that while the Balfour Declaration was the product of Zionist lobbying, the Jewish Legion initially lacked this backing. After the declaration, of course, this situation changed dramatically.

As stated earlier, the Jewish battalions had a difficult birth. Even after their formation, and later in Palestine, they still had to run the gauntlet of scepticism and downright opposition. Hostility towards the establishment of these battalions was in effect a rerun of the animus opposing the Zion Mule Corps. At that time, under its headline 'The War Office and a Jewish Battalion', the *Hebrew Standard* pointed to the great division of opinion in Great Britain over the matter.[2] Advocates of the Jewish battalion argued that its *esprit de corps* and the fighting quality of its soldiers would confer prestige on the Jewish race. Given the anti-Semitic slurs about the potential quality of Jewish fighters, this was seen as a dangerous contention by opponents of the Jewish battalion. They countered that Jewish recruits 'did not fight as Jews, but Englishmen' and that they 'fought a common foe in a common way without distrust'. One who held this latter view was the Jewish chaplain to the British forces, Reverend Michael Adler, who voiced hardy opposition to any move to separate Jewish soldiers into their own unit on any grounds.[3]

Regardless of the successful performance of the Zion Mule Corps, acerbic commentary against the formation of a separate Jewish battalion continued to flow. And it came, initially, not from a fearful Anglo-Jewish establishment, but from the dominant figure in the Zionist movement in Great Britain, Dr Chaim Weizmann. He soon changed his mind, however.

The Reverend Leib A. Falk has chronicled Vladimir Jabotinsky's protracted attempts to convince the British government and Jewish authorities alike of the desirability of a Jewish fighting force for Palestine. In a series of articles under the rubric 'With the Jewish Legion – Memoirs of a Jewish Chaplain', he discloses how Jabotinsky was often rebuffed, disillusioned, but never beaten in the pursuit of his goal. Falk, a Jabotinsky follower himself, was chaplain to Colonel Patterson's 38th Battalion of the British Fusiliers, and went with them to Palestine. Incidentally, he later acted as a rabbi in Australia, where he became an advocate of Zionism, an activity that caused him difficulties with his employer, Sydney's Great Synagogue, the bastion of Anglo-Orthodoxy in New South Wales.[4]

During 1915 and 1916, Jabotinsky's efforts got nowhere, not in London, Paris or Rome. In the British War Cabinet, opposition to a Jewish battalion was led by an assimilated Jew, Edwin Montague. He was the Secretary of State for India, and the first Jew in Great Britain to attain cabinet rank. It is said that Montague attempted to shed his Jewishness in order to rise in British society, but he was, of course, only one among a number of upper-class Jews who trembled lest their social standing be undermined.[5] Along with these were others who simply wished not to provide fodder for anti-Semitic bigotry.

On a broader canvas, even the Zionist Council in neutral Copenhagen in 1915 did not accept the idea of a Jewish army in Palestine under the British,[6] reasoning that it might be used in a manner contrary to Zionist principles. Undoubtedly, if it served in Palestine under British colours, it would be fighting against the Axis powers. A majority of delegates at the conference happened to come from Axis nations, such as Germany. The leader of cultural Zionism, Ahad Ha'Am, was not against Jewish soldiers fighting on the front line in Palestine, but he opposed the idea of Jewish units, fearing it would place Turkish Jewry in profound danger.[7]

The undeniable opposition of the British Jewish leadership to any hint of separateness was exacerbated by the presence in Great Britain of thousands of Jewish *émigrés* from lands under the tsarist rule who had not enlisted in the British forces. The fact that immigrants who were not as yet British citizens were not eligible to serve in no way diminished these leaders' profound embarrassment. These alleged 'refuseniks', mainly concentrated in such cities as London, Leeds, Manchester and Glasgow, were loath to engage in any activity that might benefit their former oppressor, Russia, then one of Britain's Allies. This justification for staying out of the war notwithstanding, it was felt that in so doing they would deliver anti-Semites fodder for their false claims that Jews were shirkers, exploiters, living off the fat of the land.[8]

This view was particularly prevalent at a time when the situation of the Allies in France and Belgium was deteriorating, resulting in an ever-increasing need for more soldiers to replace the dead and wounded. In this context, it was politically – and even morally – dangerous, to defend the *émigrés*' non-enlistment. But some, like Major Lionel de Rothschild, did so. He argued that many of them were in fact too poor to pay for naturalization, then a prerequisite for recruitment.[9] In a similar vein, the Reverend Falk suggested that a goodly proportion of them feared that if they were killed or wounded, there would be no one to care for their families. They had had little time to establish themselves financially, and there were no social services upon which their kith and kin could call for help.[10]

Russia's withdrawal from the war following the Bolshevik Revolution of 1917 proved the circuit breaker with respect to the enlistment of *émigrés*. A consequence was the concordat concluded between Great Britain and Russia, expressed in British legislative terms as the Military Service (Convention with Allied States) Act. It covered Russian *émigrés* of military age. This new law required them to return to Russia to enter its military forces, or enlist in the British military. Those who wished to leave had only to register at a local police station under the Alien Registration (Consolidation) Order of 1916. Before their actual departure, however, they had to make financial provisions for any dependant left behind. Those staying were immediately liable to serve in the British Army, with the same rights as British subjects. Decision day was 9 August 1917. After that date *émigrés* would no longer be able to play the anti-Russian card to justify their non-enlistment.[11]

The availability alone of these *émigrés*, or 'East Enders' as they were often tagged, would not have been sufficient to revive Jabotinsky's push for an all-Jewish battalion to serve in Palestine, even as a unit of the British Army. The British Zionist leader, Chaim

Weizmann's conversion to the cause over the objections of his fellow leaders on the continent was not sufficient to create this outcome. That required, in the first place, an attitudinal change in the elite of the British political class. This could not have happened without a fortuitous rethink by the government of Great Britain late in 1916, when David Lloyd George replaced Herbert Asquith as prime minister.

Despite Palestine's place in Christian Zionist thought in the nineteenth century and into the early years of the twentieth,[12] it had barely – if at all – figured in British strategy.[13] As previously mentioned, the Minister for War, Lord Kitchener, had not seen Palestine as having any great strategic importance. With a change of government, however, a new geo-strategic mindset arose. Despite some claims that this thinking was influenced by Christian philo-Zionism, concern for Palestine came from a reassessment of the British national interest in the evolving context of war. This need was multi-layered. First, there was the horrible stalemate in France and Belgium, which was haemorrhaging men at an ever increasing rate with no apparent prospect of improvement.[14] New strategies were needed to relieve the pressure on this front. What made this even more imperative was the extremely fragile domestic situation in both France and Russia, which threatened the withdrawal of both nations from the war. This would have placed an even greater military load on the shoulders of the British Empire.

Certainly, the Middle East was on the strategic radar screen with the conclusion of the clandestine Sykes–Picot Agreement in 1916.[15] This secret pact envisaged a fundamental British-French carve-up of the Ottoman lands of the Middle East, with some Russian influence allowed once the Allies had achieved victory. Apart from the situation on the Western Front, the Middle East became a strategic flashpoint for Great Britain because it harboured the Suez Canal, its imperial conduit from the Mediterranean through to the Pacific Ocean. The defence of the Suez Canal became paramount. Palestine came into view in the context of a desire to assert British power from the Levant to the Persian Gulf. Strategically, Palestine's role was to protect Egypt and its Suez Canal from an attack from the east. It was this kind of thinking that caused the British to encourage Arab peoples to rise against their rulers in the Ottoman lands of the Middle East. British influence with the Arabs was designed to undermine the potential French gains prescribed by the Sykes–Picot Agreement. With the help of Arab forces, the British were at the gates of Palestine, after the defeat of the Turks at Rafa in December 1916.[16] Further advances were stymied by the Turks, however, newly reinforced in Gaza by Germany and helped by Palestinian Arabs.

Zionist aspirations for Palestine fell well within the comfort zone of British strategic thinking. Given that a number of the Zionist leaders on the continent were German, there was a fear in Great Britain that its enemy might help establish a Jewish enclave in Palestine. Thus, the British move supporting Zionist aspirations there was in part designed to pre-empt this possibility. Because there was also some support for German patronage of a Jewish homeland in Palestine among Zionists in the United States of America, London felt it necessary to quash any American sympathy for this goal.[17] A mistaken belief was current that Jewish influence could sway government policy in both Germany and America.[18] That was why the Lloyd George government waited for the Woodrow Wilson administration's agreement with its purposes in Palestine before it would, as it were, sign on to the Balfour Declaration.[19]

As circumstances on the ground changed, so Jabotinsky's efforts on behalf of a Jewish fighting force for Palestine finally found fertile soil. He had always argued that an alliance with Great Britain would enhance Zionist claims at any peace conference after an Allied victory. Though Jabotinsky's labour bore fruit before the Balfour Declaration, there is little doubt that both were a consequence of the same political and military situation. This synergy invested the notion of a Jewish fighting force for Palestine with a particular legitimacy.

Nevertheless, nothing would have been possible without Chaim Weizmann's change of mind over the desirability of this force, and his subsequent influence with significant members of the British War Cabinet. He has been justly credited with winning over the War Cabinet to the view that Zionist and British strategic interests in Palestine were one.[20] He did this against the wishes of prominent figures both in the Anglo-Jewish establishment and the Zionist movement. The former did its best to kill off the idea of an all-Jewish battalion, even after it had been officially gazetted.

The claim that philo-Semitism influenced the Lloyd George government to favour Zionism remains moot.[21] Certainly, religious sentiment can motivate human action, and there is little doubt that such feelings existed in and around the War Cabinet. Nevertheless, in this case, if such attitudes were at work it was at the periphery of the decision-making process, grafted on to a geo-strategic policy deemed best for the interests of Great Britain and its Empire.

In July 1917, Colonel Patterson received orders to establish a Jewish battalion. Vladimir Jabotinsky immediately took charge of recruitment. To the chagrin of the anti-Zionist and anti-separatist factions within the Anglo-Jewish establishment, the battalion's existence was made official in the *London Gazette* on 23 August 1917. It was intended that this unit would not only take into consideration its recruits' religious requirements and cultural demands, but that it would bear both a name and insignia that would reflect its Jewish distinctiveness. Opponents of the battalion could not abide this overt display of special identity. As late as 30 August 1917, a private deputation of prominent Jews from London and the provinces, led by such luminaries as the Chief Rabbi of the British Empire Joseph Hertz, Lord Swaything, and Sir Sebag Montefiore, met with Lord Derby at the War Office. They beseeched him not to grant the battalion a name, or adorn it with insignia that would distinguish it as Jewish. They reiterated the argument that the 40,000 Jews then serving in the British forces did so willingly as citizens of Great Britain, not as Jews.[22] Given the distinguished nature of the lobby, it was successful. The War Office abandoned its plan for the battalion to wear both a distinctive blue-and-white ribbon and the insignia of the 'Star of David' on the hat.[23] Onlookers with anti-Semitic inclinations would have relished this example of Jewish in-fighting.

Not all of the Anglo-Jewish establishment, however, opposed the formation of the Jewish battalion. Although his direct financial ties with Palestine had ended by 1901, Baron Edmund de Rothschild had been a keen supporter of the Zion Mule Corps, believing that there should be a strong Jewish military force in Palestine. Although he said nothing explicit about the formation of the Jewish battalion in 1917, Mordechai Naor comments that it was highly unlikely that his son James would have transferred to it without his consent.[24]

On cue in the week following the Balfour Declaration, the *Hebrew Standard* spoke of its misgivings with the Jewish battalion in an editorial titled 'Jewish Yet not Jewish':

> Lord Derby's consent to abolish the title of 'Jewish Regiment' resulted from an influential deputation headed by the Chief Rabbi who argued that the reputation of Jewry should not be allowed to stand on the creation of a specifically named Jewish battalion. Such judgement would be unfair in view of the distinguished service of so many Jews

in other regiments. With the establishment of a Jewish 'title' the previous privilege of Kosher diet also goes. Now there is no certainty that the new regiment will see service in Palestine. So far no definite reason has been given for this segregation of Jewish enlistees. If its object had been to please the Jewish community, it must be voted as a signal failure, while a split in Zionist ranks has been narrowly averted according to Dr. Samuel Daiches. Most likely to nature which primarily activated the War Office was a desire to avoid possible complications in assimilating many thousands of Russian Jews into British ranks. Someone has wisely suggested that while this addition to the fighting strength might with advantage be trained together, the conscripts should ultimately be drafted into various regiments in the usual way. In the absence of any benefits at present undiscovered from the Jewish point of view, this appears to us the best course possible to pursue.[25]

Such an attitude may go some way to answer why this communal paper failed to report later the deeds of the Jewish Legion in Palestine, and Eliazar Margolin's role in it. To have done so would have required this journal – in all conscience – to admit that its prognostications had been wrong. This it never did.

10

The New Battalion

Some 120 ex-Zion Mule Corps veteran volunteers formed the nucleus of the new Jewish battalion. Their understanding was that they would be deployed only in Palestine. As a very temporary measure on recruitment they were assigned to the 20th London Battalion.[1] Jews in other sections of the British Army were given free rein by the adjutant-general to transfer, although only a few hundred actually did so. Apart from satisfaction with, and loyalty to, their current posts, the intense opposition from the Anglo-Jewish establishment deterred some from taking the plunge. Under the leadership of the Patterson-Jabotinsky team, the former members of the Zion Mule Corps were joined by *émigrés* – mainly from London's East End, who were no longer able to avoid overseas military service – to form the 38th Battalion of the British Royal Fusiliers. This first battalion of what became called the Jewish Legion was soon to be followed by another, commanded by Eliazar Margolin.

Vladimir Jabotinsky says that when he received the news that Eliazar was recuperating after his ordeal in France, he decided to visit him in his London hospital, and to secure his services for the Jewish battalions. He remembered Eliazar as the AIF officer who had visited the Jewish refugees from Palestine housed in the Gabbari camp in Egypt, and recalls his speaking to the internees there in broken Yiddish.[2] He says of Margolin: 'I knew his story well, from his brother in St. Petersburg – the editor of Effron's Russian and Jewish Encyclopedias, and still more from the legends about him in Palestine. His family had emigrated to Palestine in the first days of the "Bilu", when Eliazar was still a child.'[3] Details of Eliazar's backgound may well have come from St Petersburg, but hardly from his brother, who after all was blind and resided in Palestine. Moreover, Eliazar had arrived in Palestine not as a child but as a sixteen-year-old youth. No doubt the prospect of command sugared the request for him to join the Jewish battalions. According to Jabotinsky, Eliazar's immediate response was to prevaricate, saying, 'I am afraid ... I am afraid of Jews. One has to talk too much'.[4] Whether or not this was his actual reply is questionable; however, at least two quirky explanations may be offered. The first is that, given Eliazar was known as a man of very few words, the reported reply was a Jabotinsky joke. On the other hand, it may have been a tongue-in-cheek example of Margolin's self-deprecating humour. Whichever is the true explanation, the upshot was, as Jabotinsky put it, 'but he came'. He joined the Jewish battalions and his transfer between the Australian and British armies was facilitated by the British adjutant-general.[5]

When the notion of a Jewish battalion was first mooted, it was Patterson's view that it should be commanded by a Jew. None of sufficient rank, however, was available or willing to take the job. Eliazar Margolin was mentioned, but at the time he was in France with the AIF.[6] With no Jewish commander available, Patterson was an enthusiastic applicant, seeing the battalion's role in philo-Semitic terms as helping to promote the physical redemption of the Jewish people in the Holy Land. Anti-Semitic slogans labelling Jews as innately incapable and untrustworthy fighters had shocked his Irish Protestant sensibility. Anglo-Jewish opposition to the Jewish battalion dismayed him even more. This particular hostility was now being repackaged in a language that would have given heart to any anti-Semite: that these *émigré* recruits' performance would inevitably bring disgrace and embarrassment to British Jewry. All this baffled him. How could a Jew oppose the idea of the first all-Jewish military force to serve in Palestine since the days of Judah Maccabeus and Bar Kokhba? And especially when this challenge to the common enemy brought such benefits to the *Yishuv* and British Empire alike.[7]

The training site of the 38th Battalion, replete with eighty commissioned and one hundred non-commissioned officers, was in the West Country, with battalion headquarters established forty miles from London. Its rank and file comprised not only Jews from the Zion Mule Corps and Russian *émigrés*, but also a minority from Allied and neutral states. Only a handful were English-born. As a collection of men, the battalion was an extremely broad repository of talent and skills, and contrary to the expectations of Sydney's *Jewish Standard*, full provisions were made for the religious and cultural needs of the men. Given that a good many officers were fluent in both Yiddish and Russian, there were no difficulties communicating with the ranks. *The Times* in London wrote that the battalion 'offers the Russian Jews a chance of being with their own kind'.[8] Given that the Russians, who were being 'forced' to serve, required British naturalization, this was now granted free of charge after only three months in uniform. *The Times* speculated that it might be in prospect for the Jewish battalion 'to assist in the capture of Jerusalem'. This was indeed what the recruits hoped, but it was not to be. Indeed, the Manchester *Guardian* reported their concern that they might arrive in the Holy Land too late, and only when the war was over.[9]

Apparently, there were a few Christians among those who volunteered for the Jewish battalion.[10] Possibly they were motivated by feelings of philo-Semitism and wished to help restore the Jewish people to their ancient land. As it had been specified that the corps was to be all-Jewish, however, they were not accepted. The *London Daily News* reported that two Jewish soldiers in the AIF who had sought a transfer were informed by Patterson that if this were approved, it would be accompanied by a marked reduction in wages. As noted before, Australian soldiers earned more (six times more) per day than their British counterparts. The two Australians in question claimed that loss of pay was not an issue for them, only a desire to serve 'in the Jewish Regiment'.[11] Their names were not disclosed, nor, it seems, were their transfers effected.

The *Jewish Herald* referred to the Middle East campaign in typically exaggerated terms when it claimed that the goal of driving the Turks from the Holy Land had become a 'Maccabean inspiration' to Australian Jewish youth.[12] There was no evidence for this assertion from any observation of Jewish youth in Australia, or from any impression of the opinions of young Jewish soldiers in the trenches. Its source was a single quote from an American officer in France who had heard that some Australian Jews who had served two and a half years on the hellish Western Front wanted to transfer to the British forces in Palestine.[13] The reason for transfer had little to do with inspiration. Anyone of sane mind would surely have wished to escape the bloody nightmare of the Western Front. There was no evidence provided for any push by Jewish youth in Australia to join British forces in Palestine, nor do we know anything about whether they gave a moment's thought to redeeming Palestine as 'the Jewish land of heart's desire'. At best it could be said that the communal newspaper was indulging in wishful thinking.

On completing manoeuvres on the hillsides of western England, the 5,000 men of the 38th Battalion marched proudly through

London's West End on 3 January 1918 to the acclaim of their fellow Jews, before their departure for Egypt.[14] When the battalion left Southampton, Margolin's appointment had yet to be arranged. Once, Eliazar Margolin's participation was secured, however, the number of Jewish battalions was expanded to two.

Soon after the 38th Battalion's departure for Egypt, preparations were made to form the 39th Battalion of the British Royal Fusiliers. This was temporarily undertaken under Colonel Samuel, but on 18 March 1918, Eliazar moved to a depot at Plymouth to take charge of matters and prepare his men for combat in Palestine as quickly as possible. Unfortunately, as Yigal Elam says, much of his time was wasted, due to a lack of senior staff to train the men.[15] After much insistence from Margolin, this deficiency was rectified. Like the 38th, his camp was prepared with Jewish needs and wants in mind. There was kosher food, a library, a newspaper in Yiddish, and, where possible, no duties were allocated on the Sabbath or Jewish religious holidays.[16]

His battalion's numbers, however, had been only partially filled in England. What distinguished the 39th from the 38th was that a high percentage of its men were recruited in the United States.[17] Some were from Canada and a handful from South America. Two of its number who enlisted in the United States were David Ben-Gurion and Yitzhak Ben-Zvi, both driven from Turkish Palestine in 1915 by Djemal Pasha. At the time they were engaged in Zionist organization and activity.[18] Over a hundred of their fellows came from New York's East Side, America's equivalent of London's East End. They were also *émigrés*, foreign Jews, who had been excluded from the American draft when, on 6 April 1917, President Wilson broke with isolationism to throw in his nation's lot against Germany in Europe. Moreover, American law did not permit its citizens admittance to foreign armies.[19]

It was believed that after the war, these 'American' members of the 39th would remain in Palestine, where they would help form the 'nucleus of a Jewish Republic'. The principal recruiter in the United States was Joseph L. Cohen, who was a former President of the Cambridge University Zionist Society and founder of the Inter-University Council of New York. He hoped that many other New York 'East Siders' would follow the example of the original enlistees.[20] The likelihood of this was increased by the fact that no animosity existed there, as it did in Great Britain, towards an exclusive Jewish militia for Palestine. American Jewry had a different character, and it lacked the centralized direction and organization of British Empire Jewish communities. Moreover, the battle for the Jewish battalions had basically been won, even if the idea had not been fully accepted in Great Britain. This is not to deny that the extent of anti-Semitism in this transatlantic land was beginning to increase greatly. These new recruits paraded through the New York East Side, on the way to Boston to join others from that city, then left America, having added further volunteers in Nova Scotia, to cross the Atlantic to train in England.[21] The Americans did not join the 39th in one group, however, eventually assembling as one only later in Egypt.

Incomplete in numbers, the 39th Battalion sailed from England in April 1918 for France, left France and travelled by train to Italy, then sailed to Alexandria in Egypt. It reached its bivouac finally at Helmieth near Cairo just before Passover.[22] Camp life has been described as difficult, cramped for room, and even lacking in electric light. The situation improved when the battalion took over the space formerly occupied by their brothers of the 38th when they left for Palestine.[23] Within weeks of their arrival the 39th paraded before General Allenby, the officer in charge of the British military authority, the Occupied Enemy Territory Administration (hereafter OETA).[24] Apart from the harsh environment the men were soon subjected to constant theft of their equipment, especially rifles, by locals. As Dr Redcliffe N. Salaman, MD, medical officer of the 39th, and the only doctor to be attached to the Jewish Legion, described the situation, 'they would rob you of your pyjamas without waking you up'.[25]

In the first week of June 1918, the 38th Battalion left Egypt for the front in Palestine. The day before they left, the 39th Battalion provided their comrades with a special lunch. Margolin proposed their good health but, 'getting tied up', he called on Salaman to finish his speech.[26] From their camp, the 38th crossed the Sinai desert to Gaza, and thence into Palestine. On entering *Eretz Israel*, its accompanying chaplain, a rapturous Leib Falk, describes how beautiful the 'orchards and vineyards' of the Jewish settlements were, and expressed his excitement on seeing the red roofs of Rehovot, Eliazar Margolin's former home, near Ludd, *en route* to the battalion's camp at Sarafend.[27] It is unlikely that, at first blush, the men were as appreciative of the sights as Falk was. They were tired and tried by their journey, which had been tantamount to a forced march across a terrain for which they had not been prepared at all. Sarafend teemed with insects. Worst of all, there was a lack of water.[28] Such conditions did not help troop morale. On the other hand, Falk's commentary dwelt only on the positive. Ecstatically, he recounted how 'Numbers of Jews and Jewesses of all ages and social standings from Jaffa and neighbouring colonies whose joy on our arrival was beyond description – they came to our camp for Sabbath service dressed in festive garb.'[29]

Back in Egypt, Eliazar Margolin was once more on familiar territory. He had visited Egypt the first time he left Palestine for Australia, and had trained in its environs both immediately before and after the Gallipoli campaign.

The 39th waited for the rest of the Americans, delayed *en route*, to arrive and complete its ranks.[30] That happened only on 15 July 1918, when 300 Americans, together with another 150 men, reached camp at Helmieth. In the meantime, the word from the 38th Battalion in Palestine was that boredom had set in because they had not been engaged at the front, while a scarcity of food and water added to their discomfort.[31]

Eliazar is reputed to have told Moshe Smilansky, before he left for Australia in 1902, that he would return to *Eretz Israel* as a British soldier to help free the *Yishuv* from Ottoman rule, the baron's officers and moneylenders.[32] On a few occasions Margolin interrupted his training of the 39th in Egypt to return to *Eretz Israel* as a British officer. This had been made easy because British forces had already secured Jaffa-Tel Aviv and its environs from the Turks, including the nearby Jewish settlements.

He was reunited with his brother and sister on his first visit. After this meeting, he borrowed a horse to make a pilgrimage to Rehovot to visit the graves of his parents, which he had not seen for sixteen years. He found his old village very different from the place of penury he had been forced to abandon.[33] A London *Times* correspondent who toured Rehovot in 1918 found that this community, established by Russian and Polish Jews, included 270 Jewish workers from Yemen in its current population of 900. They had all been successfully integrated. The settlement was comprised of 'family-owned homes', sandy streets 'bordered with avenues of mulberry trees' and an array of public buildings, notably a community hall, synagogue and library. The correspondent thought that it exuded a prosperous ambience.[34]

In Rehovot Eliazar met old friends like Moshe Smilansky, whom he encouraged to help form another unit of the Jewish Legion from the Jews of the *Yishuv*. Smilansky responded with the promise 'that within a short period of time, you will have a band of soldiers of whom you will be proud'. That pledge was soon fulfilled. Encouraged by Smilansky, workers, farmers, students from the local Hebrew School, and some from Jerusalem, volunteered for a Palestinian battalion.[35] As might have been expected, the British military authorities showed no interest in another Jewish battalion, particularly at this late stage in the war, because they thought an armed Palestinian Jewish unit might stir up Arab resentment. The idea was also unpopular with some *Yishuv* leaders. The Turks' expulsion of Jews from Jaffa and its environs had already denuded the district of able-bodied men. With even fewer men in the settlements, they felt further Arab attacks might be encouraged.

After serving in France, Major James de Rothschild, the son of Baron Edmund de Rothschild, volunteered for transfer to Allenby's staff to facilitate the formation of the final Jewish battalion. In the event it was agreed by the authorities that the 40th Battalion of the British Royal Fusiliers would be commanded by Colonel F. Samuels DSO. One of its recruits, Shimon HaCohen, at the time aged only sixteen and preparing for his high school matriculation examination, later recalled: 'Our recruitment did not go smoothly at first, because the war was seemingly ended and they weren't interested in having us. But we were not going to give up our rights. We were a couple of hundred people from the Galilee, some of us from the HaShomer ... thanks to James Rothschild we were admitted ...'[36]

James de Rothschild was directly involved in its recruitment *in situ*. As was usual in any situation of recruitment, an individual's motivation for enlistment was not always as ideologically pure as some later writers might have wished to suggest. One veteran has suggested that the formation of the 40th was the consequence of the men's desire to expel the Turks for nationalist reasons.[37] Another, however, says the inspiration was more pragmatic and self-interested than altruistic, claiming that many of the young men simply wished the Turkish oppression to end.[38] In true *Yishuv* socialist fashion, a committee was organized to oversee recruitment. Each member of the committee was made responsible for a specific area of the *Yishuv* to encourage men to join the battalion.[39] When the 40th began its brief training, the Australian troops were already harrying their foe in northern Palestine and the Galilee.

The regimental flag of the 40th Battalion, presented to Chaim Weizmann and Major James de Rothschild in front of Tel Aviv's Great Synagogue, was embroidered with both the battalion's motto, '*Kadimah*' (forward), and the words in Hebrew, 'For Our People

and the Cities of Our God'. As the other two battalions had their
own *Sefer Torah* or religious scroll, so Moshe Smilansky received
another on behalf of the 40th. During the time that had elapsed
while the battalion was being formed, the men had had to rely on
local communities for such basics as food, clothing, medicine and
books.[40] Eliazar met them at Helmieth near Cairo, leading his
Americans to the accompaniment of a British army band. Redcliffe
Salaman's diary describes the scene when the approximately 800
men of the 40th arrived at Helmieth:

> On Thursday at 1 pm a long train with open cattle trucks rolled into
> the military siding at Helmieth, and, on a given signal, seven hundred
> of the most bizarre-looking ruffians jumped out, and in a thrice several
> hundred oddments had grouped themselves in perfect military pre-
> cision into their ranks and platoons under the banners resplendent
> with rampant lions and crossed triangles. Never in your life have you
> seen such a crowd ... they were in rags, but what rags! Garments of
> every nationality and shape – some children of 15 who swore they
> were adults, old men who declared they were only 44, some with
> long beards and piyout.[41]

One member of the 40th was apparently a friend of Eliazar
from his days in Rehovot. In such circumstances, he had to balance
familiarity with the respect owed him as a commander. This was
accomplished by a protocol of address which differed, as it were,
inside and outside his tent. In the former case, his friends called him
'Lazar', and for the latter, 'Colonel', as military practice dictated.

After a short stay at Kantara on the banks of the Suez Canal, for
a brief period of quarantine, the 40th left for training at Tel-Kabir.
The training, however, was of a very superficial nature. Some of the
soldiers were tutored in marksmanship, others trained for about a
month as guides, but most of the activity was restricted to drilling
and guard duty.[42] Turkish Jewish soldiers taken as prisoners-of-war
in Palestine by the Allies were given permission to join the battalion.
One former member of the 40th described them as 'patriotic' –
meaning Zionist – though possessing a 'different mentality' from
that of soldiers from Palestine. Nevertheless, they integrated well. A
group that did not, however, were the French-speaking platoon drawn
from Egypt, nicknamed the 'Alexandrons', who had been encouraged
to join by Jabotinsky. Apparently, not only were they not fired by
Zionism, they were forever complaining about their conditions.[43]

When the 39th Battalion was suddenly dispatched to Palestine on 5 August 1918, they left behind the 40th fretting about whether or not it would be permitted to follow before the war had ended. In one very distinct way the 40th differed from its brother battalions in the Jewish Legion. Being Jews from Palestine, they reflected the political and cultural divisions current in the *Yishuv*. These came to the fore very early, before they had even left Palestine, over the issue of the battalion's flag. A number of the men wanted the *HaShomer* flag to be adopted as the battalion's banner. *HaShomer* (the Watchman) was a band of men formed in 1909 by members of the Po'alei Zion Party (Zionist Workers' Party) to defend Jewish settlements against marauding Arabs. This proposal immediately generated an intense debate between its advocates and those who wanted to fly the flag with which they had already been presented in the 40th. Although the *HaShome*r emblem was rejected, it was unlikely that the matter would be allowed to end there. During their encampment in Kantara, the 40th was formally invited to meet the Jewish community of Alexandria. On leaving the train to assemble and prepare themselves to march and meet their hosts, an activist pulled out and waved the *HaShomer* flag from under his clothing. In the dispute that followed, the supporters of the current flag prevailed.[44]

The life of a commander of the Jewish battalions did not only involve military matters. Though scant records are left of Eliazar's social life, we know he was always invited to the concerts organized by his men. He was also present on 24 July 1918 on Mount Scopus, north of the Old City of Jerusalem, at the laying of the foundation stone of the Hebrew University of Jerusalem. Understandably, a number of legionnaires wished to attend this momentous event in modern Jewish history, but General Allenby denied them permission. The excuse, soon to be used all too often, was that the sight of Jewish men in uniform might arouse Arab ire. Only with great reluctance did he permit the three commanders of the Jewish battalions and Dr Redcliffe Salaman, the medical officer of the 39th, to attend. In Salaman's words, 'a great crowd of Jerusalemites and colonists ... wended their way up Mount Scopus like pilgrims'. True to his prejudices, Allenby did not allow any of the senior staff of the Jewish Legion actively to take part in the actual stone laying, lest their participation annoy or even possibly incite the Arabs. On the other hand, the Islamic representative and the Christian bishops present were involved in this activity.[45]

One commentator has described the commander of the 39th Battalion as a 'large raw-boned man, tall and powerful, and every inch a soldier'. Traits attributed to him include having a strong character, being thoroughly courageous, utterly sensible, having a dry sense of humour, but being a person of few words.[46] Other than in Russian, he never was fully confident in the languages that his peripatetic life called on him to use. Both his Yiddish and English were poor, and overlaid with a strong Russian accent. He spoke little Hebrew, though he understood it. Perhaps, because of this, and because his unit belonged to the British Army, he demanded that military orders be given in English. Eliazar has been described as a deep thinker, acutely aware of things around him, but as a man who exhibited a rural unhurriedness. Despite, at times, being irritated by his demands for precision, correctness, detail and an exemplary camp, his men regarded him affectionately as a father figure. One of his soldiers rewrote the lyrics of an American folksong in honour of Eliazar. Called 'Aryeh, Aryeh' (Lion, Lion) it read:

> I volunteered and went to Egypt
> In a train full of coal and soot
> Until we finally arrived
> (Lion, Lion, up and volunteer for the Jewish Battalion)

> In the evening we were given meat
> The meat in truth, was not fresh
> We complained to Margolin the Minister
> But he said, 'Eat and be well'
> (Lion, Lion, up and volunteer for the Jewish Battalion)[47]

It became the unofficial song of the battalion.

On 5 August the 39th moved out of camp to Kantara on the Suez Canal, which had literally become the port city for Palestine. Finally, after a few days spent training and being re-equipped, they left by train across the Sinai desert on 8 August for Palestine. There they set their tents in Sarafend, some fifteen miles from the front.

11

The AIF–Jewish Connection

From the perspective of military operations in the Middle East campaign, the Jewish battalions played a small, but not insignificant role in the war against the Turks. That said, they became involved in action in Palestine after the British forces led by General Edmund Allenby had taken possession of the City of Jerusalem. After being held up in the Sinai at the battle of Rafa, the Australian Light Horse was in the vanguard of the British push into the Holy Land.[1] It was the first time during the Great War that an Australian, General Henry Chauvel, was to be a commander at corps level. Not only did the Australians strike up a warm relationship with the Jewish settlements of the *Yishuv*, but they also became the trusted allies of the Jewish battalions.

After the catastrophe at Gallipoli, when other 'diggers' like Eliazar left Egypt for the Western Front, the Australian Light Horse stayed on to see further action in the Middle East. Whereas the rocky shores and hinterland of Gallipoli were totally unsuited to the cavalry, the terrain of the Sinai and Negev deserts was its natural element. On 3 November 1917, they led the Allenby assault against the Turks at Be'er Sheva. Their exploits in this last great cavalry charge of modern warfare have entered the annals of Australian folklore. After Be'er Sheva, Allenby took the all-important ancient port town of Jaffa, the Holy City of Jerusalem, Amman, Palestine east of the River Jordan, cleared the Galilee region of enemy troops, going on to the final victory over the enemy at Aleppo and Damascus. *En route*, the Australians suffered greatly from heat exhaustion, sunburn, uncontrollable insect infestation, a dearth of drinking water and the inevitable malaria.[2]

His own smouldering Judeophobia notwithstanding, H. S. Gullett, Australia's official observer of the Middle East campaign, was forced to acknowledge the state of mutual respect that developed between

the Australian troops and the members of the Jewish settlements.
Putting genuine congeniality aside, this affection was a matter of self-
interest on both sides. The Jewish settlers welcomed the Australians
as liberators who had freed them from Turkish oppression. The
Australian troops considered the Jewish settlements as cultural
oases and a source of food that suited their Western palates.[3] Gullett
noted:

> [The] polyglot of Jews of Deiran and Wady Hanein were the first
> communities of white European people, wearing European dress, and
> living a Western life, whom many Australians and New Zealanders
> had known since they had left home at the outset of war three years
> before ... and there began at once an association, often marked by
> affection, which was only broken by the close of war.[4]

On one hand Gullett describes the contempt, born of experience,
in which the Australians held the untrustworthy Arab;[5] on the other,
in almost dismissive tones, he describes the Jewish farmer settlers
as 'industrious but timid and servile'. Though he acknowledges that
they had lived in dire circumstances for three years under Turkish
oppression, he appears to lack any sympathy for these Jews. Rather,
he is consumed with anti-Semitic notions of Jewish financial omni-
potence which, he argues, has seemingly quarantined the Jewish
settlements against the excesses of the Ottomans. In his words, the
Turks 'would not offend the all-powerful Semitic bankers'.[6]

On 11 December 1917, five weeks after the victory at Be'er Sheva,
Allenby and his forces encircled, then entered, the Holy City of
Jerusalem. He was met by notables of the ancient city's Christian,
Islamic and Jewish communities. An Australian officer present
observed that the Jewish inhabitants spoke only in hushed tones,
which he soon comprehended was an understandable reaction to
having lived under the harsh and rapacious Turkish rule. Part of
that legacy was starvation.[7] Their joy at having been liberated was
tempered by mourning for thirty of their community – men and
women – executed by the Turkish Army before it surrendered the
city.[8]

The Turkish surrender of Jerusalem marked a weighty moment in
history. Not only had the Ottoman suzerainty over the city ended,
but for the first time since the defeat of the Crusaders its Islamic
hegemony was no more. Seen through the Jewish prism of the
day, some gave the event a distinct spiritual meaning. It occurred

on the eve of the Jewish religious festival of Chanukah, which commemorates the triumph of the Maccabees in 164 BCE over the Seleucids, who had defiled the Holy Temple. This Holy of Holies of the Jews had then been purified and rededicated.[9]

The British forces' triumph in taking Jerusalem led the Australian Jewish press and religious leaders to compare it with the Maccabean conquest. Euphoria fuelled their rhetoric. The language stood in stark contrast to the sober, bland, almost sceptical frame of mind the same press had exhibited when reporting the Balfour Declaration. The *Jewish Herald* could not contain its delight over the rescue of Jerusalem. In megaphonic tones, its headlines proclaimed: 'Jerusalem captured', emphasizing that it had happened on 'the first day of Chanukah (Kislev 26)'. It reminded its readers that Jerusalem had fallen on the same day as it had many centuries ago to Judas Maccabeus ...

> General Sir Edmund Allenby KC and his victorious troops entered Jerusalem and raised the British flag of freedom on the heights of Zion. To the religious of all creeds this remarkable co-incidence of dates on the very anniversary is a portent full of glad possibilities ... brings the Jew a sudden realisation of a long deferred hope of pathetic yearning, and the heart's sore craving for surcease from ages of untold cravings ... the future of Palestine and its famous capital under the suzerainty of free nations is for the Jew to create. Already in the 'Promised Land' again for the Jewish People ... The formulation of peace will place the seal on the compact which will lift Zion out of the realm of idealism into the spacious atmosphere of a concrete existence ...[10]

It reported the words of the British Under Secretary for Foreign Affairs, Lord Cecil: 'The Arab countries should be given to the Arabs, Armenia to the Armenians, Judea to the Jews and the real Turkey to the Turks.'[11] Indeed, the next edition, no doubt reflecting the Australian cultural ambience and time of the year, spoke of a 'Maccabean Christmas', and said that at synagogues throughout the nations prayers of thanks were intoned for 'the deliverance of Jerusalem'.[12] In words not untypical, the President of the Adelaide Hebrew Congregation in South Australia described the capture of Jerusalem as a manifestation 'of the finger of God'.[13] Prior to this moment, to the extent that Zionism had existed at all in Australia,

Jews considered the possible establishment of a Jewish homeland in Palestine in purely secular terms. Allenby's entry into Jerusalem now gave the discourse – if only momentarily – a spiritual dimension.

Whether ordinary Australian Jews were at all concerned about what was happening in Jerusalem, at least to the extent expressed by their leaders, is questionable. Assimilation in Australia had taken its toll not just on Jewish affiliation, but also on the depth of traditional Jewish knowledge.[14] Just how many really cared about these developments when their private angst was monopolized by the bloody vicissitudes of the Western Front, in particular, remains unknown. The ordinary Jew did not write for the communal press nor declaim from the pulpit. He or she was just too busy coping with the war and its domestic fallout. It is most likely that the progress of the Middle East campaign was not seen in terms of a Jewish spiritual world view, but rather in terms of the success, or otherwise, of the British forces in general, and the Australian forces in particular. Indeed, any role played by the Jewish battalions in this theatre would have been subsumed in the actions undertaken by the British Army of which they were a part. The consequence was that there was virtually no news of their performance in Australia, even in the Jewish communal press.

H. S. Gullett appears to have relished telling the readers of his chronicle, *The A.I.F. in Sinai and Palestine*, of the relatively late entry of the Jewish battalions in the Middle East campaign, and their non-involvement in General Allenby's ultimate triumph over the Turks in Damascus.[15] Certainly, it was true that when the general progressively took Gaza, Be'ersheva, Jaffa and Jerusalem, both the 38th and 39th were still training in England, and the 40th had yet to be created. Gullett expressed Allenby's intense scepticism over the Jewish battalions' fighting ability. This sentiment was not based solely on his assessment of how an untried corps would perform in the field of battle. On the record at least, Gullett seems to have disagreed with Allenby only once, and that was over one particular case of Australian insubordination, which will be discussed shortly. It was an incident which was said to have proved a valuable lesson for the men of the Jewish Legion.

Not surprisingly, in Jabotinsky's and his fellow legionnaires' eyes, the importance of their service in Palestine was diametrically different from Gullett's view. Indeed, by any objective standards, their achievements could have been assessed only after their dispatch to Palestine, that is, after Allenby's capture of Jerusalem. Moreover, their military value could, in reality, have been determined by how well they carried out their orders under the conditions they faced.

Once Jerusalem was in his hands, Allenby set his course across the Jordan River. *En route* he tried to take Wady Auja, north of Jericho, but this attack was repulsed. His next line of assault was the railway at Amman, thirty miles east of Jericho. Before he could achieve this end, however, he needed to take bridgeheads across the Jordan River. This was attempted on the evening of 21 March 1918 by a combination of forces that included English infantry and the ANZAC Mounted Division. Two days later they had overrun three bridgeheads, permitting the cavalry to cross to the Turkish side of the Jordan. *En route* to Amman, the troops battled an intensely stubborn Turkish resistance in completely unforgiving terrain and climate. They reached Amman on 27 March to find it defended by 4,000 of the enemy, entrenched and well prepared. Prior knowledge of the British assault had been passed on to the Turks by the Bedouin. The upshot was that it failed, forcing the attackers to leave not just the immediate vicinity, but to retreat across the Jordan on 31 March. By 2 April, the only bridgehead retained was at Ghorananiye. Australian historian Bill Gammage says that a quarter of all casualties sustained by Australian troops in the whole Middle East campaign were inflicted in this engagement.[16]

Four weeks later, on 29 April, British forces attempted to capture the town of Es Salt east of the Jordan, on the way to Amman. Again the attack faltered. On 18 May the Turks battered the Australian Light Horse at Damieh near the Jordan, driving them off and almost cutting the main Es Salt track. Turkish resistance stiffened to such a degree that all British soldiers were again forced back behind the Ghorananiye bridgehead. The exhausted Australian troops were quartered in the Jordan Valley to endure blistering heat, bad food, lack of water, insects, monotony and disease while awaiting further orders.[17]

Initially the 38th Battalion of the British Fusiliers was employed in a forward position twenty miles north of Jerusalem facing the Turkish lines. The Turks basically left it alone.[18] Several weeks were spent in the Jordan Valley where, like the Australians, the members of the battalion endured environmental horrors, especially malaria, which took a great toll. Jericho was described as a 'Gehenna', a living hell, because of its combination of intense heat, clogging dust, lack of water and malaria. There was a feeling among some of the men that the British High Command hoped that these conditions would provoke the men to rebel, and thus provide an excuse to get rid of them. Jabotinsky described the 'Jericho Desert', in which they resided for several weeks, as 'purgatory'.[19]

Much of what we know of Eliazar and his 39th British Royal Fusiliers in Palestine comes from the letters of Redcliffe Salaman. He notes that in the first week of August 1918, the 39th was suddenly dispatched to Palestine.[20] *En route* to their camp in Sarafend, they trained and were equipped in Kantara.[21] After crossing the Sinai desert by train they finally pitched tents in Sarafend, but there, initially, there was little to do.[22] Soon after arriving there, Eliazar again visited Rehovot, this time with Salaman.[23]

The distance from Sarafend to the front was only fifteen miles, and from there firing could be heard.[24] On 14 August orders were given for the battalion to move to the front,[25] but before doing so Eliazar, again with Salaman, travelled to Rishon Le-Zion to say farewell to his blind brother and some friends.[26]

To this point, the 39th Battalion at Sarafend was far from complete. Nevertheless, the men at Sarafend route-marched to Latrun some fourteen miles away. The trek was made more difficult because they had never before engaged in such an expedition.[27] From there they moved on another four miles to join other units *en route* to the front, including not only the 38th but also the rest of their own battalion.[28] Margolin's tour took them around the environs of the Old City of Jerusalem: the German Hospice, the Russian Church and the Mount of Olives.[29] Because of the intense heat, some of the march was undertaken at night, and they finally reached the great plain of Jericho on 13 September 1918.[30] Salaman notes that the battalion was ordered to advance in small groups strung out to create long dust-clouds in order to mislead the Turks concerning its numbers.[31] The battalion was not prepared for the environmental conditions it met, and its men suffered from extreme heat exhaustion and fatigue. One legionnaire described the scene:

> In front rides our 'Old Man' – Margolin – on his horse and looks back, sees the situation, gets off his horse and gives it to his boy. The other officers saw this and did the same, grumbling and cursing at this whole 'Jericho idea'. He continued on foot about two hundred metres before the ranks leaning on his stick, lonely in his cloud of dust, this worn-out Colonel in his Majesty's force uniform. More have fallen but he does not look back any more. The 'boys' have satisfied his wish: they are not deserting, only falling one by one. The injured get out of the wagon and return to the ranks.[32]

Though utterly wearied himself, Eliazar Margolin rode up and down the ranks, encouraging them with the words: 'Remember you are Jewish volunteers. Keep your chins up. Fill in the ranks.' They marched in silence, as it was Kol Nidre, the eve of *Yom Kippur* or Day of Atonement, the most sacred day in the Jewish calendar. In Redcliffe Salaman's words:

> We had been encamped for a couple of days outside Tel-es-Sultan, by Jericho when orders were received. The road, which was under fire, lay in the foothills and ankle deep in dust … We marched in silence. The long columns of the battalion had a ghost-like appearance as it wound silent over the moonlit track. The muffled foot-tread of the men marching through the dust was scarcely audible. From time to time one would whisper to another as if afraid of his own voice: there was a dread expectancy in the air. Never had the Day of Atonement been so celebrated. Occasionally one heard the plaintive notes of Kol Nidre arising from one group and then another. As we marched along, the thought occurred to me again and again. A peculiar people, a special battalion, and a most peculiar day on which to begin active service.[33]

The battalion was protected and sheltered from the Turkish shelling that fell around, in a great ravine with their backs against a cliff. Nevertheless, the heat was overwhelming. Tension had built in the ranks because they had not been in the fighting to date.[34] The 38th was nearby. War casualties had not affected it, but malaria and sandfly fever had reduced battalion numbers.[35]

Orders finally arrived for the third attack east of the Jordan on 19 September. The infantry brigade accompanying the Anzac Mounted Division under Major General E. W. C. Chaytor comprised two Jewish battalions and one of West Indians. The object of the push was to carry the line from the Auja bridgehead across the Mellahah and Abu Tellel defences into the hills beyond, and then on to Amman. Patterson's column – as the two Jewish battalions were called in this exercise – was tasked with taking the Umn es Shert ford, thus securing both sides of the Jordan. Once accomplished, the thrust was to continue to the town of Es Salt in the hills of Moab. Such action was the necessary precondition for Chaytor's men to sweep into Transjordan. Although the first attempt on the Umn es Shert ford failed, the second, on 23 September, succeeded. Eliazar's men were to follow up with an attack on Es Salt, several miles south of the ford. With Umn es Shert pacified, Chaytor's horsemen crossed the Jordan, followed by the Jewish fighters.[36]

Gullett considered the introduction of both the untried Jewish battalions and the West Indians at the front a matter of necessity rather than choice. He was particularly caustic about the performance of the Jewish battalions, and saw this as a poor prognosis for its foundation as a future Jewish army in Palestine:

> It was felt that the fighting spirit shown by these battalions should be some sound indication of the capacity of their race to hold Palestine in the future against the traditional and inevitable aggression of the Arabs from the east of Jordan. For this reason their employment in Chaytor's force was looked on with keen interest and sympathy. As they moved from their post they were opposed by machine gun and rifle fire, and achieved little: neither here nor in the subsequent fighting did they disclose military promise, and they suffered by contrast with both the pugnacious West Indians and gallant Patialas.[37]

On the other hand, Allenby himself wrote, in response to a note from the Secretary of the Zionist Organization of America, of the good fighting qualities of the 38th and 39th battalions at Umn es Shert.[38] It is a moot point as to whether, given his general negative attitude towards them, the commander-in-chief's reply was just a diplomatic nicety. Chaytor, in correspondence with Patterson, was to later praise the Jewish soldiers.[39] Given the fact that the attack on the Umn es Shert ford was the third of its kind, and that the previous two had been repulsed when the Jewish soldiers were not present, Gullett's observations were somewhat disingenuous and unfair.

The presence of the Australians gave the Jewish battalions confidence. There was great respect for Chaytor, and the comradeship with his Anzac Mounted Division was highly valued.[40] They had become used to overt hostility from British headquarters down to the ranks. From the Australians they experienced the opposite. One former legionnaire remembered: 'British troops in the Military Police were unfriendly. The best friends we had among the non-Jewish troops were the Australians – they were not biased, and our boys were grateful for their gifts of water and rations, plus hand shakes and a smile.'[41]

The deleterious effects of the sojourn in the Jordan Valley on the health of the Jewish battalions were exacerbated by the arduous climb up the extremely hilly ascent towards Es Salt. Eliazar's instruction was to take the town no matter the cost, and so he urged his exhausted and ill-fed men on. When they reached Es Salt, they found that the able Turkish troops had fled and were being pursued by the Anzac mounted division. Salaman says British aircraft assaults a few days earlier had undoubtedly helped contribute to the total rout of the Turks and their German advisers. The stench of the dead hung heavy in the air. The 39th bivouacked in the town square. With their arrival in Es Salt, the Jewish battalions' fighting came to an end.[42] The whole enemy front was now collapsing. As Gammage succinctly put it, 'the great chase had begun ... everywhere the enemy was demoralized'.[43]

Eliazar was appointed the military governor of the town. His task was to establish law and order, ensure its civil administration and take care of the sick and wounded. Although his role lasted just a week, it was the first time any Jew, let alone a naturalized Australian Jew, had held such a post since the Romans had ended Jewish rule in Judea, almost eighteen hundred years earlier. Among the wounded and ill who needed care were Turks, West Indians, members of the Jewish battalions and about twelve Australians. Es Salt itself, a town of about 10,000, was a principal commercial centre, its population divided between Muslims and Christian Arabs. The Christians had sided with the British forces, and because of this, felt the need to flee to Jerusalem with the 39th when they left the town.[44]

Even Eliazar's scant knowledge of Arabic was helpful in this situation, and he saw to it that the Turkish dead were buried with dignity. Conscripted Jewish Turkish prisoners were released. He admonished his men not to act as arrogant conquerors. Not that the Turks were averse to surrendering to the legionnaires, fearing castration, decapitation and torture, should they fall into the hands of the Bedouin. The legionnaires also had to be alert to the Bedouins' marauding habits and to Arab snipers. One person Eliazar encountered was his old friend Faisal, who had been used as a guard at Rehovot and on whose horse he had greeted Herzl back in 1898. Faisal was to again help Eliazar, this time to uncover where the Turks had hidden arms.[45]

Salaman says of his commander that 'it was a real treat to see how he shone when it came to doing things', and that he fulfilled his aims with great efficiency and humanity.[46] On 1 October, Eliazar was ordered to leave Es Salt, and to return to Ludd with 1,500 prisoners, including 300 Germans captured in the battle for Es Salt. Both Salaman[47] and Patterson,[48] each from his own perspective, tell of the complete failure, ineptitude and total disregard of the British military authorities for the health and welfare of the Jewish battalions, which were in a pitiful condition and ravaged by malaria. As Salaman caustically put it, the senior medical officer and military headquarters were 'too much thinking of decorations than the medical needs of the men'. No plans were in place to move the sick from Es Salt to Jerusalem, where they should have been cared for, before being repatriated to Ludd. In perhaps his first act of open defiance of his superior officers, Eliazar refused to decamp until all the sick and wounded had been hospitalized in Jerusalem. In Jerusalem, however, conditions in hospitals for Jewish patients were abysmal, and their neglect rampant. The British authorities had denied the Jewish battalions' request for medical officers, the exception being Captain Redcliffe Salaman. With Margolin's support, he established, as it were, a field hospital in the city, aided by a team of female Jewish nurses from Jerusalem, to improve the men's treatment. Patterson felt that, 'As the Senior Officer of the Jewish Battalions, not being myself a Jew, I was deeply hurt at the un-English methods adopted towards men who had done so well in the field in England's cause, and I felt that I would not be doing my duty to those under my command, and to Jewry generally, unless I protested this unfair discrimination.'[49] The ranks of his own 38th had been so depleted that he had had to ask the Australians to help care for his battalion animals. Patterson himself was extremely ill and reduced to a skeleton. He felt he had no choice but to resign over what he saw as an anti-Jewish policy, but this was refused. According to Patterson, it was to prevent him becoming a free agent, able to tell everyone in England that GHQ in Egypt was doing its best to ensure 'the Balfour Declaration was a mere scrap of paper'.[50] Major-General Louis Jean Bols, the chief-of-staff, refused to see him. When he threatened to have the situation discussed in the British Parliament, he was asked, in true bureaucratic style, to furnish his complaints in writing. Not surprisingly, all these were ignored. Even a special badge granted by the War Office, which was to be given to the Jewish battalions, had been denied them by GHQ in Cairo.[51]

In medical terms, according to Salaman, the attitude of GHQ meant that the Jewish battalions always found it difficult to obtain supplies, even in camp at Sarafend, simply because they were not brigaded or attached to any particular division. This sorely affected his patients in Jerusalem. On a general level, however, it meant that the battalions were constantly being messed about with. In part he saw this problem as of the battalions' own making, because 'they did well in whatever they were called on to do'.[52]

Certainly, the men of the 40th Battalion felt messed about. The frustration they felt was in no way diminished when they were belatedly allowed to return to Palestine. They judged that their training in Egypt had not just been kept substandard deliberately, but that this fact was then used as an excuse by the authorities for not sending them to the front in Palestine. Impatience grew into downright annoyance, which eroded discipline. When they were ultimately dispatched to the camp at Sarafend, nothing really changed; it was business as usual. Drill and guard duty were again the daily order. Not only were the men not personally challenged, but they, as Palestinian volunteers, felt demeaned and diminished. After all, they had enlisted specifically to defend the *Yishuv*. Now others were doing this job. Only a handful of skilled riders, who spoke Arabic and knew the topography and Arab settlement to the north, acted as guides to the Australian and West Indian contingents.[53]

Soon after his return to Sarafend, Margolin took time off for yet another short visit to see friends in Rehovot, which was only six miles from camp. It was to be one of many future visits. Again, Salaman went with him.[54]

After enduring heavy bombardment, the Turks surrendered northern Palestine without firing a shot. The Australian cavalry raced to the Lebanese border, and turned eastwards to the Jordan River and Syria to help complete Allenby's victory over the Turks.[55] On 11 November 1918, with the declaration of the Armistice, the Great War officially came to an end. Nevertheless, the British military suzerainty over Palestine was to remain in force until 1920, as the Occupied Enemy Territory Administration (OETA) headquartered in Cairo, with General Sir Edmund Allenby its commander-in-chief. With the Armistice came the rumour that the Jewish battalions were to be kept in Palestine as a garrison force.

Abe Troy tells the story that Lieutenant-Colonel Margolin and his medical officer, Dr Salaman, toasted the Armistice with a glass of Rishon wine: ' "To peace," said Dr Salaman. "We will pray for it," said Colonel Margolin. "I doubt, however, if total peace will come to this land for a long time. There are bound to be many clashes between Arabs and Jews; I know the Arabs all too well." '[56]

Episode Three

12

Military Zionophobia

The camaraderie between the Australian troops and the Jewish battalions was founded on a common humanity, much social contact and a shared contempt of the British officer corps. For the legionnaires, the Australians evinced none of the British personnel's anti-Semitism or snobbishness.[1] They warmed to the Australians' larrikin spirit and ridicule of military pomposity and protocol, manifest in their disinclination to salute British officers. Any simmering tension between the boys from down under – both Australian and New Zealander – and the British brass during the Middle East campaign, however, turned to overt hostility after the Armistice of 11 November 1918, when the guns of the Great War officially fell silent. In fact, the Middle East campaign had drawn to an end twelve days earlier when, having lost Syria to Allenby, the Turks finally surrendered on 30 October.

Two matters contributed to this explosion of feeling among the Anzac and Jewish forces in the immediate post-Armistice period: an extremely slow demobilization and the British High Command's policy of appeasing the Arabs, whatever the circumstances. One particular incident caused exceptional bitterness and the Anzacs' response to it was said to have taught the men of the Jewish Legion a salutary lesson on how to deal with the Bedouin.[2] This particular matter involved a problem that had long troubled the Jewish settlements: constant unchecked and unpunished Arab thievery and assault. The Anzacs dealt with this problem in their own way, which the legionnaires called the 'Australian method'. The circumstances involved, and the Anzacs' reaction, have been related in the memoir of George and Edmée Langley, *Sand, Sweat, and Camels*. These authors express the exasperation of the Anzacs with the 'Arabs of West Palestine', seeing them as: 'thieves by instinct and exceedingly crafty, those living close to the Jewish settlements specially practised and daring. They were a lazy coward squalid type of native with no allegiance either to Mohammed or themselves.'[3] No amount of theft from the Anzacs could persuade their British military superiors to punish the Arab perpetrators. Not only were they ordered to treat these Arabs with kid gloves, but when such incidents happened – as they often did, it was the victims – the Anzacs, who were accused of being in the wrong.[4]

The incident in question occurred at the Sarafend camp in December 1918 while the men were preparing for demobilization. One night, a New Zealand sergeant awoke to find an Arab trying to steal the kit bag on which his head was resting! He chased the intruder through the camp into the surrounding sand hills; the pursued thief turned, drew a gun and killed his pursuer. The following morning angry troops called on the sheikhs of the nearby Arab village of Sarafend, to which the offender had fled, to surrender the culprit. This was refused. The men expected a senior officer from Allenby's headquarters, only six miles away, to come promptly to attend the scene and take charge of the situation. As with previous acts of Arab criminality, however, no officer arrived, whereupon the soldiers themselves decided to dispense justice as they saw it. Women and children were removed from the Arab village, and placed under guard so they would not run away. The village encampment was then burnt. Males fleeing the fire were beaten, and several were killed. The Langleys explained succinctly, 'to the troops, the loss of a veteran comrade by foul murder, at the hands of a race they despised, was a crime which called for instant justice'. The Anzacs then raided and burned a neighbouring Bedouin camp before quietly filing back to their digs.[5] Gullett attributed a large part of these murderous doings to New Zealanders, although they had much sympathy and support among their Australian brothers.[6]

For once, Allenby's headquarters was aroused, but only instantly, to discipline the men. There was no interest at all in what had driven them to exact such savage revenge. Allenby demanded the names of those involved, but no one volunteered; rather, the Anzacs took collective responsibility. An enraged Allenby responded by parading the Anzac Mounted Division to rebuke it with 'direct' language, which further offended the men. The general's tirade only added fuel to the fire, and further increased the men's displeasure with 'the Old Country'.[7]

Despite Allenby's objections, Gullett personally intervened in this standoff to point out to the general that his attitude might well harm

1. Lieutenant E. L. Margolin in the uniform of the citizens' militia in Australia prior to his enlistment in 1914, source unknown.

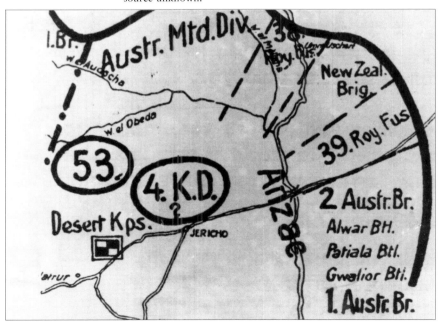

2. Enemy map showing Allied forces in the Palestine campaign (Jewish Legions Museum, Avihayil, Israel).

3. The insignia of the Jewish Legion (Jewish Legions Museum, Avihayil, Israel).

4. Margolin leading the 39th Battalion Royal Fusiliers through Ben Shemen (Archives of the Israeli Ministry of Defence, Tel Aviv).

5. Lieutenant-Colonel Margolin consulting a map of Wadi Keith on the way to Jericho (Archives of the Israeli Ministry of Defence, Tel Aviv).

6. Eliazar Margolin on his beloved horse (Jewish Legions Museum, Avihayil, Israel).

7. Flag of the First Judeans (Jewish Legions Museum, Avihayil, Israel).

8. Laying the foundation stone of the Hebrew University of Jerusalem, 1919. Margolin second from right in military uniform (Jewish Legions Museum, Avihayil, Israel).

9. Eliazar and Hilda Margolin on the steps of their Nedland home (family archive).

ברית החייל בארץ ישראל
המפקדה הראשית

ביום ה' ט"ז תמח תש"ד , (6. 7. 44) תתקיים במועדון
ברית החייל בתל אביב, נחלת בינמין 63,

אספת אזכרה לזכר של הקולונל

אליעזר מרגולין נ"ע

מפקד הגדוד העברי "ראשון ליהודה" במלחמה הקודמת

ינאמו :

הרב הראשי לתל אביב ויפו הגאון
הרי"מ טולידנו שליט"א
ה' מנחם ארבר מהגדוד העברי

תפילת האזכרה תיערך ע"י החזן מבית הכנסת הגדול
מר יהושע דלין

האספה תתחיל בשעה 7 בערב.   חיילים משוחררים ואוהדי המנוח מוזמנים.

10. The memorial service for Margolin in Tel Aviv, 1944 (Archives of the Israeli Ministry of Defence, Tel Aviv). Translation below.

Alliance of the Solder in Eretz Israel

Main headquarters

On Thursday 16 Tamuz 5704 (6.7.44)
A memorial assembly for the memory of
Colonel Eliazar Margolin ZL

Commander of the Jewish Battalion 'The First Judeans' in the former war

will be held at the Brit Hachayal Tel Aviv club, 68 Nachlat Binyamin St.

Speakers:

The Chief Rabbi of Tel Aviv and Jaffa, Rabbi Y. M. Tolidano Shatila

Mr Menachem Arber of the Jewish Battalion

The memorial prayer will be given by the chazan of the Great Synagogue (Beit Haknesset Hagadol), Mr Yehoshua Delin.

The assembly will start at 7 p.m.

All discharged soldiers and devotees of the deceased are welcome.

11. Margolin's reburial in the presence of former Legionnaires,
Rehovot Cemetery, January 1950 (Archives of Yad Itzhak Ben-Zvi,
Jerusalem).

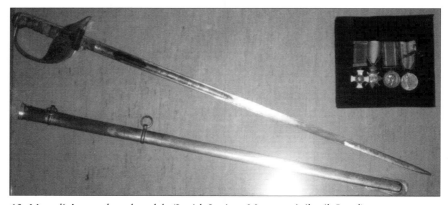

12. Margolin's swords and medals (Jewish Legions Museum, Avihayil, Israel).

13. Hilda Margolin at the Weizmann Institute, Rehovot, January 1959. Left to right: Jacob Pat, Hilda Margolin, Chaim Weizmann, Yitzhak Ben-Zvi (Archives of Yad Itzhak Ben-Zvi, Jerusalem).

14. Hilda Margolin at a ceremony honouring her husband, Jerusalem, 1950. Left to right: Yitzhak Ben-Zvi, Hilda Margolin, David Ben-Gurion, Jacob Pat (Archives of Yad Itzhak Ben-Zvi, Jerusalem).

15. Eliazar Margolin's grave, between those of his parents, Rehovot Cemetery, Israel.

16. Colonel Margolin Street, Rehovot.

imperial relations. Allenby backed down, but only slightly. As punishment, the division was relocated to the desert camp near Rafa, all leave was cancelled, and the names of its officers and men struck from the list recommended for honours and decorations.[8] One beneficial outcome for the *Yishuv* from this incident was the freeing of the road from Sarafend to the Jewish settlement of Rishon Le-Zion from the usual Bedouin interference.

Just what the Jewish battalions could learn from such an event is moot. They had no one like Gullett to defend them in the court of Allenby. They too had long endured Bedouin harassment and official inaction. If there was anything instructive that could be taken from this incident by the Jewish battalions, it was perhaps the Anzacs' attitude of 'one in, all in', of taking collective responsibility for their actions when attempting to correct a perceived wrong. Later, the legionnaires were to take similar steps when they judged that they, as a body, had also been badly treated by British military justice.

No matter how aggrieved the Anzacs felt by the appeasement policies of Allenby's officers and officials, it paled in comparison with the aggravation, cynicism, harassment and Judeophobia experienced by the Jewish battalions at the hands of the British headquarters staff from the moment they arrived in Palestine. In his book, *Israel: A History*, Martin Gilbert has suggested that Allenby appreciated the efforts of the Jewish Legion.[9] The evidence, however, simply does not support this assertion: if he did, his appreciation certainly did not filter down the chain of command in Cairo or Palestine. Patterson says that positive dispatches relating to the Jewish battalions were never allowed to appear in the Palestinian and Egyptian newspapers. This injustice was most evident in Allenby's victory speech in Cairo in December 1918, when he acknowledged the contribution to his victory in the Middle East theatre of every segment of his troops except the Jewish battalions.[10] The rank injustice of this treatment, though keenly felt, was generally suffered in silence. In reminiscing over the extreme punishment of up to seven years' gaol issued by a British military court in 1919 to men of the Jewish battalions for the charge of disobeying an order, Patterson was to write: 'All I can say is that if an Australian, English, Irish or a Scottish battalion had been treated as this Jewish battalion was treated, Divisional Headquarters could have gone up in flames and the General (viz. Major-General Louis Bols) himself would have been lucky to escape.'[11]

Pierre Van Paassen long ago made the point that those sent to manage Palestine, whether in military or civil duties, were ideologically opposed to London's official pro-Zionist policy. They had been dragged reluctantly from either Egypt or low-status imperial posts in places such as India, Kenya, Rhodesia and the Sudan, and lacked both the experience and 'the high moral character of the old-type British colonial functionary'.[12] For them, the Balfour Declaration stood in conflict with the long-term interests of Great Britain and its empire. It was considered a grave mistake, one from which Great Britain should disengage as quickly as possible. Apart from a palpable anti-Semitism among a number of the officer class, their attitude was also grounded in the strategy of using pan-Arabism to help promote British imperial ambitions in the former Ottoman lands of the Middle East. They hoped that this might happen to the detriment of Great Britain's ally, France. This policy dissonance between White-hall and its officials in Egypt and Palestine caused great problems for the Zionist cause of the *Yishuv* in general, and for the legionnaires in particular. While London might have wanted to run a Zionist line, it still relied on these officials to translate its policy into practice. Isaiah Freedman has commented that the British military administration in Palestine 'took a completely opposite line to London ... it not only breached official policy, but also Allenby's instruction on 23 October 1918 which forbade the military from interfering in any political question.'[13]

Colonel Richard Meinertzhagen, a chief intelligence officer dispatched by the Foreign Office to the British Military Administration in Egypt, indicated in 1919 the presence of a growing anti-Jewish feeling in the Palestinian administration, especially in the absence of a clear statement from London to that administration that the Arab was not to be thought of as the 'most favoured element in Palestine'.[14] His sensibilities had no doubt been sharpened by his relatively recent conversion to Zionism, been influenced by meeting, in 1917, the Aaron Aaronsohn family – whose spying for Great Britain against the Turks during the Great War had imperilled their lives – and after visiting Zionist settlements in Palestine.[15] This British officer sensed anti-Jewish antagonism across all non-Jewish communities in both Palestine and Syria. Despite his transmogrification into a Zionist, his view remained curiously overlaid by a British class and cultural snobbishness. In an epistle to Lord Curzon, he remarked that though the Judeophobia extant was traceable to a 'deliberate misunderstanding of the Jew and everything Jewish,' it had also arisen because of a lack of local contact with 'the real Jewish culture and better class of Zionist', yet to be established in Palestine. He was profoundly concerned over the immigration policy, or in his words, 'the dumping of East European undesirable Jews' there.[16]

Josiah Wedgwood, who was to enter the House of Commons, was unequivocal that at this time almost all British diplomats and military officers in Cairo who oversaw the governance of Palestine were disgusted by the Balfour Declaration. According to him, they viewed any Zionist industrial or economic development of the Holy Land as vulgar.[17] Douglas Duff, another non-Jew, one certainly not in sympathy with Zionism, and someone who had won popularity with the Arabs in the Wailing Wall violence of 1928 by preventing Jews from praying at their holy site,[18] observed that:

> For some conservative reasons, the average Englishman's sympathy seems to fly towards the Arabs. Certainly he is picaresque in his medieval virtues, he is terrible in his vices and treacheries. His houses, his clothes, his appearance, perhaps the fact that we believe he is being harshly treated as the weaker of the two protagonists in the Palestine question, tends to make many of the British espouse their cause. Maybe it is an innate hatred of all things Jewish that does this, though I do not think that, as some people believe.[19]

Such racial antagonism was confirmed by Major General Sir William Thwaites, Director of Military Intelligence for Palestine. He claimed that the British officer class dealing with Palestine feared, almost to a man, any formula that could be interpreted as favouring the Jews. In this matter, they were even prepared to defy their political masters in London. General Money, the chief administrator in Palestine, adamantly believed that the Balfour Declaration should be scrapped.[20]

A fear persisted among these officials that anti-Jewish ferment in the Ukraine might encourage a far greater number of Jews to consider Palestine as a haven of refuge. If this were to occur, it could spark insurrection against British interests, and spread throughout the Muslim world, from Egypt to Calcutta.[21] Jewish communities throughout the British Empire were extremely worried by the violent – indeed murderous – anti-Jewish riots in Eastern Europe following the Great War.[22] Such concern was felt no less by the men of the Jewish Legion in Palestine. The vicious pogroms in Poland caused Margolin's men – with his agreement – to raise a petition denouncing them. It was dispatched to Allenby with the hope he would pass the petition on to British representatives at the Peace Conference. It declared that: 'When determining the future of Poland, the rights of national minorities dwelling in that country must be safeguarded. The specific conditions under which our people live and labour necessitate that their national and political rights be everywhere guaranteed and safeguarded by the Peace Conference ...'[23]

It was not the practice of a British commander to receive a petition from his men on matters of international affairs, so its fate is not known. If it had reached Allenby, however, which seems unlikely, one particular paragraph would undoubtedly have irritated him. It read:

> We are the forerunners of a Jewish National Army, and as such we have taken up arms not only to fight for freedom in Palestine, but also to avenge our molested honour and the trampled principles of humanity and justice. We are ready to respond to the call of our outraged brethren and to shield them from the beastly attacks of marauding bands disguised in the uniforms of soldiers ...[24]

Given Allenby's disapproval of the Jewish Legion and Zionism, and his apprehensions over anything that might upset the Arabs, the notion that the Jewish battalion was 'the forerunner of a Jewish National Army' would not have made pleasing reading for him. Rather than rousing sympathy for the pathetic situation of the Jews in Eastern Europe, the spectre of Jews swarming from there to Palestine only hardened opposition to Zionist immigration, and encouraged his support for a retreat from the principles enunciated in the Balfour Declaration.

Complaints about the British military authority's maltreatment of Jews in Palestine became so numerous as to cause American Zionist leader Louis Brandeis to visit Palestine to assess the situation on the ground. Knowing that the accusations of discrimination were likely to be proven, OETA headquarters in Cairo attempted a pre-emptive strategy to head off the expected criticism. It advised London that Brandeis might well find substance in the criticisms, especially accusations that the authorities were not interpreting the Balfour Declaration in an equitable manner. The defensive tactic employed was to blame the victim, the Jews themselves. OETA claimed that the 'immoderate demeanour of a considerable proportion of the Jewish population made it necessary to carefully control Zionist activities'.[25] As expected, Brandeis did find evidence of inappropriate behaviour by British military officials. He told General Money, the chief administrator for Palestine, that he himself had witnessed examples.[26] That said, this American 'interloper', whatever his status, and his influence in London, was never going to move Money or his superior, Allenby. In a proverbial whitewash, Allenby wrote to the British Secretary of War, Winston Churchill, that he had convinced Brandeis that the dispute between his administration and the *Yishuv* was merely a case of misunderstanding.[27]

The OETA's opposition to the Balfour Declaration, and its desire that nothing should convulse its pro-Arab programme, would inevitably constrain, and make difficulties for, Eliazar Margolin's military career in Palestine.

13

The First Judeans

With the Armistice signed and sealed, the question arose of who should replace Turkish authority over Palestine – should Great Britain be left in military control of the area when the guns fell silent? While international discussion on this matter formally commenced at the 1919 Peace Conference, the reality was that no other nation, including the United States of America, felt itself in a position to challenge Great Britain.[1] Leonard Stein establishes that the British prime minister, Lloyd George, was intent on keeping Palestine.[2] As the debates at this conference indicated, the administration of Palestine would by its very nature have to juggle the competing claims of both Arabs and Zionists. During the war Great Britain had made promises to both – for the Arabs these lay in the secret McMahon correspondence of 1915.[3] Notionally, this was complicated by the Sykes–Picot Accord. Completed in 1916, this complicated matters further, given that it proposed the carve-up of the Ottoman lands of the Middle East almost exclusively between Great Britain and France.[4] This situation was further confused when the Balfour Declaration came into play on 2 November 1917. When the Jewish battalions were established to serve in Palestine, many of their men had enlisted in the belief that their corps would form the basis of a Jewish army to defend the *Yishuv*. Nevertheless, even with Great Britain in charge in Palestine, the chance for this to happen was best served by keeping alive the principles of the Balfour Declaration. This requirement was threatened by a few issues, such as the previously discussed bitter resentment of the military authorities *in situ* towards Zionism. Questions of anti-Semitism aside, this bitterness towards the Balfour Declaration was in part an attempt to keep a nascent Arab nationalism in check lest it seriously erode British strategic interests in the Middle East.

In Palestine itself, a consequence of the immediate post-Armistice friction was the tardiness of the demobilization of forces. This irritated British units across the board, but none more so than the discriminated-against Jewish battalions. As Patterson has written, many soldiers in these battalions had become so alienated by the British authorities, particularly the military police, that they gave up the idea of remaining in Palestine to form a garrison army. Many of them, who came from outside Palestine, wondered if, when demobbed, they should stay in *Eretz Israel* to help in its defence and/or development.[5]

On 2 January 1919, Salaman noted:

> The fact is that the O.E.T.A. is unfriendly to Jewish interests and will not stir itself to help, the position here is very difficult. There is a dead weight of inertia (if not hostility) against the Zionists in practically all their departments. The Zionist Commission themselves is not too strong and has no striking personality among them while Weizmann is away. Nothing can be done before the Peace Conference is ended, and the authorities won't commit themselves. They are playing for peace and quiet at any price and they know the Jews won't give trouble and the Arabs may, so they favour the latter ...[6]

One area where the OETA was active was in lobbying against any bolstering of the numbers of the Jewish battalions. On 16 June 1919, a secret note sent from Allenby, the General Officer Commanding the OETA in Cairo, to the War Office in London, read:

> I am strongly opposed to an increase in Jewish troops in Palestine: the measure would be interpreted as a preparation to enforce the claim of the Jewish community over the rest of the population. The present distrust of the non-Jewish population would be greatly increased. There have already been incidents between Jewish soldiers and non-Jewish inhabitants, especially Moslem, and an increase in Jewish troops would certainly lead to riots and widespread trouble with the Arabs.[7]

This was a response to Zionist pressure in London to prevent the disbanding of the Jewish Legion. To retain, augment, or dissolve the Jewish battalions, however, was but one issue. Another was whether any legionnaire from outside Palestine, once demobbed, should be allowed to settle as a genuine Jewish immigrant.

Christopher Sykes has blamed the Zionist Commission for making it difficult for the OETA Headquarters in Cairo to co-operate with it. An example he cites is the commission complaint that the military administration was prejudiced in not broadening the Jewish battalions into a discrete Palestinian garrison. When the 40th was ordered to Cyprus, however, it refused. This insubordination, Sykes suggests, was one reason for headquarters' reluctance to raise further Jewish units.[8] Indeed, the Palestinian battalion, the 40th, did refuse to serve anywhere other than in Palestine. Its members insisted that they had volunteered to defend only *Eretz Israel*. To be sent elsewhere would be tantamount to being exiled, and would stigmatize them in the eyes of the *Yishuv*. When they were asked to go to Cyprus, the dispute escalated to the point that the battalion was in danger of being disbanded.[9] As for the 39th, the Jewish soldiers had to wear the heat of some of its non-Jewish officers. One in particular is often mentioned, a Major Smolley, who took command of the unit when Eliazar was on leave in England. He apparently took great delight in antagonizing the 39th's American contingent.[10]

In one incident, when soldiers of the 38th considered that one of its men had been unjustly treated by a British officer, frustration turned into rebellion. They protested *en masse*, refused to disperse when ordered, and were charged with mutiny. They were represented at the resultant court martial by Vladimir Jabotinsky. Fifty-five men were given sentences of up to seven years in prison. On another occasion, some of the 39th received similar sentences merely for being absent without leave. Roman Freulich quotes Margolin as saying on returning from England that, 'when I left I had one battalion – now I have two and one of them in prison'.[11]

The general slowness of demobilization, exacerbated by the attitudes of the British officer class, severely undermined morale and discipline in all the Jewish battalions. Salaman's impression was that OETA did not want a Jewish presence in any senior position, not even under the greatly inferior conditions under which Margolin said that no one of 'ours' would work.[12] The military police seemed to take great delight humiliating Jewish soldiers especially when they were in the company of women. Jews were generally not considered culturally acceptable for posts in the military police. In Jerusalem, a city with a majority Jewish population, only thirteen men of the 126-strong military police unit were Jewish, and none of the sixteen non-commissioned officers.[13]

This prejudice was matched by the refusal of the authorities to station Jewish battalions in the traditional Jewish confessional cities of Jerusalem, Hebron, Safed and Tiberias. When a company of the

40th was deployed in Haifa, its presence was abruptly withdrawn because of Arab objections.[14] When Arab violence threatened in Jaffa in March 1919, Jabotinsky describes how:

> A company of the 39th Royal Fusiliers was doing musketry practice on the seashore, not far from the menaced area. This company was suddenly withdrawn before the course was over: the Battalion generally was relieved of all its guards and put on fatigues of a kind entrusted to native Labour corps. The C.O., Lieut-Colonel Margolin, had to explain to the men why this step was taken. The reason as set forth by him was that G.H.Q. did not want to excite the Arabs by the sight of Jewish soldiers.[15]

Such orders seem to have been intended to inflict the greatest humiliation possible on these Jewish soldiers. They found it utterly demeaning to be engaged in latrine and other menial duties, usually carried out by local Arabs, and being forced to leave the security of the Jewish population to non-Jewish soldiers. It caused a serious rethink as to why they should remain in uniform.[16] Eliazar Margolin interceded on behalf of the legionnaires, convinced the men to stay in uniform, and had the offending orders rescinded without penalty. This interference, however, would not have endeared him to fellow British officers.

The military authorities' unwillingness to upset the Arabs, whether Christian or Muslim, was well illustrated early in 1919 when, on 6 April, an order banned all Jewish soldiers from the precincts of the 'walled City of Jerusalem' between the fourteenth and twenty-second of that month.[17] That week covered the period of Passover, one of Judaism's pilgrim festivals, during which, traditionally, Jews came to Jerusalem to pray. No prohibition prevented any Christian or Muslim soldier from entering the city on their holy days. During the Passover festival, which often coincided with the Christian Easter, fiery anti-Jewish diatribes were preached in Jerusalem's churches. In this particular case, the period of prohibition did not coincide with either a Christian or Muslim holy day. Jewish soldiers were even banned from Jaffa-Tel Aviv and encouraged to take their leave in the various Jewish settlements.[18] These directions were accompanied by obnoxious harassment by the military police.[19] Jews were also generally prevented from making pilgrimages to other places, such as the grave of Rabbi Meir Baal Hananes, and celebrating at Meron the traditional Lag B'Omer festivities that split the period between the Jewish festivals of Passover and *Shavuot*, lest they upset the Arabs.[20] Any demonstration of Jewish nationalism, such as singing the HaTikvah, was also banned in public places.[21] Major-General H. D. Watson, the chief of administration in Palestine, sent word to GHQ in Cairo on 16 August 1919 expressing fear of possible Arab riots against Zionist policy.[22]

Even before the Armistice, there was much discussion in Zionist circles about the future of the *Yishuv* once it was liberated from the Turks. One topic included was defence, with plans for the Jewish community in Palestine to establish its own army. It was suggested that the three Jewish battalions combine into a Jewish brigade, with its officers promoted from the ranks, its own emblems and Eliazar Margolin as commander. In 1919, before demobilization, collectively the three Jewish battalions numbered 5,000 soldiers, a sixth of the British army in Palestine and a quarter of its infantry. Their national makeup was approximately 34 per cent American, 30 per cent Palestinian, 28 per cent English, 6 per cent Canadian, 1 per cent Argentinean, and 1 per cent former Turkish prisoners-of-war. In addition to the contempt of the OETA's minions in Palestine, boredom was another problem. Attempts were made to relieve this by activities such as inter-battalion sports. One event between the 39th and 40th, was a horse derby between officers, which featured – copying the Australians – a totalizator used to record and distribute bets.[23] The 39th also formed an orchestra, which gave numerous concerts to which Eliazar was invited.[24] Much of the time was taken up with exercises and guard duties. When an anti-British insurrection erupted in March 1919 in Egypt, only those very few in the battalions actually engaged in training programmes were called on.

It may have been a visionary idea to form a Jewish brigade of the three battalions, but it was inevitable that it would founder on the rocks of the men's intentions. Simply put, many of those who joined the 38th were not Zionists and wanted to return to England. The same was true for a good proportion of the 39th who, despite their initial statements about wanting to stay, decided to go home to the United States of America. In both cases they did so when permitted. Indeed, when this occurred during 1919, the Jewish Legion as such came to an end. The remnant of each battalion joined with the Palestinians of the 40th, to form a single unit, the First Judeans, which eventually was granted its own emblems – the *Magen David* (Star of David), and *Menorah* (Seven Branch Candelabrum) – with Hebrew as its own language of command. In charge was

Lieutenant-Colonel Eliazar Margolin. Ostensibly, this unit's job was to act as a garrison force to defend Palestine for Great Britain. Given the British military authority's attitude to the Jewish forces, it was inevitable that the two would clash. The men of the First Judeans were ideologically fully dedicated to the *Yishuv*.

It was at around this time that Eliazar Margolin was singled out in the Australian Jewish press for laudatory comment. Conspicuously absent when Jewish heroes of the Great War were being discussed and praised, suddenly, without warning, his name appeared in the *Jewish Herald* of 23 August 1919. Under a headline, 'The First Jewish Governor in Palestine – A Brave Australian Soldier' an extremely brief, and flawed, biography of 'Colonel' Eliazar Margolin followed. Though he had not been the temporary 'Military Governor of the Ramleh district in Palestine' for over a year, the impression given was that he still held that post.

Given that members of the 40th dominated the new corps, it is not surprising that the men of the First Judeans would be in total sympathy with the aspirations and mores of the *Yishuv*. Eliazar was similarly inclined. For example, the men of the 40th were used to a highly active organizing committee that met outside their camp, as gatherings of this nature were prohibited under military rules. The time and place of committee meetings were passed on by word of mouth. Sometimes up to two hundred soldiers took part in discussions about issues that affected the men, the *Yishuv*, and the relationship between the two. Representatives of the men would then seek out their commander, Eliazar Margolin, to seek appropriate solutions. The committee, where applicable, also met with Zionist officials.[25]

The destiny of the Margolin-led First Judeans was inevitably affected by the *Realpolitik* as it evolved in Palestine. As noted earlier, policy may have been determined in London but was actually interpreted on the ground by the British military authority, and after 1921, a civil authority. And that in turn relied on an assessment of how the Arabs might help – or at least not hinder – British interests in the Middle East. Post-Armistice, this was indelibly influenced by a growing Arab hostility to Zionism. They were armed well enough to carry out their threats. Salaman observed: 'The O.E.T.A. is all for peace and quiet, and as the Arab is in the majority, armed to the teeth, and much more likely to give trouble than the Jew ...'[26] He added that OETA felt 'the Balfour Declaration was a snare to grab Jewish sympathy and that the British Government will wriggle out of it'.[27]

Arab nationalist expectations elsewhere spread to Palestine, further fuelling the Arab–Jewish volcano during 1919. Beginning on 20 February 1920 there began what is remembered in Zionist historiography as the infamous, murderous Arab assault on the minuscule upper Galilee settlements of Metulla, Kefar Giladi, Khamara and Tel Hai. All were in close proximity to Arab villages. Along with a handful of colleagues, Yosef Trumpeldor, of Zion Mule Corps fame, was killed on 1 March, defending the rudimentary settlement of Tel Hai.[28] The Arab aggression in northern Palestine was soon to be followed by attacks on the Jewish Quarter in Jerusalem during the festival of Passover. There were at least a hundred and sixty Jewish casualties. Only belatedly did British troops attempt to stop the violence, and a handful of Arab rioters were arrested, slapped on the wrist, and freed the following day. What the Arabs learned from this was that they could attack Jews with little risk of punishment from the British military authority. What the Jews realized was that they could ultimately rely only on themselves for their own security.

Members of the First Judeans resented the fact that officially they were not permitted to help defend their brethren and, in some cases, their own families. In 1920 when the anti-Jewish riots began in Palestine, they demanded that they be sent to guard the various centres of Jewish population. Their plea was rejected by the military authority at Sarafend, who feared that this could lead to the killing of Arabs. The committee then went into clandestine mode, sending men to likely targets of Arab aggression. Their absences were covered by the Jewish officers, Captains Jaffe and Levy, both ex-Londoners. Non-Jewish officers were generally not taken into the men's confidence. On one occasion almost half of the Judeans were missing from roll call. It was always said that Eliazar prided himself on running an efficient camp. He was a stickler for detail, and would have been well informed had any of his men been missing, especially *en masse*. Clearly in sympathy with the sentiments of his troops, he handled matters such as this by pretending not to notice.[29]

Several months later when the situation again became difficult and information was received that the Arabs were preparing to riot, the committee approached Margolin, who in turn advised the authorities at Sarafend that a number of his men were about 'to leave', and that he wanted to send them to guard the Jewish population. This request was refused, leaving Margolin, on his return, to tell the men that he could not take responsibility for their actions if they left. He was most apprehensive that anti-Jewish riots would soon erupt, but added that if they did leave, they could not take their rifles with them. Their response was that if, in the last resort, these rifles were necessary to defend their families, they would have to disobey this order. Margolin reported the gravity of the problem facing the Jewish settlements to headquarters.[30]

On 4 April 1920 a bloody pogrom exploded in the Old City of Jerusalem. It raged for three days, and Winston Churchill, in his capacity as the Secretary of State for War, admitted in the House of Commons that it had caused at least 250 casualties, of whom nine-tenths were Jewish.[31] It was a period of murder, rape, sacrilege and pillage, aided and abetted not by British action but indifference. The British observed the anti-Jewish mayhem, and were there in sufficient numbers to stop it. Closing the city's gates to other Jews in a real sense boxed them in for murder. Jabotinsky, now demobbed from the Jewish Legion, had expected strife a few days earlier, and had to organize the defence of the Jews. When he and his two companies of mainly former legionnaires arrived at the Jaffa and Damascus Gates, however, they found them closed by the British. Only on the third day did the British military act to end the carnage, arresting Jabotinsky and some of his followers. At a subsequent military court, Jabotinsky was sentenced for 'banditism' to an incredible fifteen years' hard labour. Two Arabs caught in the act of attempting to rape Jewish women received the same sentence.[32] When the convicted legionnaires returned to Ludd, they were met and warmly received by a very sympathetic Eliazar and his Judeans in open contempt of British authority. Because of the great outcry over the harsh and completely disproportionate sentences, the convicted men were very soon released. The military authority's deliberate inaction was fed by anti-Semitic hatred as much as by a desire not to upset the Arabs. Of course, the Arab insurrection was blamed on mythical Jewish provocateurs.

Fireproofing Jewish settlements against Bedouin looters and Arab assault had long been a major preoccupation of the *Yishuv*. In the 1890s each settlement formed its own volunteer militia, and in 1909 these became more organized and extensive when *HaShomer* (the watchman) was established.[33] Nevertheless, it was the Arabs' serial attacks during 1919 and 1920 that convinced leaders of the Jewish community in Palestine that the *Yishuv* was in grave danger. The anti-Zionism and endemic anti-Semitism of the British military authority that governed Palestine meant that it would not defend Jewish lives. *HaShomer* by itself was not capable of guaranteeing the security of the Jewish population. The Jerusalem pogrom further underlined the predicament. On 15 June 1920 *HaShomer* was officially disbanded, and moves began almost immediately to create a *Yishuv*-wide self-defence force, the *Haganah*.[34]

With the Jabotinsky fiasco, the hostility and prejudice of the military authority in Palestine became so obvious that London ended its reign on 1 July 1920. OETA's military supervision of Palestine was replaced by a civil administration headed by the first High Commissioner for Palestine, Herbert Samuel. The question now was how would this change affect the daily administration of Palestine with respect to the Arab–Zionist relationship. And on this, in turn, depended the role and tenure of the Margolin-led First Judeans.

14

Civilian Rule

On 24 April 1920, the San Remo Conference, which had been convened by the principal Allied powers, decided to award the Mandate over Palestine to the occupying power, Great Britain. The agreed text was, however, confirmed by the Council of the League of Nations only on 24 July 1922, to become officially operational in September 1923. In the preamble to the documentation were included the principles of the Balfour Declaration. In essence, this meant that not only did the concept of a Jewish homeland in Palestine now have international support, but also that those same nations accepted Great Britain's supervision of its evolution. Some later commentators have suggested that in effect, Great Britain won the Mandate by default because the minds of other members of the League of Nations were concentrated elsewhere,[1] and were hence grateful to have the onerous task of administering Palestine taken off their hands. Whatever the mindset involved, however, the fact remains that the international community – as then understood – put up its hands to support the idea of a Jewish homeland in Palestine[2] for the first time since the Jewish people were exiled by the Romans in the year 70 of the Common Era. Equally important is the fact that by accepting the Mandate, Great Britain indicated its willingness to take on this task. As a result, the British administration of Palestine was to pass from the Foreign Office to the Colonial Office. Christopher Sykes comments that Palestine 'left the care of Lord Curzon, an emphatic opponent of Zionism but one who never allowed his prejudices to influence his official actions, and entered the care of the Colonial Secretary, Mr. Winston Churchill, who wished Zion well from his heart.'[3]

In the field, this change was sealed with the selection of Herbert Samuel for the post of High Commissioner for Palestine. While this choice has long been a point of controversy in the literature, for

Eliazar Margolin it was not fortuitous, for it was a decision of the High Commissioner that was to blight his life.

The Zionist leadership's initial reaction to the appointment of a Jewish High Commissioner for Palestine was understandably positive. This was particularly so in the case of Herbert Samuel, who had visited the Holy Land just two months before the decision of the San Remo Conference allocated the administration of Palestine to Great Britain. He had returned to Great Britain critical of the military administration there. Though never a formal member of the Zionist movement, Samuel became interested in the Palestine Question as early as 1914, and became a prominent lobbyist in and around the British War Cabinet in favour of a Jewish homeland in that region. With the Balfour Declaration already in existence, in 1918 he chaired the Advisory Council on Zionism, a collection of pro-Zionist British notables who charted the Zionist case at the 1919 Peace Conference. Thus, when Samuel was appointed to head the civil administration in Palestine, it was with the Zionist movement's expectations that he would immediately move to establish the foundations for the Jewish homeland.[4] One person remembered that a sense of serenity and an atmosphere of complacency descended over the *Yishuv*. It was as if the selection of Samuel would of itself lead to a great reduction, if not cessation, in Arab belligerency.[5] Of course the Arab side was not amused, and viewed the appointment with much trepidation. The *Yishuv*'s original response soon soured, however, as it became apparent that Samuel's attitude had been misjudged. His pro-Zionist tendencies became constrained by what he felt were British interests and particularly conditioned by how policies might affect the Arabs.[6] From the Zionist perspective, Samuel was quickly seen by some as an artful dodger and opportunist, taking the post of High Commissioner to ingratiate himself deeper with the British establishment. The non-Jewish Zionophile, Pierre Van Paassen, was exceedingly caustic:

> His appointment as the first High Commissioner in Palestine was one of the shrewdest moves pulled off by the imperialists in the Colonial Office. With their deep insight into the character of assimilationist Jews, the fabricators of the policy of Empire surmised that such a Jew as Sir Herbert would go out of his way, in order to reward the confidence placed in him, by being super-impartial, extra-neutral, and 125% loyal to British interests, which in this case meant slowing the

building of the house for his own people. They were not wrong in that surmise.[7]

Not seeking to second-guess the British Colonial Office, most assessments of Samuel's administration picture him as an active and loyal servant of his political masters in London. Applying political pragmatism and imperial nous, this led, ultimately, to his appeasing the Arabs. One interpretation of his actions was that he had entered Palestine seeing British and Zionist aspirations as one, and then quickly came to see them as divergent.

Samuel genuinely hoped to reduce inter-communal violence in Palestine through the formation of a joint Arab–Jewish defence force. The commander touted for the Jewish component was Lieutenant-Colonel Eliazar Margolin. Such a post would have logically followed from his leadership role in the Jewish Legion and then the First Judeans. On 23 October 1920, Eliazar attended a meeting of senior military and civilian officials, under the auspices of Samuel, to discuss Samuel's proposal for a militia to comprise of Jews, Muslims and Christians.[8] It was to be a permanent corps designed to protect Palestine. Other British troops could be called for only in extenuating circumstances. Of course, motivation for this locally raised corps was only part military. If established, it was hoped to reduce the costs for British coffers of keeping a large garrison force in Palestine. It was hoped the finances of the bi-partisan force would essentially be funded in Palestine itself. The proposal was that only a portion of the recruits would be permanent, and the rest called up for training.

Among the principal operational queries that confronted the meeting were the force's overall command, political direction, *modus operandi* in the face of Arab violence, and the location of its head-quarters. London was adamant that Palestine should bear the burden of costs, although it recognized the impossibility of this in the short term. A consensus formed that the current army in residence was not performing its professional role, because it was too engaged in policing. Samuel insisted that his new force should be for Palestine alone, already seeing the area across the Jordan River – which he called Transjordania – as extra-territorial. Transjordania would be defended exclusively by a British unit stationed there and, as it were, guard Palestine from the east. It was believed that if Palestine were to be attacked, it would be from the east. There was also the problem of how the permanent members of the Jewish militia might be usefully engaged during the winter months, when Arab attacks were far less likely.

Eliazar argued that the proposed Palestinian force should include a cavalry component. He added, however, that nothing could reasonably be achieved if those under his command were not given far better training than his Judeans had previously received. A current omission was tuition on using the machine gun. His greatest concern, however, was over the preservation of the First Judeans, whose intended life was to end on 31 March 1921. Without assurances of an extended tenure, Eliazar said that the men required for the Jewish component of the proposed force would not be available: that come 1 April 1921 – a fateful date for reasons soon to be explained – there would hardly be enough of his men left in numbers proportionate to the proposed 500 Arab Christians and Muslims.

This discussion notwithstanding, the advent of civilian rule in Palestine failed to improve the tense relationship between the men of the First Judeans and the British officer class. On the other hand, no officer was more revered than their commander Eliazar Margolin, who was too often pressed into serving as a protective buffer against other officer mistreatment. The men's warm sentiments for their leader, from the formation of the Jewish Legion through to the First Judeans, were summed up in a marching song, 'Tell me who?' Sung to the British tune, 'Inky Pinky Parlez Vous', it read:

> He is some soldier, speaks proper English
> Tell me who
> Works every morning, so visit the pride
> Tell me who
> When commanding the stick in his left,
>   his right preparing to salute
> Tell me who

As commander in the British army, Eliazar had to walk a very fine line between his role as a loyal British officer and his love for the *Yishuv*. There is no current evidence to suggest that he had any direct contact with *HaShomer* or *Haganah*; indeed, it was not in his nature to have dealings with an underground organization whose actions were likely to run counter to British authority, both military and civilian. His men, on the other hand, did have such contacts. He knew of them, and in his own way facilitated them, because he felt the *Yishuv* was in jeopardy.

Former legionnaires helped fill the ranks and train the newly established *Haganah*, and the Judeans were complicit in smuggling arms and ammunition to it. A major task given the First Judeans, as asked of the 40th Battalion of the British Royal Fusiliers before it, was to guard camp military stores. This activity provided the *Haganah* with a means of securing rifles and ammunition to help combat Arab violence.

The more the British military authorities frustrated them with their blatant pro-Arab bias, the more Margolin's men, whether in the Jewish Legion or the First Judeans, were willing to help towards the security of the *Yishuv*. One such activist, Shimon HaCohen, has recounted how he and former Jewish Turkish prisoners-of-war disobeyed military orders to travel to Jerusalem to help Jabotinsky defend the Jews of the Old City against the previously mentioned Arab violence during Passover 1920. Fully comprehending his men's frustration over being barred from Jerusalem because of possible Arab resentment, Eliazar approved leave for a number of his men to be dispersed among Jewish settlements, and to take with them arms and ammunition. HaCohen mentions one occasion when he was interrogated by Eliazar over missing explosives from the camp stores in his charge. Though his commander knew what had happened, no punishment followed.[9]

There was an unwritten rule, according to Avraham Rochel, that anyone who could steal a weapon from the arms warehouses in the camps at Ziffrin and Be'er-Yaakov, did so.[10] One group from *HaShomer*, called *Bishkilim*, took rifles, bullets and bombs, and buried them in the sand for future use. 'Creative paperwork' was devised to cover the theft. Mules were also acquired and sold, with the profits transferred to a defence fund. Sometimes the men's enthusiasm overreached them. One episode saw Eliazar's prized horse about to be purloined.

Ammunition was also prized, and bullets were even saved from rifle practice. When Eliazar inquired of Rochel about the state of the stores of which he was in charge, he responded with a list of what was supposed to be in stock. Eliazar responded that he was not deceived, and berated Rochel about the need to be far more responsible in the future. But again no penalty was incurred.[11] In such circumstances, one could well understand why the men were eager to be chosen for the boring task of guarding the camp's warehouse. Cases of ammunition were emptied and replaced with sand. Not that such deceptions were never discovered: during an exercise on the firing range, a case, supposedly of bullets, revealed only sand. Eliazar and three other British officers were present. To avoid a scandal, Charit Yoseph remembers that their commander merely turned his horse around and left with the officers in tow.[12]

When in camp at Sarafend, as has been previously indicated, Eliazar liked to ride off on his treasured white horse to visit some of his favourite places, like Rishon Le-Zion, often accompanied on these rides by Dr Redcliffe Salaman. They were among the many men from Sarafend welcomed in many a settler's home. Efrat Ben-Cohen remembers her mother, Nechama Pochatcheveski, entertaining some of these men, up to twenty at a time, who then slept on tables and floors. Under military law, rank-and-file soldiers were not permitted to socialize with officers. So whenever they saw Eliazar Margolin and Redcliffe Salaman approaching, they would jump out of the window and disappear out of respect. On the other hand, whenever Eliazar became aware of them in the house, he just chose to ignore the fact.[13]

His time spent as a commander of Jewish forces in Palestine only deepened Eliazar's allegiance to the *Yishuv* even further. Originally, he had been led to believe that the Jewish Legion would become the basis of a future Jewish army in *Eretz Israel*. The anti-Zionist and often anti-Semitic disposition of many in the British military class in Palestine did not support such a development. From his actions, it was evident that he felt the protection of the *Yishuv* was too precious a task to be left to the machinations of a hostile Palestine authority. Such a realization was manifest in his refusal to inflict punishment for the wilful misdemeanors of his men in helping *HaShomer* or the fledgling *Haganah*. His attitudes and feelings towards his military superiors with respect to the *Yishuv* were very soon to be put to the test.

15

May Day Mayhem

The Arab anti-Jewish riot in the port of Jaffa of 1 May 1921, and the week of bloodshed that followed, were to prove fatal both to Eliazar's career in Palestine, and to his hopes of permanent residence in *Eretz Israel*. On a broader front, it also provided the rationale for Great Britain, with Samuel in the vanguard, to backtrack on its Zionist policy. Arab agitators took advantage of an internecine dispute between two left-wing Zionist groups to go on a vicious anti-Zionist rampage against Jewish settlements. High Commissioner Samuel established the Haycroft Commission of Enquiry to probe the causes for the killings and assaults which ended only on 7 May.

While May Day was an important date in the socialist calendar, and was celebrated by left-wing cadres in Palestine, this 1 May 1921 was far more significant than usual. It also happened to have religious significance encompassing the Jewish Passover, the Nebi Moussa celebration for Muslims, and Easter Sunday for Orthodox Christians. This notwithstanding, the Arab violence that began on this day had nothing to do with any secular or religious festival, but was purely politically motivated.

Winston Churchill, who in January 1920 had been appointed Great Britain's Colonial Secretary, had just the day before, on 30 April, ended his short visit to Palestine, where he had been surveying the scene with respect to his government's administration there. Not surprisingly, Arab complaints against Zionist developments were forcefully put, but they apparently failed to convince Churchill.[1] The events in Palestine immediately following his departure, however, were severely to undermine his support for the principles enunciated in the Balfour Declaration, which favoured the Zionist enterprise. Tensions were indeed palpable.[2] The Arabs were angry over Jewish immigration and the purchase of land for Zionist expansion and economic development.

On May Day two opposing Jewish groups scuffled on the outskirts of the Arab quarter of Jaffa, in the Neve Shalom area near the seashore just outside Tel Aviv. The two parties in question were the communist-leaning *Mifleget Po'alim Sozialistit* (Socialist Workers' Party, called MOPSI) and the more nationalist *Achdut Avoda* (Labour Party). This internecine left dispute was immediately misinterpreted by Arab nationalists as an anti-Arab attack by Jews, and was the excuse used for their subsequent savage behaviour. They launched a murderous attack on the migrant hostel in Jaffa where Jewish newcomers to Palestine found temporary accommodation before moving on into the hinterland. The Haycroft Commission's subsequent judgment was that this was no ordinary riot, that over those seven days whenever Arabs came into contact with Jews they attacked them with ferocity. It concluded that the killing and pillage were an affront to civilized society, and that while the Jews retaliated with 'an equal savagery, they had much to revenge'.[3]

No doubt Arab anti-Zionism had been boosted by Samuel's appointment of Haj al Husseini to his newly created post of Grand Mufti of Jerusalem in 1921. This Mufti had already been sentenced *in absentia* to fifteen years' imprisonment for incitement against Jews in Jerusalem the year before.[4] Samuel hoped that his selection would provide the Arabs of Palestine with evidence that Great Britain was protecting their interests, and not just those of the Zionists. On the contrary, however, it showed the Arabs that violence against Jews could reap political rewards.

The bushfire lit by the Arabs in Jaffa took both the Mandate authority and the *Yishuv* by surprise.[5] The former initially dismissed it merely as a local affair. Only when it spread did Samuel declare martial law, on 31 May, but only in Jaffa and nowhere else. On 6 May his appeasement policy had intensified when he had further capitulated to Arab demands and suspended Jewish immigration to Palestine.

Eliazar entered the scene on the second day, 2 May, when the fighting had moved from Jaffa to the adjacent new city of Tel Aviv. A recent book by Naomi Shepherd, *Ploughing Sand – British Rule in Palestine*, dismisses the nature and significance of his role with the bland statement: 'Eliazar Margolin, an officer who had served in the Jewish regiment during the war, rallied thirty-four recently demobilized Jewish soldiers, made his way into an army camp and handed out rifles which were used against the Arabs ...'[6]

Through the prism of British self-interest, the Haycroft Commission saw Eliazar's intervention rather differently and unsympathetically:

Lieutenant-Colonel Margolin D.S.O., was stationed at Sarafend in command of No. 1 Battalion of the Palestine Defence Force. This was only a nucleus consisting of 24 N.C.O.s and 8 men from the 38th (Judean) Battalion of the Royal Fusiliers. In command of the whole defence force was Colonel-Commandant Costello V.C. whose headquarters was in Jerusalem ... Sunday evening Colonel Margolin received information of the Jaffa riots. He is a Jew and was naturally anxious about his friends, and particularly about the safety of the Tel Aviv quarter. Next morning he went by car to Jaffa and found Tel Aviv in a state of excitement and alarm, and clamouring for arms for defence. There were in Tel Aviv about 100 demobilised men of the Judean Battalions (38th Fusiliers). He went to see the Governor and found him and the Civil Secretary, Colonel Deedes, were disinclined to agree. The latter, however, had himself been in Tel Aviv and had witnessed the state of excitement prevailing there, and finally allowed 18 Turkish rifles, then in control of Mr. Jeune, to be taken to Tel Aviv, and there used for defence in that quarter only. It was understood by him that Colonel Margolin would be in charge of the men and would be responsible for them.

Meanwhile, 17 N.C.O.s of the Defence Force at Ludd, who had left camp without permission at midnight on Sunday for Jaffa with their arms, and we believe, with ammunition, were in Tel Aviv, and their presence there must have been known to Colonel Margolin. He said nothing about them when he saw Colonel Deedes at the Governorate and asked for arms, and he states he was ignorant at their having left Ludd until after Tuesday. Colonel Margolin was made responsible for the carrying out of his arrangements with Colonel Deedes, but he allowed Captain Jaffe of the Defence Force, then in Tel Aviv, to march 25 demobilised Judeans dressed in Khaki uniform down to the Port Office to take possession of the 18 rifles promised by Mr. Jeune, and to march back with them with fixed bayonets through the streets of Jaffa to Tel Aviv. This action was contrary to the arrangements made with the Civil Secretary, who intended the arms be issued at Tel Aviv, and it caused much irritation at the time. On the same day two of the absent N.C.O.s went to Sarafend in a car professing to have an order from Colonel Margolin and Captain Jaffe, to take back to Jaffa all available rifles in camp. They could, however, show nothing in writing to this effect, and Major Neill, then in charge of the Defence Force in Sarafend, refused to deliver the rifles with ammunition, and return to Tel Aviv. There were at the time 30 rifles, in addition to any firearms the inhabitants may have possessed. Colonel Margolin took no disciplinary action against the men who had broken camp ...[7]

Eliazar testified before the commission[8] that on 1 May he had left camp at Sarafend for the settlement of Rishon Le-Zion about 3.30 to 4 p.m. Before he left, a civilian had told him that riots were in progress in Jaffa, but he thought this was mere rumour, so he rode on. In Rishon Le-Zion he again heard about the riots. Indeed, someone from Jaffa had reached the settlement to confirm that there had indeed been much rioting but that Jaffa was now quiet. Margolin returned to Sarafend, and there he heard that many Jews had been killed. He could not reach the Governor or the Commander of the Military Police by phone, but he did speak with people in Tel Aviv who indicated that Jaffa was now indeed quiet. His men were upset and he had heard nothing officially. Because of this he decided to go to Jaffa himself the next day. This he did on the morning of 2 May, driving straight to Tel Aviv, and found distraught people gathering in the streets, all fearing an Arab attack and demanding weapons with which to defend themselves. Margolin was told there were around forty to fifty discharged legionnaires who, if given firearms, could defend Tel Aviv in the apparent absence of soldiers. At Government House he apprised Messrs Deedes, the Civil Secretary and Bentwich, the Judicial Secretary, of the situation.

He advised that armed demobbed legionnaires could provide Tel Aviv with the security that people craved, and they agreed. Deedes told him to return to Tel Aviv and bring back Jewish notables, and said that he would do the same with Arab leaders, the idea being to walk through the different quarters of Jaffa and soften inter-communal tensions. In Tel Aviv, Margolin ordered Captain Jaffe to gather discharged legionnaires and put them in uniform. They would be provided with firearms from Government House. When Eliazar arrived back at Government House in Jaffa with Meir Dizengoff, the Mayor of Tel Aviv, he found that the arms did not exist. A Major Jeune had eighteen old Turkish rifles in his office, and if it were agreed to by the Governor, Eliazar could have them. No ammunition was available, however, so the Governor gave Eliazar an order for 200 boxes to be supplied by the police. Then, in the company of Deedes and an entourage of important people, he left for the troublesome Manshiye Quarter.

In Tel Aviv, Eliazar told Jaffe to go to Major Jeune's office for the pledged Turkish rifles, and that he would bring the requested ammunition from the Council Hall. His men then set about defending Tel Aviv. Responsibility for his men's conduct was his. Jaffe divided the city into districts and assigned men to secure them. Eliazar stayed in Tel Aviv. Later on the Monday, Colonel Biron arrived and asked Eliazar if he was the commander of this 'unorganized army'. Eliazar's response was that he was not the commander of any army, but that with the permission of Governor Deedes he had taken over the defence of Tel Aviv. As Colonel Biron was Eliazar's military superior, he had then taken charge. That night Eliazar stayed on guard with friends and next day he travelled to Jerusalem to meet with Commander Costello and apprise him of what had happened.

The commission was sceptical concerning Eliazar's claim that he had not known that his men had left Sarafend without his or anyone else's permission or when they had actually gone missing.[9] One of his men, however, recalls that was the case, and says that when Eliazar first arrived in Tel Aviv, they had hidden from him fearing he would punish them. But once in Tel Aviv, Eliazar had set up his own headquarters in Gruzenberg Street, leaving Captain Jaffe in charge. Former legionnaires in their old uniforms assembled in front of the Gymnasium Herzlia, and then moved on to the main street in Neveh Shalom to receive their rifles. That night Captain Jaffe, with, he thought, around sixty men, comprising discharged and serving legionnaires, was tasked with defending both Tel Aviv and Neveh Shalom.[10] Another person involved recalls that, although not a legionnaire, he was given their uniform, a rifle, and assigned to patrol the alleyways.[11] The prevailing sentiment was that the British were fundamentally pro-Arab. Some even felt that the British had helped the Arabs to prepare for the riots. On 2 May alone, thirteen Jews had been killed and twenty-six wounded, while ten Arabs died and eleven were injured. Most of the Jews had died from stabbings and blows, and the Arabs from bullets. One of the first Jews to die was the Labour Zionist leader, Y. H. Brenner. When Deedes and the Arab notables from Jaffa came to Tel Aviv to the gymnasium to view the bodies of Jewish dead killed by their Arab brothers, Margolin prevented an assault on them by an extremely angry group of Jews. He demanded that the crowd disperse immediately to allow the delegation to continue its visit unhindered.[12]

Believing that his soldiers had helped ensure the safety of Tel Aviv, Eliazar ventured to Jaffa to assess the situation. A story is told that en route he came across a British officer who had arrested a group of Jewish settlers because they had ignored his direction to disband. Eliazar explained to his fellow officer that the men had refused his request because they did not speak English, and therefore could not understand his order. The officer rejected Eliazar's plea for their release on the grounds that this could happen only if directed to do so by his own commanding officer. And as this order was as yet not forthcoming, he could not release the offenders. He finally capitulated, however, under Eliazar's unusual display of public anger, but he promised to lodge a complaint over the matter with his superiors. To which, Eliazar was said to have replied calmly, but determinedly, 'OK, first carry out my orders and then complain.' He then left Jaffa to return to Tel Aviv.[13]

Whether the recall is accurate or not, a Lieutenant Bradshaw testified before the Haycroft Commission that he had arrested the men, that Eliazar had demanded their release, but then Deedes had come along to tell him to do his duty. Eliazar's interpretation was that he:

> ... was walking behind Mr. Deedes who was coming back from Manshiye and Tel Aviv after returning from Sharona. Looking towards Tel Aviv I saw five to seven boys, fourteen to twenty years of age, standing by a wall with two sergeants with rifles standing over them. One sergeant had a long rope in his hand was about to arrest them. At first I did not see the officer and I said to the sergeant, 'What are you doing?' He answered, 'We are carrying out an order.' I asked, 'Do you mean to shoot to kill them?' He answered, 'No, we were gathering them up to guard over.' I asked: 'What did they do?' and his answer was 'They attacked Arabs.' In all Tel Aviv there wasn't an Arab to be seen but many Jews stood there and watched. I was born in Russia, and so were many of the citizens of Tel Aviv who were on guard. There is no doubt this reminded them of the pogroms carried out against the Jews of Russia by Russian officers and they must have thought this was a sign that this was going to happen here too. I have always said that the British reign is a just one. I told this to the officer who came just then, and I added, 'this will make a bad impression'. They then put their arms down, and the prisoners were taken to an automobile. They weren't my men. They were fourteen to twenty years of age ...[14]

Whatever Eliazar's knowledge or intentions, back at administrative headquarters in Jerusalem, news of his and his men's independent actions was not well received. Samuel and his cohorts did not believe that the security of the *Yishuv* was in any way at stake. It is related that at 3 p.m., on the third day – 3 May – of the continuing conflict, Eliazar was informed by telephone by a very junior officer that he was being called to account, and that in the future he would not be allowed into Jaffa in uniform. Coming as it did from a junior officer, Eliazar considered this call offensive and degrading. His response was, 'I am an officer, I do not receive orders from any [viz. lower-ranking] officer, and will not submit to them.'

Several hours later he was called to Jerusalem to meet with his superiors, whose attitude towards him was cold and hostile. For a long time they had seen the presence of the Jewish battalions as an encumbrance, barely tolerated, and wished them to be disbanded. On arrival in Jerusalem, Eliazar realized that his and his men's actions had now provided the pretext for just that. He is said to have told his interrogators that, as a Jew, he was not prepared to sit back and wait while they, through their inaction, allowed a Russian-like pogrom to occur in British-governed Palestine.[15] No doubt his decision to act had been informed by his observation, since his arrival in Palestine, of the way both military and civil British administrations treated the Jewish community, let alone the men of the Jewish battalions. In an article in the *Jewish Chronicle* on 12 October 1948, Ya'akov Dori, who became the first Chief of Staff of the Israel Defence Force, wrote that Eliazar, under whom he had served defending Tel Aviv in 1921, was of the view that the Jewish soldiers had had every right to go to the aid of their beleaguered people.

Eliazar must have been expecting the worst, and it came. After hearing that the First Judeans as a group would be subject to court martial, he insisted that as their commander, the buck stop with him. He unequivocally took total responsibility for their actions. Samuel then gave him Hobson's choice: either submit to a personal court martial or quit his commission and leave Palestine immediately. In taking the latter course, he was merely bowing to the inevitable. Nevertheless, for Eliazar the emotions involved in this decision must have bordered on the unbearable. Without ceremony, he instantly resigned his commission, and was granted an honourable discharge. That night he spoke to a gathering of his own, now former officers and soldiers. In the words of one who was present, he told them:

> Men! I am no longer your colonel. You must now accept orders from Major Neil. I ask you to stay faithful to your duties, as you did when I gave you orders ... for going to Yaffo without military order you have been severely punished. But don't worry, all this has to do with me and I have assumed full responsibility. Keep on being devoted brave soldiers and faithful Jewish Legionnaires to your people until the last moment.[16]

What angered him most was that, as he had feared, the First
Judeans were to be disbanded. He had been told by the Governor
of Jaffa that the presence of the First Judeans had provoked the
Arabs and thus increased the bloodshed. The bloody events in Jaffa,
however, had occurred before Eliazar's men had made their presence
felt. Apparently, Samuel was of a similar mind as this Governor, and
as a consequence cancelled his plan for the joint Arab–Jewish defence
force.

The indecision over the establishment of this force had already
seen the numbers of the First Judeans at Sarafend dwindle badly.
Before being finally dismissed, however, they had to endure one more
indignity. The authorities wanted a speedy conclusion to the First
Judeans' tenure and its members dispersed, as their presence was a
reminder of the civil authority's ineptitude and possible culpability
over the Arab riots. They wanted the affair hushed up. Samuel and
those around him were not willing to wait for the publication of
the commission's findings as to the true cause of the disturbances
that raged in Jaffa on May Day 1921, then flowed on to Tel Aviv,
Peta Tikva, Rehovot, K'far Saba and Ein Hai, until they were finally
snuffed out by British army action. Nor were they interested in what
aspects of their attitude and that of the police had permitted matters
to get so much out of hand.

The Haycroft Commission was still distilling the evidence presented
before it when the British sergeants attached to the First Judeans were
granted three months' wages in compensation, but the ranks were
offered nothing. An officer from HQ arrived to tell them that their
unit had been disbanded and they would soon have to leave camp.
The men would have none of it, telling him that they did not merely
accept collective responsibility for what had happened in Tel Aviv,
but were justly proud of their actions. They also complained bitterly
about discrimination over pay. Observing the steel in the men before
him, the officer promised to reconsider the matter of compensation
on the same terms granted the British NCOs. The very next day,
another officer arrived to pay them on the terms requested.

The men then went to bid farewell to Eliazar, who was preparing
to leave for Australia. An impromptu send-off was arranged in his
honour and was attended by a large crowd, which included a few
British officers. He is reported to have said:

> Soldiers and Visitors! I am not sorry for what I have done. We all,
> you and I, have carried out the duty which lies upon us: to defend

our brethren, no matter where and under what circumstances. I am
a national Jew and I will not permit that Jews be a target for all in
our very own country. It is for this reason that I agreed to join the
Jewish Legion. We had a fine dream, the dream of a Jewish army. It
is a pity that we cannot achieve this dream at this time. I am leaving
the country not of my own choosing, but you, who are left behind,
must carry on; I am sure, the dream will come true one day. I want
you to know that it was a privilege to be your Commander; never
had a Commander better soldiers.[17]

He thanked his audience, saying, 'I have given up my reign (viz.
command), but not on my love for the country, so goodbye. See
you again.' The men returned to camp, demilitarized it, then joined
the civilian population. On 31 May 1921, the life of the Jewish
battalions officially came to an end.[18]

Margolin's departure for Australia had been delayed for a few
days in order for him to give evidence before the Commission of
Enquiry, chaired by Sir Thomas Haycroft, Chief Justice of Palestine.
Though hearings commenced on 7 May, its findings were not
presented until October 1921. Eliazar was interrogated on the
general subject of Arab–Jewish relations. He was asked whether he
had detected a difference in this climate between the era when he
had first resided in *Eretz Israel* in the 1890s and his second arrival
in 1918 with the 39th British Royal Fusiliers. His reply was that
the real change in atmosphere had occurred in the past eighteen
months to two years as a result of a heightened and more belligerent
Arab anti-Jewish propaganda. Much of it suggested that the Jews
wanted to rid Palestine of Arabs. He thought the Arabs were interpreting Zionism wrongly, and that this misunderstanding came from
the fear that Jewish migration would leave no room for them. Eliazar
rejected the idea put to him that the presence of Jewish Bolshevists
in Palestine promoted Arab hostility. Apart from his aforementioned
role in the May Day explosion, he was questioned as to whether he
had considered the effects on the Arabs when he had counselled
Deedes that his men should be armed. He replied in the negative,
saying his only concern was the defence of Tel Aviv.[19]

The Mayor of Tel Aviv, Meir Dizengoff, sent a note to Eliazar
before he departed:

In the name of the citizens of Jaffa and Tel Aviv and at the time
of your leaving Eretz Israel, our very sincere thanks and greatest

admiration for the part you have played in our lives and for all you have done for us and for the whole Jewish community of our country. From the very day of your arrival here as Commander, in our times of sorrow, you felt for us and at the time of joy you were happy with us. You came to us, in particular, as a redeemer and liberator at a time of the difficult days of the last riots suffered by the Jewish population of Jaffa. We wish you a happy and successful journey and will be looking to your return to our Country crowned with success and ready to take up amongst us permanent residence as the commander of the Jewish Unit for the establishment of which you have fought hard. In appreciation please accept this album with photographs and the creation of the First all Jewish City, which is so dear to you. In the name of the whole Jewish community we say to you: may blessing be with you on leaving us and may you be blessed on your return.[20]

Margolin left Sarafend for Ludd, then travelled on to Egypt, to return to Australia towards the end of May.

A correspondent to the newspaper *Ha'aretz* in 1940 remembered how sad and depressed Eliazar had been when they had met in Port Said just before his ship departed in the northern summer of 1921. His face was gloomy, and his bitterness over having to return to Australia palpable.[21]

News of the Jaffa riot was not publicly acknowledged by the Australian Jewish communal press until the *Jewish Herald* reported it on 24 June 1921, that is almost seven weeks after the event. Nothing was said of Eliazar's role and that of the First Judeans' defence of Tel Aviv. Picking up the message from London, this newspaper merely reiterated Samuel's statement, that severe punishment would be meted out to anyone the Haycroft Commission found culpable. Although a self-proclaimed pro-Zionist communal newspaper, the *Jewish Herald* remained silent about the predicament of the Jews of Palestine, and restricted itself to a mindless exercise in semantic technicalities, ranting against anyone who dared call the incident on May Day 1921 a pogrom. It would have supported the use of this term if the ruling authority itself had engaged in the assault or had authorized it. This definition, however, neglected to acknowledge either the fact that senior Arab police officers had been in the vanguard of the attack on the civilian Jewish population, or the civil authority's early indifference to the unfolding tragedy. This had been tantamount to giving the rampaging Arabs de facto

support. Instead of indignation or moral umbrage, this Jewish newspaper dismissed this unfortunate affair with the statement that it was
'the test to which most peoples are placed that determine to make
a stand for their National Home'. No critical words were allowed
even to hint that the Jewish community in Australia was anything
but utterly loyal to the British motherland and its empire.

The May Day riot subsequently led Samuel to abandon his own
plan for a joint Arab–Jewish force, and his clampdown on Jewish
immigration and land purchase in *Eretz Israel*, was an aspect of his
radical reassessment of British policy in Palestine. Arab concerns
had to be placated, and this meant backtracking on the Zionist
tenets of the Balfour Declaration.[22] It would not be an exaggeration
to say, that by deciding to defend his fellow Jews against Arab
attacks in the manner in which he did, Eliazar Margolin played a
part in this revision of British policy.

16

A Distasteful Affair

On 5 May 1921, the upper chamber of the Australian Parliament in Canberra bore witness to a vicious personal attack on Eliazar, which included an attack on his military competence. Was this incident motivated by racial prejudice, xenophobia, plain jealousy, or some combination of these? The latter is probably closer to the mark, and was part of a broader campaign by those who felt that they had not received their deserved promotion during the Great War. Certainly the perpetrator of this defamation – under the cover of parliamentary privilege – was one very willing to shoot the malicious bullets of others.

The attack occurred at a time when Palestine was still being convulsed by serial Arab anti-Jewish aggression, when Eliazar was still in the Holy Land, and just after he had received Samuel's edict of choosing between a court martial or leaving *Eretz Israel*. Conveniently for this accuser, Eliazar was not in Australia to defend his reputation. This timing notwithstanding, it is extremely doubtful whether what was happening in Palestine at the time had any influence on what occurred in the Australian Senate. Distance, and poor communications about matters in the Middle East, usually routed to Australia via London, assured ignorance of them. Whether any local anti-Semitism tinged the allegations is moot. What is not is that the tirade was voiced by a very senior Australian officer, still in the army reserve, who should have known better. It was also replete with factual error.

The offender was Senator 'Pompey' Harold Edward Elliott from the State of Victoria, a retired brigadier-general (though elevated in 1926 to major-general), who like Eliazar had served in Gallipoli and on the Western Front with great distinction.[1] Though at no stage did he malign Eliazar by name, everyone knew of whom he was speaking. The issue arose on 5 May 1921 in the Senate's debate on the Defence Bill. Both major Melbourne broadsheets, the *Age* and the *Argus*, reported the incident the next day. Elliott cited an unnamed 'foreign-born' officer as an example of his general objection to the AIF's practice during the Great War of appointing outsiders over the heads of incumbent battalion officers, who he thought were entitled to take precedence in command. He referred to a 'Polish Jew' appointed from elsewhere to take charge of the 14th Battalion over other well-credentialled officers, including Australia's Victoria Cross winner, Captain Jacka. The offending officer, he said, spoke poor English, was culturally inadequate when dealing with Australian soldiers, and to add insult to injury, had not even 'gone into the line'.[2] Eliazar was a Russian-born, not a Polish-born Jew, but such distinctions would probably have been too subtle for his accuser. It was true that his English was far from the King's finest; nevertheless, none of his men had complained that they had been mystified by it. On the contrary, they had commended his leadership and caring attitude. And, of course, he had indeed entered 'the line' with the AIF both in Gallipoli and at the Western Front where the fighting was thickest.

Unfortunately for Elliott, he was immediately followed in the debate by another decorated soldier, this time a representative from Eliazar's home state of Western Australia. This was Senator Drake Brockman, who had also risen to the rank of brigadier-general, and who just happened to have been one of Eliazar's commanding officers, and thus had been in an excellent position to have observed him. He corrected Elliott on a number of points of fact, such as Eliazar's place of birth and his years of residence in Western Australia before enlisting. Moreover, he assured the House that Margolin had been dependable and devoted as his second-in-charge in the 16th Battalion. Gilding the lily somewhat to blunt the ferocity of Elliott's slander, he pictured Eliazar as a gallant educated man, who though he spoke English with a slight accent, could also converse in French, German, Russian and 'Gippo'. In no way was this man a poor communicator. Two points were emphasized. The first was Eliazar's winning the DSO at Gallipoli, and the second, his intense desire that the 14th Battalion be successful on the battlefield in France when he took charge of it, albeit temporarily, from Drake-Brockman. He said that Eliazar had accidentally fallen into one of the shell holes that riddled the environs of the Battle of Messines, badly injuring his knee. He refused advice to seek medical treatment and he had left the front only under orders to go to hospital. Drake-Brockman advised his audience of Eliazar's command of a Jewish regiment raised in Great Britain to serve in Palestine after he had been invalided out of the AIF. He explained that his subject was 'a loyal officer to Australia, and loyal to me. I have the greatest admiration for him and would consider myself contemptible if I did not stand up for him. When last I heard of him he was Governor of Jerusalem.'[3]

Of course, Eliazar had never been Governor of Jerusalem, merely the temporary Military Governor of Es-Salt and areas of immediate proximity. Drake-Brockman was immediately followed by a fellow Senator from Western Australia who informed the House that he had met Eliazar, and had also found him to be an honourable and educated person, and that if the House wanted further evidence of his great qualities and experience, he could provide it.[4]

Undoubtedly caught by surprise by the strength of the counter fire, Elliott resorted to blaming others for his misrepresentations. Unfortunately, he had acquired a history during the war of maligning other officers. One biography says of him that 'he had a habit of putting into his written reports criticisms of superior officers or reflections on other troops which caused trouble, and that this, more than any other, was the reason for not rising to higher command during the war'.[5] In the face of his fellow Senators' utter rejection of his assertions, Elliott refused to retract his claim that Captain Jacka and other officers had been wronged when overlooked for command. He declared no personal knowledge of Eliazar or of his career, and said that if his statements had erred in fact, then for that he was sorry. Claiming to have been misled over this matter, he assured the House that this had not been the intent of those whom he had represented in this matter.[6] Two glaring omissions from this explanation were any semblance of an apology to Eliazar Margolin, or any reason as to why it had been necessary to highlight his religion.

On 7 May 1921, that is, on the very day the Haycroft Commission in Jerusalem opened its proceedings – ostensibly to determine the cause of Arab violence against Jewish settlement in Palestine – the *contretemps* which had erupted in the Senate now moved to the pages of the mainstream Australian press. The *Argus* published two telling letters in defence of Eliazar. The first was from John Monash himself, of whom it had been reported that he would be appointed either as Governor-General or Military Governor of Palestine, tasked with implementing the Balfour Declaration. On this matter in 1919, Eliazar had written from Palestine to Monash, then in England, that

Zionists in *Eretz Israel* were very interested in him. Monash, however, had no intention of playing any role in Palestine, preferring to return to Australia to further his civilian career.[7] He was to acknowledge that whatever he knew of Zionism had been greatly influenced by three friends, Dr Leon Jona, Lizette Bentwitch and Eliazar Margolin.[8] In his epistle to the paper, Monash wrote:

> The success of the A.I.F. was due in large measure to a spirit of comradeship, tolerance, and mutual co-operation which its leaders constantly laboured to foster. It seems to me, therefore lamentable that aspersions should now, without knowledge or inquiry, be cast by a senior officer on a man having a distinguished record, and who is not present to defend himself. Colonel Margolin has been described during the current Senate debate as an 'illiterate Polish Jew'. To all who know him, the implied calumny is ridiculous. This officer served with great distinction under me during the first three years of the war. He is a gallant, cultured gentleman of fine physique, and an engaging personality, ardently loyal to Australian soldiers and ideals. He ably commanded the 16th Battalion during the closing months on Gallipoli. During the dark days of September and October 1915, it was his courage and determination which upheld the morale of his battalion amid dire sickness and a horrible environment. He served subsequently, and until armistice in the Palestine campaign, and is at the present time, Commanding Officer of the 38th Battalion of the Royal Fusiliers.[9]

Even Monash fell into an error of fact over which battalion of the Royal Fusiliers Eliazar had commanded.

A second testimony came from an anonymous former member of Margolin's 16th Battalion:

> I am sure I shall be voicing the opinions of all my comrades of the 16th Battalion and many others who had the honour to come into personal contact with 'Margie' – Colonel Margolin. This officer embarked with 'the old 16th', and saw the Gallipoli campaign right through, and though wounded on at least one occasion, stuck to his post when many of his brother officers were being evacuated with lesser wounds. He was undoubtedly a Jew, as was another highly honoured comrade of ours – General Monash – and his knowledge of Turkish and Russian languages made him a very valuable asset to the 14th Brigade on Gallipoli. He was, at all times, all for his men, who were absolutely incapable of further effort, back in the line. He

was a thorough soldier, a gentleman, and a good Australian, and it was chiefly due to Colonel Pope and Major Margolin that 'the old 16th' had such a fine record – second to none – for comradeship. It was with great pleasure I read the remarks of Brigadier-General Drake-Brockman in defence of the major, and all members of 'the 16th' are very grateful to him. Senator Elliott [sic] showed a deplorable lack of fair play in condemning one of his former comrades, as, on his own admission, he 'did not know this officer, and had been misled'. Before making a charge of this nature in future, he would be well advised to ascertain the true facts. I presume, as a senator, he would have no difficulty in obtaining access to the files in base records.[10]

It was one thing for Elliott to attempt a partial *mea culpa* in the Senate, it was another when a prominent figure, such as Monash, took him to task in the press. Any hint of conciliation immediately disappeared. In response to the letters, he undoubtedly concluded that the best mode of defence was to attack. Hence his own riposte to the *Age*:

In the case of Colonel Margolin, I desire to point out that the name of this officer was not mentioned by me at any time. The incident to which I referred was, apparently, identified by General Drake-Brockman, who in his reply somewhat misguidedly, in my opinion, mentioned the name in the Senate. For this I am not to blame, as he could have equally well dealt with the matter without referring to the officer by name. In regard to the character given to this officer by General Monash and others I am personally not prepared to comment, since I have never met the officer in my life. I resent, however, the statement that I made my aspersion on anybody 'without knowledge or inquiry'. In point of fact, I investigated the complaint made to me in the presence of the representative of the 'Sun' newspaper for several hours, and examined a number of witnesses. The incident occurred while Colonel Margolin was in the 4th Division, and not under General Monash's command, who then commanded the 3rd Division. I was, therefore, unaware that he knew anything in the case. In answer to another letter, I would add that the service records of officers are quite properly not open to the inspection of Senators. In the course of the same enquiry, however, another senior officer, a man now occupying a permanent position in the instructional staff of Australia, was mentioned as having been dismissed by General Monash from the 3rd Division about the same time, and I did thereupon inquire from Sir John Monash as to his opinion of this officer, and may state that his opinion thoroughly bore out the evidence which had been placed before me by the same witness, which established pretty conclusively the fact that a senior permanent officer twice removed from his command for incompetency by Sir John Monash was re-employed in another battalion by Sir William Birdwood, when he proved a more hopeless failure than ever, and that he was subsequently 'whitewashed' and restored to his position in the Australian Military forces.

Neither Sir John Monash nor General Drake-Brockman have contravened these facts – a) that Lieutenant-Colonel Margolin, a foreigner, though of some considerable length of residence in Australia, and a man who to a stranger might well appear illiterate by reason of the peculiar English he spoke, was placed in command of a battalion which had no knowledge of him at a time when they had several distinguished officers serving in the regiment, and who might well infer from that fact that they were deemed unfit to fulfil the duties of commanding officer; b) that this officer did fail during the time he was in command of the battalion to in any sense lead the battalion, and in fact did not during this period of duty visit the front line at all. (It is now stated that this was due to an injury to the knee, but I may point out that the officers concerned may have been quite unaware of its origin, and they might well, from the surrounding facts have discredited its existence); c) that on leaving the battalion on that occasion for hospital he did not return to it throughout the war, and as far as I can learn was never re-employed with the A.I.F. In regards to his subsequent service, I believe that it is the case that he was appointed to the command of a Jewish battalion raised in London for service in Palestine under the name of the 38th Battalion of the Royal Fusiliers, which was, and is still, employed on garrison duty in Jerusalem. When on top of this event the battalion had, as above stated, another undoubtedly unworthy officer placed in command of it, the sense of wrong felt by its officers in such circumstances can be well understood, and might well lead to their forming erroneous conclusions in regard to the first officer.[11]

The *Age* merely observed that the affair had 'left the Minister dumb', and suggested that the then Minister for Defence had no stomach for an inquiry into army procedures.[12] This Anglocentric newspaper seemed itself to evince a sympathy for the investigation. It had no comment on the specific issue of the personal attack on Margolin, including the reference to his religion. Hilary Rubinstein has pointed out that for all the patriotism Jews showed towards Australia during the First World War, and despite the highest esteem in which a person like John Monash was generally held, editorials in the mainstream press would still question their loyalty to Australia.[13]

Elliott's letter revealed the presence of a group of disgruntled Australian army officers who were suspicious, even envious, of the success of those who spoke with a heavy foreign accent. Such persons were an easy oriflamme around which disaffected butterflies could gather. Indeed, the affair raises the question as to whether this prejudice in any way influenced the army's refusal to restore Eliazar to active duty after his successful recuperation in London in 1917. After all, he was well enough to be accepted into the British Army to serve in the Middle East theatre.

The events in the Senate were covered by the *Australian Jewish Herald*, formerly the *Jewish Herald*, under the rubric, 'Lieut-Colonel Margolin DSO – A Slandered Hero'. Included was a reprint of the two aforementioned supportive letters to the *Argus*, but no accompanying analysis was offered. The *Jewish Observer* of 24 May opined that Elliott might have fared much worse had he made his remarks outside the chamber in the presence of members of the 16th Battalion. It cited two instances that showed why Eliazar had been so popular with his men. The first occurred when the 16th was training at Broadmeadows in Victoria before embarkation to Egypt. The payroll failed to arrive, thereby seriously affecting those who wished to take leave prior to departure. Eliazar advanced cash from his own private funds to enable them to leave camp to say farewell to their families. The second was in Gallipoli, when the 16th was ordered to change position without having received the requisite supply of sandbags. His reaction was swift. He 'bore down on headquarters, and by stint of forcible language of which he was a most capable exponent, caused headquarters to change its tune and tumble over one another in excess of zeal to oblige one with such a fluency of expression; the result of a supply of sand bags being increased comfort and safety for the men.'

Despite these few examples, the incident in the national parliament appears to have been generally ignored by the then Australian Jewish community, which generally kept its head down and sought to avoid public controversy.

The evidence shows that Eliazar was a loyal and caring leader of men, and that they returned these sentiments in kind. If only because of this, Elliott's calumny in the Senate was quite bizarre. Why such a character assassination should have occurred almost three years after the Armistice is uncertain. We do not know if Elliott, or indeed those whom he claimed to represent, considered that Eliazar's 'foreignness' or religion would lend public credibility to their cause.

Just as Eliazar could not have been aware of this distasteful affair before he left Palestine, we do not know how it affected him when he did learn of it. What is certain is that Elliott's attack in the Senate in no way diminished the warm feelings of Eliazar's former comrades towards him.

17

Return to Sender

Just as there was a suggestion in 1902 that Eliazar had travelled to London before settling in Australia after leaving Palestine the first time, so it has been said that when virtually dismissed from *Eretz Israel* after the May Day riots in 1921, he visited that selfsame British capital before returning to Western Australia. In the first case, the purpose had been to enlist for the Boer War, and in the second, to seek a post in the Palestine police, or an administrative role in the civil administration of *Eretz Israel*.[1] As implausible as the first seemed, the second was similarly so. Apart from the previously mentioned observation of one who saw him in Port Said just before his departure for Australia, the fact that the High Commissioner for Palestine had just dismissed Eliazar from his bailiwick meant that it would have been most unlikely that anyone in London would have countermanded that decision by appointing him to any position there. No doubt he returned directly to Perth a saddened man. Moshe Smilansky says that his first letters back to Palestine after his return were suffused with yearning and bitterness,[2] though none of these communications appears to have survived to confirm this. The question now was to what degree his history would affect his relationship with his former comrades-in-arms, and the Western Australian Jewish community.

After Eliazar's return, in 1922, the very year the British Mandate over Palestine as such came into being, *The British Jewry Book of Honour* was published. According to the Chief Rabbi of the British Empire, Rabbi Dr J. Hertz: 'This permanent written record of the part played by Anglo-Jewry in the Great War will help lovers of the Truth in their warfare against the malicious slander that the Jew shrinks from sacrifices demanded of every loyal citizen in the hour of national danger.'[3]

It was thought that Judeophobia would melt away in the face of the facts of Jewish bravery and heroism during the Great War: that the *Book*'s tabulations of those who had fought for the Allied cause would once and for all demonstrate Jewish loyalty to the British Empire and the individual nations it comprised. No doubt its principal target was the prevailing anti-Semitism in Great Britain. Nevertheless, the rhetoric of anti-Semitism was still known in Australia.[4] Indeed, the Jew remained an ever-present scapegoat for any social difficulty, and at times was singled out for special notice. Praise was heaped on Lieutenant-General Sir John Monash who, in a compendium piece, declared that the Jewish soldiers, 'by their valour, their fortitude, and their devoted sacrifice have combined to achieve a story of Jewish service to our Country, which still further enhance the prestige of every British citizen of the Jewish faith, as second to no other in patriotism or readiness and ability to bear his full share of all the burdens of the State.'[5]

Another piece was on Lieutenant-Colonel Eliazar Margolin, pictured, and with a brief romantic biography by none other than Vladimir Jabotinsky, who spoke of his role in both the Australian and British armies.[6] Missing in this account, however, was Eliazar's brush with the Palestine authorities, while there were no criticisms of the British military and civil authorities' negativism in the Holy Land towards the Jewish battalions. This was to be whitewashed and forgotten. The Jewish Legion was something the Anglo-Jewish establishment in Great Britain felt was worthy of veneration. Previously, the objections to it were based on a fear that it might raise the bar of anti-Semitism. Now it was being used, as it were, in a hope that it might purge that prejudice. Eliazar's 'indiscretions', along with other unmentionable matters, were now locked away in the cupboard. Interestingly, this memorial to Jewish heroism was published at the time when Winston Churchill, with Herbert Samuel in the driving seat, was instigating a claw-back from the pro-Zionist principles of the Balfour Declaration.

As the new orthodoxy was from the hand of the English-Jewish establishment, it was something with which the Antipodean Anglo-Jewish-led communities could be comfortable. The inevitable question was, did the reconstructed interpretation propagate, or enhance, Eliazar's reputation down under, and especially in its Jewish communities? Most people would not have heard of him until the infamous Senate affair, and even that interest, in the scheme of things, was but fleeting. With the Great War long past, it is questionable if anyone in Perth, let alone on the other side of the Nullarbor, really cared. The answer seems to have been 'no', if the Australian Jewish communal press, which failed to respond with any excitement to the *Book*'s publication, is taken as the gauge.

Back in Australia, Eliazar returned to Collie to resume his activities at the soft drinks factory. He found that while he had been away, however, someone else had replaced him, and he moved to Perth. He bought a share in the company, United Buses, which plied the route between Perth and Fremantle. Later, United Buses became a limited company with Eliazar as its managing director. Further, he invested in a profitable service station in Nedlands and established a tyre retreading company, said to have been the first to introduce full cycle retreads.[7]

In his maturity, Eliazar married a non-Jewish lady on 24 July 1926, in a civil ceremony at the Perth District Registrar's Office. His bride was Hilda Myrtle England. She had grown up in Boulder, the daughter of a miner. Unfortunately, her father had been killed in a mining accident, leaving his widow with five children. Hilda won a scholarship to St Hilda's boarding school in Perth, and then went on to study to be a teacher. She subsequently returned to Boulder, later joining the staff of the National Australia Bank, where she became Australia's first woman bank teller. 'Margy' had become a member of the Board of Visitors to Lemnos, the army hospital where Hilda's sister Vera was a nursing sister after her return from wartime duties in England. And it is most likely that that was where Eliazar and Hilda first met. There was another connection, however, linked to Hilda's brother, Ernest Roy England, who had served with great distinction in both Gallipoli and France, winning the MC and bar plus the DCM, under 'Margy'. Eliazar had great affection and admiration for his brother-in-law.[8] At the time of their marriage, Eliazar was fifty-one and Hilda thirty-two. According to the Post Office Directory of 1929, they lived at 62 Tyrell Street, Nedlands. While they had no children, they showed devotion for their three nephews, of whom they saw a great deal.

Despite his social work among his former digger mates, Eliazar led a basically quiet and essentially private life. Until his marriage, he had seemed to shy away from close personal relationships. While concern for his digger mates was a prime concern of his life, he seemed reluctant to share his innermost personal feelings with others. His marriage with Hilda, however, was an extremely happy one. They shared a great sense of humour, and much laughter permeated their home. A family member remembered Eliazar as a gently spoken man, seeming always in good humour.[9] No doubt this jocularity masked his gnawing feelings for *Eretz Israel*.

'Margy' not only joined the Western Australian Returned Soldiers League (RSL), and was on that organization's executive for twenty years, he also chaired its financial and hospital visiting committees. He helped establish the Nedlands' sub-branch of the RSL and was its inaugural president. Further, as previously mentioned, he was the RSL's representative to the Lemnos Repatriation Hospital, and helped found the Perth Legacy Club, which provided care for diggers and their families damaged by war. Abe Troy, who first met Eliazar in the late 1920s, says that it was natural for this single man of forty-six years, on his return from Palestine, to spend much of his time with the RSL. At his mature age, and after his full commitment to the military he loved, he had, like many others, initially found it extremely difficult adjusting to civilian life. Before his marriage, the RSL and its associated instrumentalities constituted his family. In Troy's words, he genuinely took 'a paternal interest in the affairs of the returned soldier'.[10] For many years Eliazar was conspicuous in the vanguard of that great event in the Australian secular calendar, the annual Anzac Day march through the main streets of Perth. He was also, in the words of the Lord Mayor of Perth, 'the most efficient and courteous Marshall of the Dawn Service in King's Park'.[11]

It seems that his private sorrow was so evident in letters he sent back to Palestine in the early years after his return to Western Australia that friends there lobbied people close to the Mandate authority to allow him back. Individuals with influence apparently promised help, but did nothing.[12] Eliazar's popularity in *Eretz Israel* may well have been seen by those officials as a potential thorn in their side. As a leader of men, and a committed Zionist, his presence might prove a centre of social instability. Moreover, he would be an embarrassing reminder of the events of May Day 1921, something the government of Palestine wanted to forget. In 1928, when the Arabs were again on a bloody and murderous rampage against the *Yishuv*,[13] his friends in Palestine wanted him back as an organizer and commander in the *Haganah*.[14]

On 27 May 1931, when the Great Depression in Australia was biting hard, a request passed from the office of W. Glukin, a lawyer in Tel Aviv, to the Rt Hon. Baron James de Rothschild who had helped recruit the Palestine regiment, the 40th Battalion of the British Royal Fusiliers, and served in the Jewish Legion:

Dear James

We take the liberty to call your attention to the following which we think will interest you. Colonel Lazar Margolin is well known to you. After demobilization of the Jewish Legion he went back to Australia not being able to find something to do in Palestine. He was a good farmer in Rehovot and hard working before leaving Palestine for the first time for Australia. In the last ten years he tried hard in Australia and was not successful there. He is married now.

He is the type that would not ask anything for himself. He has a sister in Rishon le-Zion and she spoke to us about his sad condition. She asked us to try and do something to bring him back to Palestine. Under present conditions there is no chance to get any position for him.

We heard, however, that PICA is colonizing now some Palestinians on the basis of orange groves to pay out in terms of years. Would it not be possible to colonize Colonel Margolin on the same terms? He would be one of the ablest colonists.

We wanted to talk to Mr. Henri Frank but he left the country before we could reach him. Knowing, however, your good opinion of Colonel Margolin, we dare trouble you with this subject. We hope you will consider this matter, and do whatever is possible, and pardon us for bothering you.

'PICA', to which this note referred, was the Palestine Jewish Colonization Society originally established by Baron Edmund de Rothschild. From 1924 to its conclusion in the 1950s it was headed by his son, James. It helped in the establishment of Jewish settlement in pre- and post-state Israel.[15] From this missive, it can be seen that Eliazar knew nothing of the content of the letter. How he would have reacted, especially now he was married, can only be imagined. We don't know if Rothschild or one of his minions replied.

Smilansky says that once he was back in Australia, nothing more was heard of Eliazar in Palestine. As evidenced from the above letter with respect to PICA, however, this cannot be true. Perhaps it was just a case of Eliazar losing contact. During the Second World War, Smilansky recounts that he heard of his friend, when Australian soldiers, fighting once more in the Middle East, brought personal regards from him. An old friend of Eliazar from Rehovot told Smilansky a tale of how Eliazar had grown decidedly old and bent, and that his application to join the Second AIF had been rejected.[16] Even if he had been in good health, which he seemed to enjoy at the time, the Australian Army would not have recruited a person well into his sixties.

Following the Great War, much of the non-religious Jewish cultural life in Perth revolved around the Western Australian Zionist Association.[17] It commemorated the Balfour Declaration, Zionist events, and celebrated Zionist luminaries such as Theodore Herzl, whom Eliazar had met back in 1898; Vladimir Jabotinsky, who recruited him to the Jewish Legion; and the poet Chaim Nachman Bialik. Whenever available – and that was not too often – Eliazar would be asked to speak. Though he was far from being an orator, Troy recounts that: 'In a simple, deep, heavily Russian-accented English interspersed with Hebrew, Margolin would relate a story or two of his association with the liberation of Palestine from the Turks by the British, and his association with the exploits of the Jewish Battalions of the Royal Fusiliers with whom he was closely involved.'[18] He was able to 'touch the hearts' of his receptive Zionist audience when he spoke of life in the very early days of the *Yishuv*. Although enjoying much respect among Zionists, and a vice president of the Western Australian Zionist Association, he was not an activist.[19] Many of its meetings were held in Yiddish[20] in which Eliazar was not at all fluent. He did have an involvement with the Jewish scouts, but in what capacity is not known.

Eliazar's tenuous relationship with the Western Australian Jewish community, its Anglo-Jewish leadership, and Judaism generally, was undoubtedly further strained when he married outside the faith. His synagogue attendance was limited to the Anzac Day service, which the Reverend D. Freedman, Chaplain to the Jewish soldiers in first AIF and Rabbi of the Perth Hebrew Congregation, made a public event. Resplendent in his medals, Eliazar Margolin was given pride of place.[21] Even in this situation, however, tensions emerged. Indeed, it is told, and it echoes with the ring of truth, that at one service, a congregant objected to Eliazar's partaking in the sacred task of 'being called to the Reading of the Torah', the scroll which comprises the 'Five Books of Moses', because he had married outside the faith.[22]

Only rarely did Eliazar offer his name to activities within the Jewish community. In 1943, just eight months before he died, he lent his name to a push to establish a Council to Combat Anti-Semitism in Western Australia, to contest the anti-Semitic literature circulating in Perth.[23] There was also a drive to break the Anglo-Orthodox dominance over the Western Australian community's approximately 2,000 Jews,[24] and to make communal practices far more democratic through the formation of a Council of Jewish Affairs. Divisions had long simmered between the community's

'Anglo' and 'foreign' elements. What had tipped the balance was the arrival, especially in 1937–39, of German and Austrian Jews used to a different communal structure.

The United Australia Party Government, led by Joseph Lyons's United Australia Party, had agreed in 1938/39 to an intake of 15,000 European refugees seeking to escape a rampant Nazism. The government's move had nothing to do with any humanitarianism; rather, it was on the advice of Australia's High Commissioner in England, Lord Bruce, that such an intake would win goodwill in London and Washington. Bruce was not concerned for the fate of European Jewry, and had been a vocal supporter of the 1939 McDonald White Paper out of a fear that Jewish refugee immigration to Palestine would upset the Arabs, who had to be appeased.[25] Originally Bruce suggested Australia take 30,000 refugees, but a reluctant Lyons government agreed to only 15,000 from the many thousands of applicants. Ultimately, some 8,000 arrived before the Second World War erupted, and of these only around 5,000 were Jews.[26] Between 1937 and 1939 a handful of these refugees made their home in Western Australia, bolstering the number of 'foreigners'.[27]

Eliazar was enticed, very reluctantly, into tense discussions between those who wanted a more democratic community, and the bastion of Anglo-Orthodoxy, the Perth Hebrew Congregation. He allowed his name to be put on the ballot for the selection of the inaugural Western Australian Council of Jewish Affairs. Eighteen people were nominated for the five-person executive, including Eliazar, but in the subsequent ballot he polled eighth, and consequently was not elected.[28] Given his age, and reluctance to engage in communal activity, this defeat was a relief.

The year following, on Wednesday 2 June 1944, Eliazar Lazar Margolin died, at the age of sixty-nine, after collapsing in his office at the headquarters of United Buses in Claremont. Rushed immediately to the John of God Hospital, he failed to recover, dying of a cerebral haemorrhage. Out of respect, flags on Anzac House in Perth were flown at half-mast. A senior member of the RSL paid tribute: 'Although born outside the British Empire, Colonel Margolin was intensely British and a large number of Diggers apart from his old comrades of the 16th will mourn his loss. He was a great soldier and a Digger comrade.'[29]

His body was taken to the Chapel of Donald Chipper and Son, undertakers, in Hay Street, Perth. There it is said some kind of Jewish ceremony took place, though its nature, given Eliazar's lack of interest in religious proprieties, what was about to occur is obscure. From the undertakers, the funeral procession moved slowly through the Perth streets, halting at the entrance gate of the Karratta cemetery. There the casket was transferred to a gun carriage, which carried it to the cemetery's crematorium. In death, as in life, Eliazar maintained his distance from Judaism, choosing cremation over a traditional Jewish burial. Because of this, no rabbi or rabbinical appointee conducted the proceedings.

Former members of the 16th Battalion had gathered outside the cemetery gates, then marched to the crematorium. There the service was conducted by E. S. Watt, the Acting State President of the RSL in Western Australia. The crowd of mourners was large, and included Brigadier Hoad, representing General Office Command in Western Australia, politicians, both the executive and RSL sub-branch members, and Jewish friends of the deceased. In his oration, Watt stated:

> The 16th Battalion and men who wore the navy blue and white shoulder patch of that famous unit always filled a very big place in Colonel Margolin's heart. He was intensely proud of the Battalion and his fellow Diggers: so much so, that after all these years, one could not think of Colonel Margolin without thinking of the 16th or the 16th without the Colonel ... He was a man of outstanding physical and moral courage – never flinched in action, nor ever afraid to speak his mind when speaking was called for. He was a rare combination of a man of action, who was a reader and thinker, with it all, he had the modesty and unfailing courtesy, which does so benefit a man of war.[30]

The Minister of Mines, A. H. Panton, placed a red poppy – an Australian traditional symbol of remembrance for the military fallen – on the casket, adding that: 'There would be no great opposition to Jewish immigration in the West at least, if Australia could be assured of getting a fair proportion of Jews as "Margy". He remained a true and loyal Australian, never afraid to change his mind. He died as he wished, with his faculties unimpaired – virtually with his boots on.'[31] Others then followed, also placing their own poppies on the coffin.

Inadvertently, Panton's words unfortunately used what has been called the 'some of my best friends are' statement often used by the anti-Semite. There is little doubt his reference to 'opposition to Jewish immigration' related to the great fear, current in Australia at the time, of the immigration of Jewish refugees seeking to flee Nazism before the Second World War. Strong opposition to this immigration, particularly that from Eastern Europe, existed, both on cultural and economic grounds, especially throughout the 1930s, when Australia was in the grip of the Great Depression.[32] Anti-Semitic sentiments were heard in Western Australia, as elsewhere in Australia.[33] In essence, it was considered that those of similar origins to Eliazar's would neither assimilate in Australia's Anglo-Saxon society, nor be loyal subjects of the nation and British Empire. As Watt explained, however, Eliazar was different. Indeed, this man of unassuming manner was an extremely distinguished soldier and a highly distinguished citizen, and 'belonged to that illustrious band of people from overseas who have come to Australia and put more into our social life than was ever possible for them to take out … in all his business doings, he was infected with the highest ethics … he remained a true and loyal Australian.'[34]

The proposition that Eliazar 'was a great soldier, a citizen, and a Digger comrade', was later supported in an open letter to the *Boddulin*, addressed to his widow by an unnamed former comrade in the 16th Battalion:

> Dear Mrs Margolin
> … I must admit it is also with a glow of pride, that I could associate myself with such a good soldier. Margy (as you are already aware, all the boys used to call him) was a highly esteemed man, in the 16th, especially so in the B Company where I first came into contact with him. I shall never forget one night as we were going up the line digging, all tracking after the other in a single file dark as black as coal. We came to a turn in the trench, and a voice said as we passed, keep your head down boys. I could see no one. I said to my mate, as we struggled with our picks and shovels etc, who was that? He replied it was Margy. Snipers were busy and he is warning us, as we pass. It is printed on my mind because Margy had such a low voice, and it came so unawares. Of course this was only a little incident among hundreds, but it impressed my mind I suppose. I used to see him in Perth occasionally and I always pulled him up and had a word with him. He was so pleased to think you would stop him, and he would also seem to enjoy a chat with any of the lads. The last time I saw him a few months ago, I was talking to him and he remarked I do not think my life has been in vain. I said certainly not, the boys of the 16th know that.[35]

The blast of the Last Post, then reveille, ended proceedings, and as Eliazar's body moved to be consumed by fire, all present joined in a rendition of a verse of the Christian hymn, 'Abide with Me'.

The absence of a traditional Jewish burial robbed those in the Western Australian Jewish community of the chance to bid farewell to Eliazar formally. To satisfy this need, a memorial gathering was organized on 4 July 1944, under the joint auspices of the Jewish National Fund (JNF), the Council of Jewish Affairs and the Western Australian Zionist Association. Also present were members of the RSL and representatives from his beloved 16th Battalion.[36] The President of the JNF eulogized him in the manner of others, as a man of action who had possessed outstanding moral and physical courage, and in reference to the heinous events of the time added: 'he was the personification of those qualities which are inherent in Russian people which have given them strength and faith to endure the triumph over the Nazi invaders of their beloved countries.'[37]

Eliazar was described as 'a staunch Jew in whom the true spirit of the Maccabees burned strong', the ethos which ultimately led to the deliverance of European Jewry from their current trial and persecution. Extolled as a man of the British Empire, though never at the expense of forgetting his Jewishness, he was even compared to the great American Zionist and jurist, Louis Brandeis, who had declared 'a Jew who is conscious and proud of the traditions of his people is by the same token a better citizen and man of the country where he lives'.[38] With the horrors of the Second World War extant, Eliazar confided: 'to liquidate my business would take me from 12–15 months, but should there be a desire for my services, I would be willing to accept anything that is asked of me and be prepared to leave immediately.'[39]

The deceased was described in terms that would have profoundly embarrassed him. Not only was he – along with Vladimir Jabotinsky and Yosef Trumpeldor – said to have carried on the spirit of the Maccabees, but was placed only second to John Monash as Australia's greatest Jewish soldier. It was suggested that a grove of trees be planted in *Eretz Israel* in his honour.[40]

A telegram from Benzion Patkin of Melbourne on behalf of the Executive of the Zionist Federation was read: 'Profound sympathy for loss of Colonel Margolin. The pioneering work of Margolin in Palestine in the early years of settlement is judged by wonderful results achieved. It eventually created the possibility for Jewish mass migration to Palestine.'[41]

When Margolin left Palestine in 1921, after his meeting with his men for the last time, he did so with *HaTivah* (The Hope), the anthem of the Zionist movement, ringing in his ears. This gathering closed with yet another bugle blast of the Last Post.

Eliazar's comrades and friends in *Eretz Israel* were not going to allow his passing to go without any recognition. A memorial gathering was held for him by the *Brit Hachayal Be-Eretz Israel* (the Soldiers' Organization in Israel) on Thursday 6 July 1944 at 7 p.m., in their rooms at 68 Nachlat Binyamin Street in Tel Aviv. Among those who spoke of their comrade were the Chief Rabbi for Tel Aviv and Jaffa, Rabbi Y. M. Toledano Shalita, and a former legionnaire, Menachem Arber.[42]

In January 1945, the Returned Soldiers' and Airmen's Imperial League of Australia, Western Australia Branch, received a letter from Field Marshal Birdwood. It read:

> It is with great regret I have just heard of the death of my old friend and comrade Colonel E. L. Margolin M.C. and D.S.O. whom I remember so well in the last war as a member of the magnificent 16th W.A. Battalion, A.I.F. I write to you to say how grateful I will be if you will kindly convey my deep sympathy to his family and to my old A.I.F comrades on the great loss I feel we have all sustained ...[43]

18

Homeward Bound

Not long before Eliazar died, he willed his military decorations, sword and medals to Avihayil, a settlement established by veterans of the Jewish Legion near Netanya. They were to be part of the collection in its museum, *Beit Hagdudim*, dedicated to the deeds of the Zion Mule Corps and the Jewish Legion. He also extracted from his wife the promise that as soon as a Jewish state was established in Palestine, he would be buried there. Approximately three and a half years after his death, on 14 May 1948, a former member of Eliazar's 39th Battalion of the Royal Fusiliers, David Ben-Gurion in Tel Aviv, declared that longed-for Jewish entity into being, after obtaining international support at the United Nations.[1] True to her husband's wishes, Hilda Margolin successfully negotiated with the Israeli authorities to allow his ashes to be returned to the land that he always felt to be his home. In Israel, this event was organized under the auspices of the relatively newly established Jewish State's Department of Defence.

On 19 January 1950, the very day that the remains of Eliazar Margolin came home to rest in his beloved *Eretz Israel*, his biography appeared in the Revisionist newsletter, *Herut*, written by Vladimir Jabotinsky, who had so long before recruited him into the Jewish Legion. Accompanying the ashes of her husband, Hilda had sailed from Australia on the *Campidulio*, stopping in Greece before reaching the Israeli littoral. Hilda's execution of her husband's wish, his reburial in Israel, was an event of major and poignant significance in the new Jewish State. Thus, nothing was to be left to chance: the event in its entirety was to be thoroughly and thoughtfully choreographed.[2]

The ship arrived on time at the port of Haifa. At 7.45 a.m., a welcoming party, which included Mr Ya'acov Patt, in charge of the Department for Special Duties in the Ministry of Defence, the head of the Coast and Borders Division, together with four former comrades of the Jewish Battalions, went on board to meet Hilda. Eliazar's ashes were placed in a large wooden coffin draped in the blue-and-white flag of the Jewish State, and bedecked with his sword, medals of honour and service hat. The veterans then took the coffin, and placed it on board police boat CG14 to be conveyed to the wharf opposite the police station. There, Eliazar's former comrades transferred the coffin to a military car, and then passed the first of a number of welcoming honour guards along the way, this time of Israeli navy and police, who presented arms.

Many Haifa residents crowded the entrance of the port as the funeral procession left for a short memorial service at the Haifa Council chambers. The procession halted at a number of places that had figured significantly in Eliazar's life during his sojourn in Palestine. Heading the entourage was an escort of police motorcycles, followed by the military car bearing the coffin, the vehicle conveying Hilda, an honour guard and a few friends of the deceased. The Mayor of the City delivered a short oration at the Haifa Council before the motorcade proceeded for a brief pause at the Kiryat Eliyahu military base at Sarafend, where Eliazar's battalion had camped, and then moved on to Avihayil, the settlement of former members of the Jewish Legion. Here, a memorial service was held in the presence of Yitzhak Ben-Zvi, Knesset (Israeli Parliament) member, battalion comrade, and destined two years later to be the second President of the State of Israel (after Chaim Weizmann). From there, the coffin travelled to the Ohel-Shem Hall (cemetery parlour) in Tel Aviv. Another company of soldiers and police presented arms before the coffin was borne into the hall and placed on a stand headed by the battalion menorah alight with four candles. The ceremony was conducted by Tel Aviv's Chief Administrator, Chaim Alperin.

Wreaths were laid by the Mayor of Tel Aviv and former fellow defender of the city against Arab riots, Mr Y. Rokach, and – only recently arrived – Australia's diplomatic representative to the fledgling State of Israel, O. W. C. Fuhrman, who in common with Eliazar had served in Gallipoli and on the Western Front.

Leaving the Ohel-Shem Hall, the slow motorcade passed through the streets of Tel Aviv, on to Ziffrin, where the three Jewish Battalions and the First Judeans had camped, and then moved on to Rehovot, arriving at two o'clock in the afternoon. There the cortege was met by a large crowd, comprising local residents and an entourage from all over the country, led by his friend Moshe Smilansky. Words of commemoration were uttered by Mr Ben-Zion Horovitz, the Mayor of the Rehovot Council, followed by the recital of the *Kaddish*, the Jewish memorial prayer, intoned by Chazan David Resnik. Given Eliazar's secular burial in Perth, this was probably the first time this traditional Jewish dirge had been chanted in his memory. Those present then filed past the coffin to pay their respects to the deceased.

At half past three that afternoon, Israel's prime minister, David Ben-Gurion, arrived from Jerusalem to bid a personal farewell to his old commander. The casket was then transferred to a newly dug grave in the Rehovot cemetery next to Eliazar's beloved parents, who had been buried alongside each other half a century earlier. Moshe Smilansky declaimed the final panegyric. There followed a volley of gunfire in military salute, a rendition of *Aryeh, Aryeh*, and two minutes of silence to reflect on the life of Lieutenant-Colonel Eliazar Lazar Margolin. He had finally come home to *Eretz Israel*, and now at last his spirit could be at rest.

After the funeral, in a study of Rehovot's famous Weizmann Institute, Hilda met Israel's first President of the Jewish State, Chaim Weizmann, with Prime Minister Ben-Gurion present. Weizmann of course, after some very early hesitancy, had become a strong advocate of the Jewish Legion, and subsequently, the First Judeans. Hilda told her hosts that Eliazar had predicted that she would receive a royal welcome in Israel, though this had had to await the conditions laid down by his will, that is, the establishment of a Jewish State in Palestine. Clearly, he had foreseen that day eventuating during her lifetime. She presented Weizmann with her husband's sword and decorations, willed as a gift to the Jewish State. It was his own patriotic military salute to the land of his longing. Hilda confided that after her stay in Israel she also intended to travel to England to meet some of Eliazar's former colleagues in the Jewish Legion. Among them would be Colonel Fred Samuels, who had commanded the 40th, and Eliazar's trusted friend and medical officer of the 39th, Dr Redcliffe Salaman.[3] Only a very brief report of Eliazar's funeral appeared in London's *Jewish Chronicle* on 27 January 1950.

On 1 February 1950 some ninety veterans of the Zion Mule Corps and the Jewish Legion gathered at the Menorah Club in Jerusalem to exchange reminiscences. It was a solemn occasion, honouring the moment when Hilda officially presented Eliazar's gift to the State of Israel. Receiving the memorabilia was the Chief of Staff of the Israel Defence Force, Yigael Yadin, on behalf of the army. He, in turn, presented them to the Menorah Club, which had been established by ex-servicemen of the First World War. One member, Prime Minister Ben-Gurion, stated that the task of the veterans was yet to be completed, and that they were still required to 'instil a pioneering spirit into the ranks of the youth and people of the State'. He fondly recalled Lieutenant-Colonel Margolin's share in nurturing the first seeds of the Israeli Army.

Hilda told her audience that she had been greatly moved by the kindness of her reception since her arrival in Israel. She repeated her appreciation of the warmth shown towards her, and mourned the fact that she had had to experience it alone. In her view, her husband had indeed received an 'honoured burial'. Of the veterans who had come from Avihayil, other settlements and also Haifa and Tel Aviv, there were the only two surviving officers of Lieutenant-Colonel Margolin's battalion in Israel, Captain T. Cousin of Jerusalem and Lieutenant P. Phillips of Haifa.

A few months later, the *Palestine Post* published a letter from Hilda reiterating her thanks for her kind welcome in Israel, adding that she had been inspired by what had been achieved by the new polity of the Jewish State in the face of the profoundly difficult strategic and social problems it was being forced to endure on a daily basis.[4]

Maintaining contact with the Jewish State, Hilda sent good wishes to Yitzhak Ben-Zvi in 1953 on the occasion of his appointment to follow Chaim Weizmann as Israel's second president.[5] She was to bequeath $4,000 to the *Beit-Hagdudim* Museum in Avihayil. Eliazar's sword, medals and oil portrait are on open display there today.

In August 1956, in Rehovot, President Ben-Zvi attended the unveiling of a memorial stone over the grave of his former commander with the words: 'We shall never forget the sterling services to the Jewish people and to this country, in addition to his excellent achievements.'[6]

After her husband died, Hilda lived with her two older unmarried sisters, Charlotte and Vera. She moved to a hostel in Shoalwater after their deaths. She passed away there at the age of ninety-six. Right up to that time, Hilda travelled to Perth for the annual reunion of the 16th Battalion, of which she was patroness.

19

Hawaja Nazar

If one takes Moshe Smilansky at his word – and there is no reason to doubt him – in the early years of Rehovot, he was for a time a lodger in the Margolin home. He was thus in a comfortable position from which to observe Eliazar in his young adulthood. Indeed, he claims to be his prime mentor on matters of Zionism, Jewish history and Jewish culture.[1] A pioneer farmer and labour organizer in the *Yishuv*, he says, on the other hand, that it was Eliazar who encouraged him to be involved in the establishment of the Palestinian battalion of the Jewish Legion.

Smilansky is famed, above all, as the writer of short stories about the first decades of the *Yishuv*, the subjects of which, according to I. M. Lask, were 'the early settlers, their hopes, dreams, disappointments, and achievement'.[2] A prime target of his concern was Jewish–Arab relations, and his Arabs were often painted with warm and sympathetic strokes. One of his numerous works was the tale 'Hawaja Nazar', written before the First World War, which found its English voice in a collection published in 1936 called *Palestine Caravan: A Collection of Stories*.[3] *Hawaja Nazar* was the soubriquet, according to Smilansky, given to Eliazar Margolin by the Arabs out of their respect for him.

This story is concerned solely with one actor, Eliazar, in his First *Aliyah* existence before his first departure for Australia in 1902. Although he is the subject, however, the story is fictional not historical, and as such is a vehicle for the author's interpretations and world view. The question remains that, though the tale may be quint-essential Smilansky, to what degree does it actually describe the real Eliazar?

The tale opens in the newly founded Rehovot, with an Arab attack on an eighteen-year-old new immigrant from Russia who is attempting to enter the settlement. This recent arrival has come alone from the Jaffa port, the point of immigration for Jews entering *Eretz Israel*. Overcoming his attackers, the youth deals justly and humanely with them. Because of this, one of his assailants, an Arab employed to guard the settlement, describes his conqueror as *Hawaja*. As mentioned earlier, *Hawaja* means 'a man, by the prophet of Moses'. *Nazar* is a wordplay on the youth's name, Lazar. The pseudonym, which becomes *de rigueur* among Eliazar's fellow pioneers, was bestowed on him by the Arabs because of his ability 'to ride like a Bedouin and shoot like an Englishman'. They greatly revered both horsemanship and marksmanship from the saddle. It was these traits that brought him fame throughout the *Yishuv*, particularly when he was forced to defend Rehovot and its environs against marauding and thieving. Moreover, *Hawaja Nazar* often roamed the Palestinian landscape in Bedouin garb, learning the ways of the Arabs. Though his relations with them are characterized as giving and receiving respect, the *Hawaja* is never seduced by Arab or Bedouin ways. In dealing with them, he always maintains a sceptical distance.

Smilansky's *Hawaja* is only half-Jewish, and that aspect attenuated at best. Certainly, he is totally devoid of any knowledge of his Jewish heritage. His father is Jewish, but not his mother, who died in his infancy. In traditional religious terms, according to which Jewishness is dictated by the maternal line, this youth is a Gentile, not a Jew. At least early in his stay he hears his father's plea ringing in his ears, begging him to return to Russia. None of this fits the real Eliazar. There is no doubt about the Jewishness of both his parents, and thus his own. Moreover, it was at their cajoling that he accompanied them, his blind brother and unwed sister, to immigrate to Palestine.

Hawaja Nazar is described as 'a mountain of a man', and Eliazar was indeed tall compared with many of his confrères from the cities and *shtetls* (villages) of Eastern Europe. And both the fictional and historical Eliazar showed a great capacity for work, organization, leadership and a proven capacity to defend the settlement of Rehovot.

Despite his father's efforts to have him educated in Jewish ways, he arrived in Palestine with, at best, a modicum of Jewish learning and interest in it. Whether or not his parents had flirted with Zionism in Russia, the young Eliazar must have heard the word discussed within the family milieu some time before they set out for the unknown Palestine rather than the 'goldeneh medinas' in Western Europe, the United States and perhaps even Australia. On the other hand, Smilansky's character first hears of Palestine only via an inadvertent dip into the Bible, and of Zionism on board ship *en route* to Palestine. *Hawaja Nazar* and Eliazar acquired their Jewish culture and love of *Eretz Israel* in Palestine itself.

The description of *Hawaja Nazar*'s personal development in Rehovot and travels throughout Palestine is to establish the basis for his ultimate pilgrimage-cum-spiritual odyssey in search of Zion. For him, this is not the physical or metaphysical Jerusalem of traditional Judaism, but the River Jordan of his imagination. As the early practical Zionists had to run the gauntlet of aggressive scepticism in Eastern Europe, no scoffers, even those who had seen the actual Jordan, could dissuade him from wandering through the wilderness in pursuit of his goal. In his mind's eye, the River Jordan is a full-flowing raging torrent of water throughout its length.

In keeping with the story of the Moses-led Exodus from Egypt, this traveller meets obstacles and experiences, no doubt designed to threaten his resolve, indeed, his very faith. Here, Smilansky's negative attitude to traditional Judaism comes to the fore. Along the way, the hero seeks to affirm the triumph of the new *Yishuv* of practical Zionism over the old *Yishuv*, with its passive and pious Jews ever waiting for God to redeem the Jewish People. Emblematic of his contempt for the latter are the pious mendicant residents, depicted as dirty and smelly, of the decaying ancient Jewish city of Tiberias. It is a scene that our intrepid traveller seeks to escape. There is no doubt that Eliazar always had his problems with orthodox Judaism, even in its Anglo manifestation in Australia. It never reached the heightened scorn felt by the *Hawaja*, however. Even so, it would be fair to say that both experience a pantheistic ecstasy that derives from the raw physicality of the land, as it did from the human camaraderie of *Eretz Israel*. This was unquestionably the source of Eliazar's Zionism.

Firm in his own Zionist faith, the meagre reaches of the River Jordan do not cause him to waver. Any burden of doubt is lifted when he finds that section of the river which becomes an expansive, free-flowing stream. Though a non-swimmer, an ecstatic *Hawaja* dives into the strong currents, just as many of the *Yishuv*'s practical Zionists impetuously attempted to till an unknown soil despite lacking any knowledge of agriculture. Returning to the surface, *Hawaja* dives under a second time, but on his third attempt he is fatally trapped by underwater weeds, and drowns. When these hostile plants finally release his lifeless body to rise to the surface, the *Chevra Kadisha* or Jewish Burial Society is called. They discover that he had not been circumcised. This places him outside the covenant of Israel, and thus he cannot be interred in a Jewish cemetery, only outside it. Great anger grips the narrator of the story – obviously Smilansky – who bitterly cries out that it is the drowned man, the practical Zionist, and not the religious men of the *Chevra Kadisha*, who are the future of the Jewish People. Indeed, the story ends with the waterlogged body suddenly swaying or 'shuckling', in the manner of a traditional Jew at prayer, and then being swept by the river's current downstream, disappearing face downwards. The story ends with the telling words, 'Jordan had taken him'. Zion had taken his soul for eternity.

The story was written before the First World War, at a time when many who attempted to farm *Eretz Israel* saw their efforts turn sour in a difficult and harsh environment. Just like *Hawaja Nazar*'s first two dives, early successes were short-lived, and just like him, were devoured by their own dream. There can be little doubt that Eliazar Margolin had had his periods of exhilaration, but these had been crushed under the hammer of a brutal economic reality. And just as *Hawaja Nazar* floated away, so too was he forced to divorce himself from his acquired love of *Eretz Israel*, 'looking down', facing the land to which he always hoped to return. Zion had consumed him.

Eliazar had made two attempts to remain permanently in *Eretz Israel*, and had been forced to leave. On the third occasion, unlike in *Hawaja*'s case, his spirit was welcomed home. No doubt Smilansky, who died just a few years after Eliazar was reinterred in the Jewish State, would have regarded his *Hawaja* as having finally triumphed.

20

Postscript

There continues to be much discussion in contemporary anthropological and historical literature about the degree of congruence or dissonance between what is called the 'collective memory' of any particular group, and actual historical events.[1] This is the same for the nation. What the nation – or indeed the community – believes occurred not only helps to define its current identity, but its future presence. Over the passing of time, this process is one of inclusion and exclusion. What is in and what is out, is a complex mix of political and social forces mixed into, and affecting, the contemporary mood. Once a particular view becomes fixed, as it were, into the fabric of a culture, it is difficult to budge – even in the face of compelling evidence.

The Anzac story has become perhaps the pivotal mythical force in Australia. Many people's names criss-cross this now moral tale. One on whose journeyman's back the legend was brokered, however, was Eliazar Margolin. Along with those of many other co-creators, his name has gone 'missing in action'. Several reasons have been proffered for this, but given the notion that if one doesn't acknowledge one's own, then others can't be expected to, there has been a major failure of Australian Jewry to recognize and celebrate Eliazar's uniqueness as an Anzac Zionist. In Perth, he was acclaimed by his digger mates and Zionists alike, but for quite separate reasons, and never the twain did meet. The former appreciated his role in the AIF, and his work in post-war welfare efforts under the aegis of the RSL and Legacy. Among the latter he attained fame as a pioneer and defender in, and of, the *Yishuv*. Each aspect was, as it were, compartmentalized, and never wholly celebrated together, as a synergy. Doubtless, within the Western Australian Jewish community, the possibility of this ever happening was severely undermined by Eliazar's own difficulties with traditional Judaism.

In Israel, Eliazar's reputation did not face these problems, and he has a definite place in the nation's pre-state history. It may well be that Moshe Smilansky's *Hawaja Nazar* did not resemble the incarnate Eliazar Margolin, but on the other hand, his readers knew of whom he was writing. Two elements provided him with a legitimacy in *Yishuv* history and folklore, the first as a pioneer builder and the second as a military commander of Jewish forces defending the Zionist cause *in situ*. What certainly helped was the fact that a number of his men in the Jewish Legion became the political and military supremos when one of them, David Ben-Gurion, declared the Jewish State into being in 1948. His deeds and – after his death – his memory, were celebrated by some of the most powerful leaders of the nation. Eliazar was part of their experience. Hence, it is not surprising that Eliazar Margolin is not memorialized anywhere in Australia, as he is in Israel. Particularly, he has pride of place in the museum dedicated to the Zion Mule Corps and Jewish Legion at Avihayil near Netanya. In Rehovot, not far from where he and his parents are buried, a street bears his name.

When all the words about Eliazar have been exhausted, we are still left with the remarkable story of an outstanding personality, someone who courted no public attention, let alone fame. He was essentially a shy person who failed to match his military achievements in civilian life. This notwithstanding, whether in the persona of *Hawaja Nazar*, or *Lazar*, or 'Margy', as the diggers affectionately called him, he was a most loved figure. Though he was never religious in the traditional Jewish sense, Lieutenant-Colonel Eliazar Margolin DSO, this Anzac Zionist, surely would not have objected to the description of his life as a testament to the commandment of the Hebrew Prophet Isaiah: 'Learn to do well: seek justice, relieve the oppressed, judge [procure justice for] the fatherless, plead for the widow.'[2]

Glossary

Bar Kokhba: The leader of the Jewish revolt against Rome in Judea 132–35 CE.

Bund: Jewish Socialist Party founded in Russia in 1897. Ideologically devoted to the Yiddish culture that envisioned an autonomous secular Jewish nationalism in Eastern Europe, the party strongly opposed Zionism.

Chaver: (Hebrew) A friend or colleague.

Cheder: A Jewish religious elementary school.

Diaspora: Lands of the dispersion of the Jewish people worldwide, prior to, but particularly after, the Second Temple period.

Digger: Colloquial affectionate term for an Australian soldier, especially those of the First World War.

Eretz Israel: 'The Land of Israel', a term of biblical origin, which following the destruction of the Second Temple became the appellation for 'the Promised Land'. It was also the name for the area of Palestine administered by the British after the First World War until 1948.

Haluka: Financial charity collected from Jews around the world to help support their religious brethren in the Holy Land.

Haganah: Organized Jewish defence force in Palestine from 1920 until the formation of the State of Israel in 1948.

Ha Shomer: An organized body of settlers in the period 1909–20 whose purpose was to defend settlements of the Jewish community in Palestine against attack by local Arabs and marauding Bedouins.

HaTikvah: 'The Hope', the anthem of the Zionist movement composed by Naphtali Herz Imber around 1878, that became the national anthem of the State of Israel.

Kaddish: Jewish memorial prayer.

Kol Nidre: (Aramaic for 'all vows') the solemn prayer that commences the Yom Kippur evening service.

Lag b'Omer: Religious celebrations and commemoration that falls between the principal festivals of Passover and Shavuot.

Pale of Settlement: Area in tsarist Russia to which Jewish settlement was restricted.

Passover: The religious festival that commemorates the Exodus of the Jews from slavery in Egypt and the first political murmurs of the Jews as a people.

Yeshiva: A Jewish religious college of higher learning or secondary school.

Yiddish: A hybrid language of the Jews of Eastern and Central Europe written in the Hebrew script. Its linguistic influences are German, Hebrew and some Slavic languages.

Yishuv: The Jewish community in Palestine – 'the old', the pious religious settlement over centuries, and 'the new', the modern settlement from the 1880s to the establishment of the State of Israel in 1948.

Yom Kippur: Traditionally the most solemn day of the Jewish religious calendar. It is a day of fasting, prayer, inner contemplation and the seeking of personal repentance.

Zionism: The political and cultural movement of the nineteenth and twentieth centuries to re-establish the Jews of the Diaspora in their ancient biblical home in the Holy Land.

Notes

Prologue

1. Eliazar is often spelled in texts as 'Eliezer'. The spelling here, however, is how the name appeared on his application for Australian naturalization.

Chapter 1

1. *Palestine Post*, 4 January 1950.
2. Gouttman, 'The Two Faces of Fuhrman'.
3. Gouttman, 'First Principles'.
4. *Encyclopedia Judaica*, vol. 9, p. 788.
5. *Jewish Herald*, 4 February 1921.
6. Honig, *Zionism in Australia*, pp. 48–50.
7. The burial occurred on 19 January 1950.
8. Australian National Archives, A1838/2, item 175/10/8/1, Fuhrman in Tel Aviv to Department of External Affairs, Canberra, 23 April 1951.
9. *Australian Dictionary of Biography, 1891–1939*, vol. 8, pp. 592–3.
10. Zerubavel, *Recovered Roots*, pp. 13–161.
11. See Chapter 16, 'A Distasteful Affair'.
12. Adler, *British Jewry Book of Honour*.
13. Price, *Jewish Settlers in Australia*, Appendix VI.
14. Rutland, *Edge of the Diaspora*, pp. 216–19.
15. Gouttman, 'Between Two Stools', p. 717.
16. Rouse, *Australian Liberalism and National Character*, pp. 8–11.
17. Clendinnen, *Reading the Holocaust*, p. 6.
18. H. Rubinstein, *The Jews in Australia*, pp. 471–528; W. D. Rubinstein, *The Jews in Australia*, pp. 379–479.
19. Cathcart, *Defending the National Tuckshop*.
20. Bartrop, *Australia and the Holocaust*. See also Rutland, *Edge of the Diaspora*, pp. 216–19.
21. Gouttman, 'The Australian Left and Anti-Semitism', pp. 24–5.
22. Bartrop, *Australia and the Holocaust*.
23. Bartrop, 'The "Jewish Race" Clause'.
24. Gouttman, 'A Jew and Coloured Too!'.
25. Rutland, *Edge of the Diaspora*, pp. 232–43.
26. Ibid., p. 185.
27. H. Rubinstein, *Chosen*, pp. 78–81.
28. Serle, *John Monash*, p. 325.
29. Ibid. p. 491. See also Rutland, *Edge of the Diaspora*, p. 144, among others.
30. Encel, 'Anti-Semitism and Prejudice in Australia', pp. 40–1.

31. Several institutions were badly damaged, for example the synagogue in the Sydney suburb of Bankstown was never rebuilt.
32. S. N. Herman, 'A Framework for a Social Psychological Analysis', in Y. Bauer. (ed.), *Present-Day Antisemitism* (Jerusalem: Vidal Sassoon International Center for the Study of Anti-Semitism, Hebrew University of Jerusalem, 1988), pp. 283–96.
33. Mossenson, 'History of Jews in Western Australia', p. 672.
34. H. Rubinstein, 'Australian Jewish Reactions to Russian Jewish Distress', *JAHS*, IX(6), 1984: 444–56. See also Gouttman, 'Brothers and Sisters', pp. 359–72.
35. Honig, 'Some Notes on the "Palestinian" Immigrants in Melbourne', pp. 63–4.
36. Mossenson, *Hebrew, Israelite, Jew*, p. 79.
37. Crown, 'Demography, Politics, and the Love of Zion', pp. 226–31.
38. Mossenson, *Hebrew, Israelite, Jew*. See also Honig, *Zionism in Australia*, p. 17.
39. Crown, 'Demography, Politics and the Love of Zion', p. 226.

Chapter 2

1. National Archives of Australia, Series A1, Item 1904/6208, Eliazar Margolin, Statutory Declaration.
2. *Encyclopedia Judaica*, vol. 4, p. 423.
3. Ibid.
4. *Israel Shelanu*, 29 November 1985 (Hebrew), one of the stories of *Eretz Israel* entitled, 'The Emigrant Who Became Commander', about Eliazar Margolin – the Commander of the 39th Battalion of the Royal Fusiliers, one of three battalions in the First World War.
5. Smilansky, *Palestine Caravan*, pp. 148–81.
6. Smilansky, *Mishpachat-Ha'adama*, pp. 167–76.
7. Ibid.
8. Ibid.
9. Ibid.
10. Ibid.
11. H. M. Sachar, *The Course of Modern Jewish History* (New York: Dell Publishing, 1977), pp. 240–6.
12. H. Rubinstein, *Chosen*, p. 79.
13. Crown, 'Demography, Politics, and the Love of Zion', p. 219.
14. S. Avineri, *The Making of Modern Zionism – The Intellectual Origins of the Jewish State* (New York: Basic Books, 1981), pp .47–55.
15. M. M. Kingsley, *The Reaction of Orthodox Judaism to the Rise of Secular Jewish Nationalism 1919–1939*, PhD thesis, University of Melbourne, 2000.
16. Levin, *While the Messiah Tarried*, p. 219.
17. *Encyclopedia Judaica*, vol. 16, pp. 1037–40.
18. See Avineri, n.14, pp. 73–82.
19. *Encyclopedia Judaica*, vol. 16, p. 1040.
20. Ibid. vol. 14, p. 444.
21. Ibid. vol. 4, pp. 492–3.
22. Ibid. vol. 14, p. 44.
23. Ibid. vol. 7, p. 1268.
24. Rabbi Dr J. H. Hertz, *The Pentateuch and Haftorahs*, second edn (London: Soncino Press, 1976), p. 96.

Chapter 3

1. *Encyclopedia Judaica*, vol.12, p. 1323.
2. Benbassa, 'Zionism in the Ottoman Empire', pp. 128–9.

3. Aaronsohn, 'Vines and Wineries in the Jewish Colonies', pp. 31–2.
4. Ibid., p. 39.
5. Ibid., pp. 43–4.
6. *Encyclopedia Judaica*, vol. 9, p. 788.
7. Aaronsohn, *Rothschild*, pp. 215–21.
8. *Encyclopedia Judaica*, vol. 9, p. 788.
9. Aaronsohn, *Rothschild*, pp. 231–5.
10. Ibid., pp. 223–5.
11. Smilansky, *Mishpachat-Ha'adama*, pp. 167–76.
12. Ibid.
13. Ibid.
14. Ibid.
15. Ibid.
16. W. Laqueur, *A History of Zionism* (New York: Schocken, 1978), pp.109–10.
17. Latai, *The Complete Diaries of Theodor Herzl*, 29 October, Jerusalem, p. 742.
18. Smilansky, *Mishpachat-Ha'adama*, pp. 167–76.
19. Ibid.
20. Ibid.
21. Naor, 'Edmond de Rothschild and Zionism', p. 187.
22. Smilansky, *Mishpachat-Ha'adama*, pp. 167–76.
23. Mossenson, *Hebrew, Israelite, Jew*, p. 32.
24. Rubinstein, *Chosen*, pp. 13–16.
25. *Splinters*, June 1944, p. 4. *Splinters* was the newsletter of the Nedlands sub-branch of the Western Australian Returned Soldiers', Sailors', and Airmen's Imperial League of Australia.
26. National Archives of Australia, Series K269, 'Collector of Customs, Western Australia, Inward Passenger Manifests', p. 2. The ship originally sailed from the German port of Bremen to Fremantle, Western Australia.

Chapter 4

1. *Australian Dictionary of Biography*, vol. 1891–1931, p. 408, contributor Suzanne Welborm. Eliyahu Honig penned his brief biographical snapshot in Geoffrey Wigoder (ed.), *New Encyclopedia of Zionism and Israel*, vol. 2, K–Z, (London and Toronto: Herzl Press), p. 917. Hilary Rubinstein does have a very brief biographical count and picture of Margolin in *The Jews in Australia*, pp. 402–4. The note in *Encyclopedia Judaica*, vol. 11, pp. 961–2, dwells mainly on Eliazar's contribution to the *Yishuv*.
2. National Archives of Australia, Series K269, 'Collector of Customs, Western Australia, Inward passenger Manifests'.
3. Ibid., Series A1, item 1904/6208, 'Margolin, Eliazar'.
4. Ibid.
5. Longmore, *The Old 16th*, p. 4.
6. A. G. Korsunski Memorial Lecture, G. Korsunski Carmel School, Perth.
7. The contributor, Suzanne Welborn, says that she also conferred with Mrs Margolin.
8. This was confirmed by the contributor, Eliyahu Honig, to the author on 16 July 2000.
9. A. G. Korsunski Memorial Lecture.
10. Ibid.
11. Smilansky, *Mishpachat-Ha'adama*, p. 172.
12. Ibid.
13. Mossenson, *Hebrew, Israelite, Jew*, p. 33.

14. Price, *Jewish Settlers in Australia*, Appendix 1.
15. Mossenson, *Hebrew, Israelite, Jew*, p. 34.
16. Ibid., pp. 34–5.
17. Ibid., pp. 42–3.
18. Crown, 'Demography, Politics, and the Love of Zion', pp. 226–30.
19. R. Gollan, *Radical and Working Class Politics: A Study of Eastern Australia 1850–1910* (Kingsgrove, NSW: Melbourne University and Australian National University, 1967); R. N. Ebbels, *The Australian Labor Movement 1850–1907* (Melbourne: Cheshire-Lansdowne, 1965).
20. S. A. Alomes, *A Nation at Last? The Changing Character of Australian Nationalism 1880–1988* (Sydney: Angus and Robertson, 1988), pp. 12–38.
21. Crown, 'The Initiatives and Influences in the Development of Australian Zionism', p. 329, entry in the endnote.
22. Rubinstein, *Chosen*, p. 43.
23. Ibid., p. 45.
24. Ibid., pp. 126–7.
25. Crown, 'Demography, Politics and the Love of Zion', p. 227.
26. Andrews, *A History of Australian Foreign Policy*, pp. 11–13.
27. Ibid., p. 6.
28. Clarke, *Australia*, pp. 189–91.
29. Grey, *A Military History of Australia*, p. 76.
30. National Archives of Australia, Series B2455, 'Personnel Dossiers for 1st Australian Imperial Forces Ex-service Members'.
31. Grey, *A Military History of Australia*, p. 78.
32. Ibid., p. 68.
33. Ibid., p. 85.
34. Ibid.

Chapter 5

1. National Archives of Australia, Series B2455, 'Personnel Dossiers for 1st Australian Imperial Forces Ex-service Members'.
2. Ibid.
3. Ibid. The District Commandant of the 5th Military District recommended Eliazar for his commission on 20 November 1914.
4. Grey, *A Military History of Australia*, p. 77.
5. Longmore, *The Old 16th*, pp. 17–19.
6. S. A. Alomes, *A Nation at Last? The Changing Character of Australian Nationalism 1880–1988* (Sydney: Angus and Robertson, 1988), pp. 39–72.
7. Lewis, *Our War*, p. 2.
8. Beaumont, *Australia's War 1914–18*, p. 2.
9. Ibid., p. 3.
10. P. Maclean, 'War and Australian Society', in Beaumont, *Australia's War 1914–18*, pp. 66–74.
11. Grey, *A Military History of Australia*, pp. 85–6.
12. Rubinstein, *Chosen*, p. 153.
13. Ibid., p. 154.
14. Adler, *The British Jewry Book of Honour*, p. 21.
15. Rutland, *Edge of the Diaspora*, p. 134.
16. Ibid.
17. Adler, 'Experiences of a Jewish Chaplain on the Western Front (1915–1918)', *The British Jewry Book of Honour*, pp. 33–58.
18. P. Masel, 'David Isaac Freedman', *Australian Jewish Historical Society Journal*,

XI(5), 1992: 752. Rabbi Freeman served as chaplain-major at Gallipoli and in France, Belgium, Egypt and Palestine.
19. J. S. Levi, *Rabbi Danglow* (Melbourne: Melbourne University Press, 1995), pp. 94-103.
20. Cesarani, 'An Embattled Minority', p. 65. For another view, W. Rubinstein, *A History of the Jews in the English-Speaking World*, pp. 192–223.
21. Grey, *A Military History of Australia*, pp. 108–10.
22. Beaumont, 'The Politics of a Divided Society', *Australia's War 1914–18*, pp. 54–7.
23. Mossenson, *Hebrew, Israelite, Jew*, pp. 88–9.

Chapter 6

1. Longmore, *The Old 16th*, p. 19.
2. Grey, *A Military History of Australia*, p. 88.
3. Winter, *25 April 1915*, pp. 3–7.
4. Ibid.
5. Grey, *A Military History of Australia*, p. 89.
6. Winter, *25 April 1915*, p. 3.
7. Longmore, *The Old 16th*, p. 32.
8. Sachar, *A History of Israel*, pp. 89–91.
9. Ibid.
10. Brugger, *Australians and Egypt*, pp. 57–63.
11. Jabotinsky, *The Story of the Jewish Legion*, pp. 33–4.
12. Ibid., p. 35.
13. Van Paassen, *The Forgotten Ally*, pp. 49–64.
14. Ibid. p. 63.
15. Grey, *A Military History of Australia*, p. 89.
16. Woodruff and McGregor, *The Suez Canal and the Australian Economy*, pp. 8–9.
17. Beaumont, 'The Anzac Legend', *Australia's War 1914–18*, pp. 149–80.
18. *Jewish Standard*, 28 April 1916.
19. Longmore, *The Old 16th*, p. 32.
20. Cutlack, *War Letters of General Monash*, p. 28.
21. Longmore, *The Old 16th*, p. 32.
22. Grey, *A Military History of Australia*, pp. 90–1.
23. Cutlack, *War Letters of General Monash*, pp. 33–5.
24. Ibid., p. 37.
25. Ibid., p. 46.
26. National Archives of Australia, Series B2455, 'Personnel Dossiers for 1st AIF Ex-service Members', E. L. Margolin, K1143/1, Casualty Form-Active Service.
27. Grey, *A Military History of Australia*, p. 93.
28. National Archives of Australia, Series B2455, 'Personnel Dossiers for 1st AIF Ex-service Members', E. L. Margolin, K1143/1, Casualty Form-Active Service.
29. Longmore, *The Old 16th*, p. 57.
30. C. E. W. Bean, *The Official History of Australia in the War of 1914–18*, vol. 2, (Sydney: Angus and Robertson, 1941), pp. 107, 109, 206.
31. Longmore, *The Old 16th*, p. 63.
32. Ibid.
33. Ibid., p. 88.
34. Cutlack, *War Letters of General Monash*, p. 67.
35. *Jewish Herald*, 3 December 1915.
36. Cutlack, *War Letters of General Monash*, p. 78.

37. Grey, *A Military History of Australia*, p. 94.
38. Longmore, *The Old 16th*, p. 84.
39. Cutlack, *War Letters of General Monash*, p. 98.
40. Ibid., p. 116.
41. Ibid., pp. 96–102.
42. Longmore, *Carry On*, p. 26.
43. National Archives of Australia, Series B2455, 'Personnel Dossiers for 1st AIF Ex-service Members', E. L. Margolin, K1143/1, Casualty Form-Active Service.
44. Sachar, *A History of Israel*, pp. 91–2.
45. Zerubavel, *Recovered Roots*, pp. 41–6.
46. *Jewish Herald*, 10 March 1916, letter from AIF 2Div.HQ, Mudros 24/12/15.
47. Ibid., 24 March 1916.
48. Ibid., 10 March 1916.
49. Bean, *The Australian Imperial Force in France*, p. 833.
50. National Archives of Australia, Series B2455, 'Personnel Dossiers for 1st AIF Ex-service Members', E. L. Margolin, K1143/1, Casualty Form-Active Service.
51. Ibid.
52. Ibid., letter he sent to the Commandant, AIF HQ, London, from the Australia Club, Piccadilly, 13 December 1917.
53. Jabotinsky, *The Story of the Jewish Legion*, p. 102.
54. National Archives of Australia, Series B2455, 'Personnel Dossiers for 1st AIF Ex-service Members', E. L. Margolin, K1143/1, Casualty Form-Active Service.

Chapter 7

1. *Jewish Herald*, 8 September 1916.
2. A. D. Crown, 'Demography, Politics and Love of Zion: The Australian Jewish Community and the Yishuv, 1850–1948', in W. D. Rubinstein (ed.), *Jews in the Sixth Continent* (Sydney: Allen and Unwin, 1987), p. 230.
3. W. Laqueur (ed.), *The Israel–Arab Reader: A Documentary History of the Middle East Conflict* (New York: Bantam Books, 1971), pp. 17–18.
4. *Hebrew Standard*, Editorial, 16 November 1917.
5. Ibid., 4 January 1918.
6. *Jewish Herald*, 8 March 1918.
7. Ibid.
8. *Hebrew Standard*, 4 June 1918.
9. *Jewish Herald*, 3 November 1916, speaking of the bravery of soldiers in France, which he sent on 22 August 1916.
10. Letter from David Mossenson, 28 January 1999.
11. *Jewish Herald*, 29 June 1917 Editorial.
12. Ibid.
13. Ibid., 26 January 1916. Lord Rothschild argued that Jewish enlistment numbers and performance during the war dispelled any notion of Jewish cowardice.
14. Ibid., 14 November 1917 Editorial on Conscription.
15. Ibid., 26 July 1918.
16. Serle, *John Monash*, pp. 254, 277, 325, 373.
17. Adler, *The British Jewry Book of Honour*, pp. 9–11.
18. Ibid. The contributors included the Chief Rabbi of the British Empire J. H. Hertz, General John Monash, Rufus Isaacs the Earl of Reading, Field Marshal Earl Haig, Viscount Northcliffe, the Marquis of Crewe and Winston Churchill.
19. Ibid., p. ix.

Chapter 8

1. *Encyclopedia Judaica*, vol. 10, p. 69.
2. Sachar, *A History of Israel*, p. 91.
3. Ibid.
4. M. Mintz, 'Pinchas Rutenberg and the Establishment of the Jewish Legion in 1914', *Studies in Zionism*, 6(1), 1985:24.
5. *Encyclopedia Judaica*, vol. 10, p. 70.
6. Sachar, *A History of Israel*, p. 91.
7. Mintz; see n.4.
8. Sarner, *The Jews of Gallipoli*, pp. 13–14.
9. *Jewish Herald*, 18 June 1915.
10. Sarner, *The Jews of Gallipoli*, pp. 13–14.
11. Mintz; see n.4, pp. 15–26.
12. Falk, 'With the Jewish Battalions in Palestine'.
13. *Hebrew Standard*, 18 August 1915 Editorial, 'Englishmen First – Jews After'.

Chapter 9

1. W. Laqueur, *The Israel–Arab Reader: A Documentary History of the Middle East Conflict* (New York: Bantam Books, 1971), document 7, pp. 17–18.
2. *Hebrew Standard*, 29 January 1915.
3. Ibid.
4. Rutland, *Edge of the Diaspora*, p. 172.
5. Stein, *The Balfour Declaration*, pp. 497–501.
6. Ibid., p. 487.
7. Ibid., p. 494.
8. *Jewish Herald*, 29 June 1917 Editorial.
9. Ibid., 17 March 1916.
10. Falk, 'With the Jewish Battalions in Palestine'.
11. *Jewish Herald*, 29 June 1917 Editorial.
12. Tuchman, *Bible and Sword*, pp. 175–266.
13. Eliav, *Britain and the Holy Land*, pp. 21–102.
14. Grey, *A Military History of Australia*, pp. 97–109.
15. Gilbert, *Exile and Return*, p. 90.
16. Karsh, *Empires of the Sand*, p. 190.
17. Kimche, *The Unromantics*, pp. 7–17.
18. Ibid., p. 20.
19. T. Tomes, *Balfour and Foreign Policy: The International Thought of a Conservative Statesman* (Cambridge: Cambridge University Press, 1997), pp. 206–9; Stein, *The Balfour Declaration*, pp. 605–20.
20. Kimche, *The Unromantics*, pp. 24–30.
21. Sykes, *Cross Roads to Israel*, p. 22.
22. Ibid.
23. Ibid.
24. Naor, 'Edmond de Rothschild and Zionism', p. 196.
25. *Hebrew Standard*, 9 November 1917 Editorial.

Chapter 10

1. Patterson, *With the Judeans in the Palestine Campaign*, p. 31.
2. Jabotinsky, *The Story of the Jewish Legion*, p. 34.
3. Ibid., p. 102.

4. Ibid.
5. Ibid.
6. Ibid., p. 88.
7. Patterson, *With the Judeans in the Palestine Campaign*, p. 31.
8. Cited in the *Jewish Herald*, 3 November 1917.
9. Cited in ibid., 23 March 1918.
10. Ibid., 3 November 1917.
11. Ibid., 16 November 1917.
12. Ibid., 24 July 1918.
13. Ibid.
14. Ibid., 19 April 1918.
15. Elam, *The Jewish Legion in World War I*, p. 231.
16. Ibid.
17. *Jewish Herald*, 11 June 1918.
18. Bar-Zohar, *Ben Gurion*, pp. 30–1.
19. *Jewish Herald*, 18 October 1918.
20. *Hebrew Standard*, 24 May 1918.
21. Ibid.
22. Salaman, *Palestine Reclaimed*, letters 15, 20, 29 April 1918, pp. 1–6.
23. Ibid., letter 31 May 1918, p. 12.
24. Ibid., letter 15 May 1918, p. 6.
25. Ibid., letter 12 May 1918, p. 6.
26. Ibid., letter, 7 June 1918, p. 14.
27. Falk, 'With the Jewish Battalions in Palestine', 18 October 1929, p. 12.
28. Ibid., 1 November 1929, p. 12.
29. Ibid.
30. Salaman, *Palestine Reclaimed*, letter 4 July 1918, p. 22.
31. Ibid.
32. Smilansky, *Mishpachat-Ha'adama*, p. 172.
33. Ibid., p. 173; see also Salaman, *Palestine Reclaimed*, letter 28 July 1918, p. 41.
34. Cited in *Hebrew Standard*, 14 June 1918.
35. Jabotinsky, *The Story of the Jewish Legion*, pp. 111–12.
36. Ministry of Defence, State of Israel, Tel Aviv, testimony files (Hebrew), 'Jewish Legion', Shimon HaCohen, 17–28, p. 4.
37. Ibid., B. Sonin, 196.70, 25 January 1952, p. 1.
38. Ibid., S. D. Jaffe, 198.33, p. 1.
39. Ibid., B. Sonin, 196.70, 25 January 1952, p. 1.
40. Ibid.
41. Salaman, *Palestine Reclaimed*, letter 13 July 1918, p. 23.
42. Ministry of Defence, State of Israel, Tel Aviv, testimony files (Hebrew), 'Jewish Legion', B. Sonin.
43. Ibid., S. D. Jaffe, 198.33, p. 1.
44. Ibid.
45. Salaman, *Palestine Reclaimed*, letter 28 July 1918, p. 31.
46. Freulich, *Soldiers in Judea*, p. 173.
47. *Israel Shelanu* (Hebrew), Friday, 29 November 1985, 'The Emigrant Who Became a Commander/Stories of Eretz Israel'. The lyrics were written by A. Rubinstein.

Chapter 11

1. Gammage, *The Broken Years*, pp. 128–30.
2. Ibid. pp. 131–46.

3. Gullett, *The A.I.F. in Sinai and Palestine*, p. 479.
4. Ibid.
5. Ibid. p. 477.
6. Ibid.
7. *Jewish Herald*, 22 March 1918.
8. Ibid., 5 April 1918.
9. J. Comay, *The World's Greatest Story: The Epic of the Jewish People in Biblical Times*, (New York: Holt, Rinehart and Winston, 1978), pp. 310–16.
10. *Jewish Herald*, 14 December 1917.
11. Ibid.
12. Ibid., 28 December 1917.
13. R. M. Gouttman, 'Response of Adelaide Jewry to Twentieth Century Anti-Jewish Atrocities', *Australian Jewish Historical Society Journal*, XII(2), 1994:363.
14. Rutland, *Edge of the Diaspora*, p. 146.
15. Gullet, *The A.I.F. in Sinai and Palestine*, pp. 686, 719.
16. Gammage, *The Broken Years*, p. 135.
17. Ibid., p. 135–6.
18. Jabotinsky, *The Story of the Jewish Legion*, pp. 123–9.
19. Ibid., p. 130.
20. Salaman, *Palestine Reclaimed*, letter 5 August 1918, p. 43.
21. Ibid., letter 7 August 1918, p. 4.
22. Ibid., letter 10 August 1918, p. 45.
23. Ibid., letter 12 August 1918, p. 46.
24. Ibid., letter 13 August 1918, p. 49.
25. Ibid.
26. Ibid., letter 15 August 1918, p. 50.
27. Ibid., letter 16 August 1918, p. 51.
28. Ibid., letter 18 August 1918, p. 51; 29 August 1918, p. 55.
29. Ibid., letter 13 August 1918, p. 64.
30. Ibid., letter 17 September 1918, p. 66.
31. Ibid.
32. *Ha-Aretz* (Hebrew), 12 September 1932; the legionnaire's name was not given.
33. Salaman, *Palestine Reclaimed*, letter 17 September 1918, p. 66.
34. Ibid., letters 17, 22, 29 September 1918, pp. 67–72.
35. Patterson, *With the Judeans in the Palestine Campaign*, p. 127.
36. Ibid., pp. 123–34.
37. Gullett, *The A.I.F. in Sinai and Palestine*, p. 715.
38. Patterson, *With the Judeans in the Paelstine Campaign*, p. 189.
39. Ibid., p. 192.
40. Ibid., p. 125.
41. Freulich, *Soldiers in Judea*, p. 113.
42. Salaman, *Palestine Reclaimed*, letter 21 October 1918, p. 83.
43. Gammage, *The Broken Years*, p. 136.
44. Ibid., p. 87.
45. Smilansky, *Mishpachat-Ha'adama*, p. 175.
46. Salaman, *Palestine Reclaimed*, p. 88.
47. Ibid., letter 24 October 1918, pp. 94–7.
48. Patterson, *With the Judeans in the Palestine Campaign*, pp. 167–71.
49. Ibid., p. 169.
50. Ibid., p. 170.
51. Ibid., p. 171.
52. Salaman, *Palestine Reclaimed*, p. 98.

53. Ministry of Defence, State of Israel Tel Aviv, testimony files (Hebrew), Jewish Legion, S. D. Jaffe, 188.33, p. 3.
54. Salaman, *Palestine Reclaimed*, letter 3 November 1918, p. 101.
55. Gammage, *The Broken Years*, pp. 137–8.
56. A. Troy, 'The Life of Colonel Eliazar Margolin', A. G. Korsunski Memorial Lecture, G. Korsunski Carmel School, 19 September 1982, p. 12.

Chapter 12

1. Gammage, *The Broken Years*, pp. 121, 140–1; Gullett, *The A.I.F. in Sinai and Palestine*, pp. 207–8.
2. Gilner, *War and Hope*, p. 162.
3. Langley, *Sand, Sweat and Camels*, p. 172.
4. Ibid., p. 173.
5. Ibid., pp. 173–4.
6. Gullett, *The A.I.F. in Sinai and Palestine*, pp. 788–9.
7. Langley, *Sand, Sweat and Camels*, p. 172.
8. Ibid., p. 174; see also Gullett, *The A.I.F. in Sinai and Palestine*, pp. 789–90.
9. M. Gilbert, *Israel: A History* (London: Black Swan, 1999), pp. 36–7.
10. Patterson, *With the Judeans in the Palestine Campaign*, pp. 187–8.
11. Ibid., p. 225.
12. Van Paassen, *The Forgotten Ally*, p. 121.
13. Sachar, *The Rise of Israel*, Introduction by Isaiah Friedman.
14. Ibid., Col. Meinertzhagen to Lord Curzon, 26 September 1919, Doc. 49, p. 148.
15. Ibid.
16. Ibid.
17. Stein, 'Josiah Wedgwood and the Seventh Dominion Scheme', p. 141.
18. Duff, *Palestine Picture*, p. 155.
19. Ibid., p. 195.
20. Sachar, *The Rise of Israel*.
21. Ibid., Doc. 26, p. 77, fifth meeting of the Advisory Committee to the Palestine Office at the residence of the Right Honorable Herbert Samuel, 10 May 1919, p. 77.
22. Gilbert, *Exile and Return*, p. 121; between 1917 and 1921 pogroms criss-crossed Eastern Europe in the wake of the Soviet Revolution and the subsequent civil war between the Red and White armies.
23. Salaman, *Palestine Reclaimed*, letter 14 March 1919.
24. Ibid.
25. Sachar, *The Rise of Israel*, Doc. 40, p. 131, Colonel French (Cairo) 31 July 1919.
26. Urofsky, *American Zionism from Herzl to the Holocaust*, p. 265.
27. Sachar, *The Rise of Israel*, Doc. 42, p. 133.

Chapter 13

1. Stein, *The Balfour Declaration*, pp. 605–8.
2. Ibid., p. 614.
3. Karsh, *Empires of the Sand*, pp. 208–15.
4. Ibid., pp. 224–41.
5. Patterson, *With the Judeans in the Palestine Campaign*, p. 220.
6. Salaman, *Palestine Reclaimed*, letter 2 January 1919, p. 152.
7. Sachar, *The Rise of Israel*, Doc. 28, 6 June 1919, p. 98.
8. Sykes, *Cross Roads to Israel*, p. 31.

9. Ministry of Defence, State of Israel, Tel Aviv, testimony files (Hebrew), Jewish Legion, S. D. Jaffe, 198.33; Gilner, *War and Hope*, p. 303.
10. Freulich, *Soldiers in Judea*, p. 145; Patterson, *With the Judeans in the Palestine Campaign*, p. 224.
11. Ibid.
12. Salaman, *Palestine Reclaimed*, letter 3 March 1919, p. 195.
13. Sachar, *The Rise of Israel*, Doc. 50, 7 October 1919, Jabotinsky's petition for mercy addressed to the king on the alleged anti-Semitic attitude of the British military authorities.
14. Ibid., pp. 3–4.
15. Ibid., p. 4.
16. Ibid.
17. Ibid., pp. 4–5.
18. Ibid.
19. Ibid.
20. Gilner, *War and Hope*, p. 300.
21. Sachar, *The Rise of Israel*, C.Z.A. 3/91, Doc. 45, 22 August 1919, p. 140, Military Governor, Jerusalem to David Eder; Doc. 46, 24 August 1919, p. 141, Zionist Commission to Military Governor of Jerusalem.
22. Ibid., Doc. 47, p. 143.
23. Salaman, *Palestine Reclaimed*, letter 26 December 1918, p. 145.
24. Ibid. Such as at Rishon LeZion, letter 16 February 1919, p. 186.
25. Ministry of Defence, Jewish Legion, testimony S. D. Jaffe, 193.33, p. 2.
26. Salaman, *Palestine Reclaimed*, letter 20 January 1919, p. 171.
27. Ibid., letter 3 February 1919, p. 173.
28. Zerubavel, *Recovered Roots*, pp. 39–41.
29. Ministry of Defence, Jewish Legion, testimony S. D. Jaffe, 193.33, p. 2.
30. Ibid.
31. Gilbert, *Exile and Return*, p. 129.
32. Patterson, *With the Judeans in the Palestine Campaign*, pp. 262–73.
33. Sachar, *A History of Israel*, pp. 80–2.
34. *Encyclopedia Judaica*, pp. 1064–5.

Chapter 14

1. Lindemann, *Esau's Tears*, p. 420.
2. Stein, *The Balfour Declaration*, pp. 652–63.
3. Sykes, *Cross Roads to Israel*, p. 54.
4. E. Friesel, 'Herbert Samuel's Reassessment of Zionism in 1921', *Studies in Zionism*, 5(2), 1984:213–15.
5. Ministry of Defence, Tel Aviv (Hebrew), Jewish Brigade, testimony Elimelech Avner, 1.41-Zelig, p. 1.
6. Freisel, see n.4, pp. 217–19; see also A. Nutting, *The Arabs: A Narrative History from Mohammed to the Present* (London: Hollis and Carter, 1964), pp. 323–4.
7. Van Paassen, *The Forgotten Ally*, p. 124.
8. Ministry of Defence, Tel Aviv, File 63/6, Minutes of Meeting 21 October 1921, Defence Forum. Present were High Commissioner Samuel, Mr W. H. Deeds, Brigadier-Colonel Byron, Colonels Evans, Margolin and Bramley, and Mr Smallgood.
9. Ibid., Jewish Legion, testimony 17.28 (Hebrew), Shimon Hacohen, p. 5.
10. Ibid., testimony 175.7 (Hebrew), Avraham Rochel, p. 1.
11. Ibid.

12. Ibid., testimony 22.26 (Hebrew), Joseph Charit, p. 1.
13. Archives, *Yad-Ben-Zvi*, Jerusalem, Appendix 54, Efrat Ben-Cohen interviewed by Shimon Rubinstein over her mother Nechama Pochatchevski in his book 'And Nevertheless Moshe Malal and Yoseph Amuzig were the First Executed by Order of the King in the 20th Century', Jerusalem, 2000.

Chapter 15

1. Gilbert, *Exile and Return*, pp. 132–3; see also Sykes, *Cross Roads to Israel*, p. 59.
2. E. Friesel, 'Herbert Samuel's Reassessment of Zionism in 1921', *Studies in Zionism*, 5(2), 1984:219.
3. Disturbances in May 1921 – Report of the Commission of Enquiry, presented to the British Parliament, October 1921. The commission comprised Thomas Haycroft (Chief Justice of Palestine) as chairman, H. C. Luke and J. N. Stubbs.
4. Sachar, *A History of Israel*, p. 370.
5. Friesel, n.2, p. 220.
6. Shepherd, *Ploughing Sand*, p. 58.
7. Disturbances in May 1921, see n.3
8. Archives, Israel Ministry of Defence, Tel Aviv, Margolin testimony, 2303, Ha'aretz (Hebrew), 7 June 1921, file number 20–22.
9. Ibid., 2305, 8 June 1921, file number 23.
10. Ibid., S. D. Jaffe testimony (Hebrew), Jewish Legion, 198.33, p. 8.
11. Ibid., Zvi Nadav testimony (Hebrew), Jewish Legion, 35–5.
12. Ibid.
13. Ibid.
14. Ibid., *Ha'aretz* (Hebrew), 8 June 1921.
15. Ibid., S. D. Jaffe testimony, 198–33.
16. Ibid.
17. A. Troy, 'The Life of Colonel Eliazar Margolin', A. G. Korsunski Memorial Lecture, G. Korsunski Carmel School, 19 September 1982, cites the quote from the book on the Jewish Legion (Hebrew) by Y. Biber published in 1978.
18. Ministry of Defence, Tel Aviv, *Ha'aretz* (Hebrew), 7 June 1921.
19. Ibid., 8 June 1921.
20. England Family Archive, Perth, Western Australia.
21. *Ha'aretz* (Hebrew), 2 January 1940.
22. Freisel, n.2, pp. 223–36.

Chapter 16

1. *Australian Encyclopedia*, vol. 3 (Terry Hills, NSW: Australian Geographic, 1996), pp. 1182–3.
2. *Age*, 6 May 1921.
3. *Argus*, 6 May 1921.
4. *Age*, 6 May 1921.
5. *Australian Encyclopedia*, n.1, p. 1183.
6. *Argus*, 6 May 1921.
7. Serle, *John Monash*, p. 414.
8. Ibid., p. 487.
9. *Argus*, 7 May 1921.
10. Ibid., signed 'Late 16th BTN, AIF'.
11. *Age*, 9 May 1921.
12. Ibid., under the headline 'News of the Day'.

13. Rubinstein, *Chosen*, p. 167, citing as an example the editorial in the *Argus*, 14 February 1920.

Chapter 17

1. Smilansky, *Mishpachat-Ha'adama*, p. 175.
2. Ibid.
3. Adler, *The British Jewry Book of Honour*, p. ix.
4. Rubinstein, *Chosen*, pp. 153–67.
5. Adler, *The British Jewry Book of Honour*, p. x.
6. Ibid., Jabotinsky's title piece, 'The Jewish Units in the War', p. 60.
7. A. Troy, 'The Life of Colonel Eliazar Margolin', A. G. Kosunski Memorial Lecture, G. Korsunski Carmel School, Perth, 19 September 1982.
8. Correspondence with Mrs Ruth England.
9. Ibid.
10. Troy, n.7.
11. England Family Archive, letter from the Lord Mayor of Perth to Hilda Margolin, 3 June 1944.
12. Smilansky, *Mishpachat-Ha'adama*, p. 175.
13. Gilbert, *Exile and Return*, p. 151.
14. Smilansky, *Mishpachat-Ha'adama*, p. 175.
15. *Encyclopedia Judaica*, vol. 13, p. 495.
16. Smilansky, *Mishpachat-Ha'adama*, pp. 175–6.
17. Mossenson, *Hebrew, Israelite, Jew*, p. 134.
18. Troy, n.7.
19. Ibid.
20. A letter from Nate Zusman to the author, 30 March 1999.
21. Letter to author from Dr D. Mossenson, 28 January 1999.
22. Ibid.
23. Mossenson, *Hebrew, Israelite, Jew*, p. 155.
24. Lippmann, 'Australian Jewry', p. 7. The numbers of Western Australians identifying themselves in the Commonwealth Census in 1933 were 2,105, and in 1947 grew to 2,294.
25. Gouttman, 'First principles', pp. 285–6.
26. For a full account of pre-Second World War Jewish refugee immigration, read P. R. Bartrop, *Australia and the Holocaust, 1933–45* (Melbourne: Australian Scholarly Publishing, 1994).
27. Mossenson, *Hebrew, Israelite, Jew*, pp. 142–5.
28. Zusman, 'The W.A. Council of Jewish Affairs', p. 156.
29. England Family Archive, Perth, W.A.
30. Ibid.
31. Ibid.
32. Rubinstein, *Chosen*, pp. 168–70.
33. Mossenson, *Hebrew, Israelite, Jew*, pp. 141–2.
34. *Listening Post*, 15 June 1944.
35. *Boddulin*, 15 August 1944, in the England Family Archive, Perth, W.A.
36. England Family Archive.
37. Ibid.
38. Ibid.
39. Ibid.
40. Ibid.
41. Ibid.
42. Ibid.
43. Ibid. The letter was sent 22 January 1945.

Chapter 18

1. J. C. Hurewitz, *The Struggle for Palestine* (New York: Shocken Books, 1976), pp. 284–314.
2. *Ha'aretz* (Hebrew), 20 January 1950.
3. England Family Archive, Perth, W.A.
4. *Palestine Post*, 22 March 1950.
5. England Family Archive, Perth, W.A.: a note from President Ben-Zvi thanking Hilda for her congratulatory message, 18 March 1953.
6. *Jerusalem Post*, 23 August 1956.

Chapter 19

1. Smilansky, *Mishpachat-Ha'adama*, p. 168.
2. Jewish Agency Collection, *Tehilla and other Israeli Tales* (London and New York: Ram's Horn Books, Abelard-Schuman Ltd, 1956), p. 73.
3. Smilansky, *Palestine Caravan*, pp. 145–81.

Chapter 20

1. Winter and Sivan, *War and Remembrance in the Twentieth Century*, pp. 1–40.
2. Dr J. H. Hertz, *Pentateuch and Haftorahs* (London: Soncino Press, Edition 2, 1976), p. 753; *Book of Deuteronomy*, Chapter 1, 'Devarim', Verse 17.

Bibliography

Books

Aaronsohn, R., *Rothschild and Early Jewish Colonization* (New York: Rowan and Littlefield, Latham-Boulder Press; Jerusalem: Hebrew University Magnes Press, 2000).

Adler, Rev. M. (ed.), *The British Jewry Book of Honour* (London: Caxton, 1922).

Aldington, R., *Lawrence of Arabia* (London: Penguin, 1971).

Andrews, F. M., *A History of Australian Foreign Policy: From Dependence to Independence* (Melbourne: Longman Cheshire, 1979).

Bartrop, P., *Australia and the Holocaust, 1933–45* (Melbourne: Australian Scholarly Publishing, 1994).

Bar-Zohar, M., *Ben Gurion: The Armed Prophet* (New Jersey: Prentice-Hall, 1967).

Bean, C. E. W., *Gallipoli Correspondent: The Frontline Diary of C. E. W. Bean* (Sydney: Allen and Unwin, 1983).

— *The Story of ANZAC*, vol. 2 (4 May 1915 to the Evacuation of the Gallipoli Peninsula) (St Lucia: University of Queensland Press, 1981).

— *The Australian Imperial Force in France*, vol. 3, 1916 (St Lucia: University of Queensland Press, 1982).

Beaumont, J. (ed.), *Australia's War 1914–18* (Sydney: Allen and Unwin, 1995).

Bentwitch, N. and H., *Mandate Memoirs, 1918–48* (London: The Hogarth Press, 1965).

Ben-Zvi, I., *The Exiled and the Redeemed* (Philadelphia: Jewish Publication Society of America, 1963).

Ben-Zvi, R. Y., *Coming Home* (Tel-Aviv: Massada P.E.C. Ress Ltd, 1963).

Biale, D., *Power and Powerlessness in Jewish History* (New York: Shocken Books, 1987).

Boas, H., *The Australian YMCA: With the Jewish Soldiers of the Australian Imperial Forces* (London: Garden Press, 1919).

Brugger, S., *Australians and Egypt 1914–1919* (Melbourne: Melbourne University Press, 1980).

Caplan, N., *Palestine Jewry and the Arab Question 1917–1925* (London: Frank Cass, 1978).

Casper, B., *With the Jewish Brigade* (London: Edward Goldston, 1947).

Cathcart, M., *Defending the National Tuckshop: Australia's Secret Army Intrigue of 1931* (Melbourne: McPhee Gribble/Penguin Books, 1988).

Clarke, F. G., *Australia: A Concise Political and Social History* (Sydney: Harcourt Brace Jovanovich, 1992).

Clendinnen, I., *Reading the Holocaust* (Melbourne: Text, 1998).

Cutlack, F. M. (ed.), *War Letters of General Monash* (Sydney: Angus and Robertson, 1934).

Davis, M., *Zionism in Transition* (New York: Herzl Press, 1980).

Duff, D., *Palestine Picture* (London: Hodder and Stoughton, 1936).

Elam, Y., *The Jewish Legion in World War I* (Hebrew) (Tel Aviv: Israel Defence Force, Ministry of Defence, 1973)

Elbogen, I., *A Century of Jewish Life* (Philadelphia: Jewish Publication Society of America, 1946).

Eliav, S., *Britain and the Holy Land 1838–1914* (Jerusalem: Yad-Izhak Ben-Zvi/Magness Press, 1997).

Freulich, R., *Soldiers in Judea: Stories and Vignettes of the Jewish Legion* (New York: Herzl Press, 1964).

Gammage, B., *The Broken Years: Australian Soldiers in the Great War* (Ringwood: Penguin, 1975).

Gilbert, M., *Exile and Return: The Emergence of Jewish Statehood* (London: Weidenfeld and Nicolson, 1979).

Gilner, E., *War and Hope: A History of the Jewish Legion* (New York: Herzl Press, 1969).

Grey, J., *A Military History of Australia* (Cambridge: Cambridge University Press, 1999).

Gullett, H. S., *The A.I.F. in Sinai and Palestine: The Official History of Australia in the War of 1914–18*, vol. 7 (St Lucia: University of Queensland Press, 1984).

Heikal, M., *Secret Channels: The Inside Story of the Arab–Israel Peace Negotiations* (London: HarperCollins, 1996).

Honig, E., *Zionism in Australia: 1920–39, the Formative Years* (Sydney: Mandelbaum Trust, Sydney University, 1997).

Idriess, I. L., *The Desert Column* (Sydney: Angus and Robertson, 1932).

Jabotinsky, V., *The Story of the Jewish Legion* (New York: Bernard Ackerman, 1945).

Kaplan, R. D., *The Arabists: The Romance of an American Elite* (New York: Free Press, 1993).

Kark, R., *American Consuls in the Holy Land, 1832–1914* (Detroit, MI: Magnes Press and Wayne State University Press, 1994).

Karsh, E. and I., *Empires of the Sand: The Struggle for Mastery in the Middle East 1789–1923* (Cambridge, MA: Harvard University Press, 2001).

Kaufman, M., *The Magnes–Philby Negotiations, 1929: The Historical Record* (Jerusalem: Magnes Press, 1998).

Kimche, J., *The Unromantics: The Great Powers and the Balfour Declaration* (London: Weidenfeld and Nicolson, 1968).

Kipen, I., *Ahad Ha-Am: The Zionism of the Future* (Sydney: Mandelbaum Trust, University of Sydney, Studies in Judaism No. 9, 1997).

Kristianson, G. L., *RSL: The Politics of Patriotism* (Canberra: A.N.U. Press, 1966).

Langley, G. F. and E. M., *Sand, Sweat and Camels* (Victoria: Hinkler Books, 1995).

Levin, R., *While the Messiah Tarried: The Jewish Socialist Movements 1871–1917* (New York: Shocken Books, 1977).

Lewis, B., *Our War: Australia during World War I* (Melbourne: Melbourne University Press, 1980).

Lindemann, A. S., *Esau's Tears: Modern Anti-Semitism and the Rise of the Jews* (Cambridge: Cambridge University Press, 1997).

Longmore, C., *Carry On: The Traditions of the A.I.F.* (Perth: Imperial Printing Co., 1940).

Longmore, L. C., *The Old 16th: Record of the 16th Battalion A.I.F. During the Great War, 1914–18*, History Committee of the 16th Battalion Association, Perth, 1929.

Malthus, C., *ANZAC: A Retrospect* (New Zealand: Whitcombe and Tombs, 1964).

Morton, F., *The Rothschilds: A Family Portrait* (London: Penguin, 1964).

Mossenson, D., *Hebrew, Israelite, Jew: The History of the Jews of Western Australia* (Perth: University of Western Australia Press, 1990).

Patterson, J. H., *With the Zionists in Gallipoli* (London: Hutchinson, 1916).

— *With the Judeans in the Palestine Campaign* (London: Hutchinson, 1922).

Price, C. A., *Jewish Settlers in Australia*, Social Science Monograph No. 23 (Canberra: Australian National University, 1964).

Pynt, G. (ed.), *Australian Jewry's Book of Honour, World War II* (Netley, SA: NAJEX, 1973).

Reinherz, J. and A. Shapiro (eds), *Essential Papers on Zionism* (New York: University Press, 1996).

Rouse, T., *Australian Liberalism and National Character* (Victoria: Kibble Books, 1978).

Rubinstein, H., *The Jews in Australia: a Thematic History, Vol. 1, 1788–1945* (Melbourne: William Heinemann, 1991).

— *Chosen: The Jews in Australia* (Sydney: Allen and Unwin, 1987).

Rubinstein, W. D., *The Jews in Australia: A Thematic History, Vol. 2, 1945 to the Present* (Melbourne: William Heinemann, 1991).

— *A History of the Jews in the English-Speaking World: Great Britain* (London: Macmillan, 1996).

Rutland, S. D., *Edge of the Diaspora: Two Centuries of Jewish Settlement in Australia* (Sydney: Collins Australia, 1988).

Sachar, H. M., *A History of Israel: From the Rise of Zionism to Our Time* (Oxford: Blackwell, 1977).

— (ed.), *The Rise of Israel: A Documentary Record from the 19th Century to 1948*, vol. 11 (New York and London: Garland, 1987).

Salaman, R. N., *Palestine Reclaimed: Letters from a Jewish Officer in Palestine* (New York: George Routledge and Sons, 1920).

Sarner, H., *The Jews of Gallipoli* (Cathedral City, CA: Brunswick Press, 2000).

Serle, G., *John Monash: A Biography* (Melbourne: Melbourne University Press, 1980).

Shepherd, N., *Ploughing Sand – British Rule in Palestine* (London: John Murray, 1999).

Smilansky, M., 'Hawaja Nazar', in *Palestine Caravan: A Collection of Stories* (BLDSC, 1936), pp. 145–81.

— *Mishpachat-Ha'adama* (Hebrew), Part 3, 1950–51.

Sofer, S., *Zionism and the Foundation of Israeli Diplomacy* (Cambridge: Cambridge University Press, 1998).

Stein, L., *The Balfour Declaration* (London: Vallentine-Mitchell, 1961).

Sykes, C., *Cross Roads to Israel: Palestine from Balfour to Bevin* (London: Mentor, 1967).

Talmon, J. L., *Israel Among the Nations* (London: Weidenfeld and Nicolson, 1979).

Taylor, A. R., *Prelude to Israel: An Analysis of Zionist Diplomacy 1897–1947* (London: Darton, Longman and Todd, 1961).

Tehilla and Other Israeli Tales (short stories) (London: Ram's Horn Books, Abelard-Schuman, 1956).

Teveth, S., *Ben-Gurion: The Burning Ground, 1886–1948* (London: Robert Hale, 1987).

Tuchman, B., *Bible and Sword: How the British came to Palestine*, (Basingstoke: Macmillan, 1982).

Urofsky, M. I., *American Zionism from Herzl to the Holocaust* (New York: Anchor/Doubleday, 1975).

Van Paassen, P., *The Forgotten Ally* (New York: Dial Press, 1943).

Wasserstein, B., *The British in Palestine* (Oxford: Blackwell, 1991).

Weizmann, C., *Trial and Error* (London: East and West Library, 1950).

Winter, D., *25 April 1915: The Inevitable Tragedy* (St Lucia: Queensland University Press, 1994).

Winter, J. and E. Sivan (eds), *War and Remembrance in the Twentieth Century* (Cambridge: Cambridge University Press, 1999).

Wistrich R. and D. Ohana (eds), *The Shaping of Israeli Identity: Myth, Memory and Trauma* (London: Frank Cass, 1995).

Woodruff W. and L. McGregor, *The Suez Canal and the Australian Economy* (Melbourne: Melbourne University Press, 1957).

Zerubavel, Y., *Recovered Roots: Collective Memory and the Making of an Israeli National Tradition* (Chicago: University of Chicago Press, 1995).

Articles

Aaronsohn, R., 'Vines and Wineries in the Jewish Colonies – Introducing Modern Viticulture in Nineteenth Century Palestine', *Studies in Zionism*, 14(1), 1993:31–51.

Bartrop, P. R., 'The "Jewish Race" Clause in Australian Immigration Forms', *Australian Jewish Historical Society Journal*, XI(1), 1990:69–78.

Benbassa, E., 'Zionism in the Ottoman Empire at the End of the 19th Century and the Beginning of the 20th Century', *Studies in Zionism*, 11(2), 1990:127–40.

Cesarani, D., 'An Embattled Minority: The Jews in Britain during the First World War', *Immigrants and Minorities* 8 (1, 2), March 1989:65.

Crown, A., 'Demography, Politics, and the Love of Zion: the Australian Jewish Community and the Yishuv, 1850–1948', in W. D. Rubinstein (ed.), *Jews in the Sixth Continent* (Sydney: Allen and Unwin, 1987), pp. 216–61.

— 'The Initiatives and Influences in the Development of Australian Zionism, 1850–1948', *Australian Jewish Historical Society Journal*, VII(6), 1979:315–36.

Crown, A. and N. Radford (eds), 'Early Australian Zionism: An Annotated Index of Records in the Central Zionist Archives' (Jerusalem: Monograph 9, Archives of Australian Judaica, University of Sydney, 1993).

Encel, S., 'Anti-Semitism and Prejudice in Australia', *Without Prejudice*, 1, 1990 (Melbourne: Australian Institute of Jewish Affairs), pp. 37–48.

Falk, Rev. L. A., 'With the Jewish Battalions in Palestine – Memoirs of a Jewish Chaplain', series of articles in the *Maccabean*, Sydney, 15 February–15 November 1929.

Freedman, Rev. D. I, 'Diary – 1918', Archive of Australian Judaica, University of Sydney.

Gouttman, R., 'First Principles: H. V. Evatt and the Jewish Homeland', in W. D. Rubinstein (ed.), *Jews in the Sixth Continent* (Sydney: Allen and Unwin, 1987), pp. 262–302.

— 'The Two Faces of Fuhrman', *Menorah*, later *Australian Journal of Jewish Studies (AJJS)*, 4(1, 2), 1990:66–77.

— 'The Australian Left and The Jews', *Without Prejudice*, Australian Institute of Jewish Affairs, 2 February 1991.

— 'The Australian Left and Anti-Semitism', *Without Prejudice*, 8, 1991 (Melbourne: Australian Institute of Jewish Affairs).

— 'Jerusalem from the Antipodes: A Political View, 1947–1967', *Australian Journal of Jewish Studies*, 6(2), 1992:69–103.

— 'Brothers and Sisters: A Response of Adelaide Jewry to Anti-Jewish Atrocities in the First Half of the 20th Century', *Australian Jewish Historical Society Journal*, XII(2), 1994:358–72.

— 'Between Two Stools: The Rise and Fall of a Small Jewry's Newsletter', *Australian Jewish Historical Society Journal*, XIV(4), 1999.

— 'The Balfour Declaration: Philosemitism?', *Journal of Judaism and Civilization*, 3, 2001:12–27.

Honig, E., 'Sir John Monash and His Zionism', *Menorah, Australian Journal of Jewish Studies*, 4 (1, 2), 1990:78–92.

— 'Some Notes on the "Palestinian" Immigrants in Melbourne, 1900–1930', *Australian Jewish Historical Society Journal*, XII(1), 1993:63–8.

Lippmann, W. M., 'Australian Jewry: Can It Survive?', *The Bridge*, January 1973, p. 7.

Mossenson, D., 'Century of Endeavour', *Australian Jewish Historical Society Journal*, XI(5), 1992:723–37.

— 'History of Jews in Western Australia – a Personal Insight', *Australian Jewish Historical Society Journal*, XI(4), 1992:669–74.

Naor, M., 'Edmond de Rothschild and Zionism', *Studies in Zionism*, 7(2), 1986:185–98.

Silvertown, C., 'The Righteous Colonel and the Jewish Legion', *Jewish Quarterly*, 3(2), 1985:37–40.

Stein, J. B., 'Josiah Wedgwood and the Seventh Dominion Scheme', *Studies in Zionism*, 11(2), 1990:141–53.

Stern, S., 'Memoirs of Early Israel: A Diary of Events from the Turn of the Century', *Australian Jewish Historical Society Journal*, XIV(4), 1999:141–53.

Zusman, N., 'The W.A. Council of Jewish Affairs: A Milestone in the History of W.A. Jewry', *Australian Jewish Historical Society Journal*, X(3), 1988:151–8.

Press

Age
Argus
Bulletin (Sydney), 28 June 1944
Hebrew Standard
Jerusalem Post
Jewish Herald (then *Australian Jewish Herald*)
Mail (Fremantle), 19 November 1931
Palestine Post
Reveille (Sydney), August 1944

Reference

Australian Dictionary of Biography (eds B. Naine and G. Serle) (Melbourne: Melbourne University Press, 1981).

Australian National Archives, Canberra, A.C.T., Personnel Dossier, 1st AIF Ex-Service Members.

Encyclopedia Judaica (Jerusalem: Keter, 1972).

England Family private papers, Perth, Western Australia.

Freedman, Rabbi I., 'Diary 1918', Archives of Australian Judaica, Fisher Library, University of Sydney.

Patai, R. (ed.), *The Complete Diaries of Theodor Herzl* (New York: Theodor Herzl Foundation, Thomas Yoseloff Publishers, 1960).

The Jubilee of the Jewish Legion, 1917–1967, American Friends of Avichail Cultural Centre, Avichail, Israel.

Troy, A., 'G. Korunski Memorial Lecture', Perth, Western Australia, 1982.

Wigoder, E. (ed.), *New Encyclopedia of Zionism and Israel*, vol. 2 (New York: Herzl Press, 1994).

Index

Aaron Aaronsohn family, 102
Aaronsohn, Ran, 19–20
Abrahall, Major, 34
Abu Tellel, 92
Achdut Avoda (Labour Party), 122
Addel Rahman Blair, 46
Adelaide Hebrew Congregation, 88
Adler, Reverend Michael, 37, 69
Advisory Council on Zionism, 116
Aegean Sea, 44, 46–7
Age, 133, 136–7
Aleppo, 86
Alexander III, Tsar, 15
Alexandria, 41, 44, 45, 46, 80, 84
Alien Registration (Consolidation)
    Order, 71
Allenby, General, 80, 82, 84, 86,
    87, 88, 89, 90, 93, 96, 99,
    100–1, 102, 104, 105, 107
Alperin, Chaim, 152
American Jews, 79–80, 81
Amman, 86, 90, 92
Anglicans, 35
Anglo-Jewry *see* British Jews/Anglo-
    Jewry; Australian Jews: Anglo
    Jews among
Anglo-Orthodoxy, 9, 10, 36, 70,
    145, 146
Anglo-Palestine Bank, 62
Anti-Semitism, 6–8, 37, 38, 40, 58,
    59–60, 61, 71, 77, 80, 87,
    102, 113, 141, 147–8
Anzac Cove, 46–7
Anzac Mounted Division, 90, 92,
    93, 94, 100

Anzacs, xi, 45, 48, 99–100, 101, 159
Arabs, x, 8, 20, 21, 22, 23, 72, 73,
    82, 87, 96, 99–100, 102, 103,
    106, 109, 110, 111, 112, 113,
    116, 117, 118, 119, 137, 143,
    155, 156
May Day riots, 121–31
Arber, Menachem, 150
Argus, 133, 134–6, 138
Armistice (1918), 96, 99, 106
'Aryeh, Aryeh', 85, 153
Asquith, Herbert, 72
Auja bridgehead, 92
Australia
    lack of recognition for EM in, ix,
        3–12, 53, 54, 58, 159
    anti-Semitism in, 6–8, 37, 38, 40,
        59–60, 141, 147–8
    botanical link with Jews in
        Palestine, 3, 20
    EM decides to go to, 25
    EM travels to, 26
    EM lives in, 27–33
    attitudes during Great War,
        35–40
    and Gallipoli legend, 44
    Jewish press in, 53–4, 55–7, 111,
        130–1 *see also* names of
        newspapers
    Zionism in, 54–7
    EM returns to, 130
    EM attacked in Senate, 132–9
    later part of EM's life in, 140–6
    EM's death in, 146
    EM's funeral in, 146–9

see also Australian Imperial
    Force/Australian forces;
    Australian Jews
*Australian Biographical Dictionary,
    The*, 28
Australian Convalescent Home,
    Cobham, 50
Australian Imperial Forces
    (AIF)/Australian troops, ix, xi,
    4, 33, 34–5, 36, 37–8, 41, 42,
    44–8, 50, 51, 52, 54, 60, 77,
    78, 86–7, 90, 93, 96, 99, 133,
    135, 159
    see also Anzac Mounted
    Division; Australian Light
    Horse
Australian Jewish Herald (formerly
    Jewish Herald), 138 *see also*
    Jewish Herald
Australian Jews, 4–6, 8–9, 10, 11,
    29–32, 35–7, 38, 39–40, 44,
    53, 54, 55, 56–7, 58, 59–60,
    65, 78, 88, 131, 138, 140,
    141–2, 145–6, 149, 159
    Anglo-Jews among, 7, 8–9, 10,
    29, 30, 31, 36, 55, 58, 65,
    88–9, 145, 146
Australian Labor Movement, 31
Australian Light Horse, 54, 86, 90
Australian Senate, 7, 132–4, 138,
    139
Australian Zionist Federation, 4
Austria-Hungary, 44
Austrian Jews, 146
Avihayil, 151, 152, 154, 160
    Beit Hagdudim museum, 151, 154

Baker, Major E. K., 45
Balfour, Arthur James, 55, 69
Balfour Declaration, x, 55, 56, 57,
    69, 73, 74, 88, 95, 102, 103,
    104, 105, 106, 111, 115, 116,
    121, 131, 134, 141, 145
Balkans, 44
Bar Kokhba, 4, 49, 161
Bean, C. E. W., 46, 50
Beaumont, Joan, 35
Bedouin, 21, 22, 23, 90, 94, 99,
    100, 101, 113, 156

Be'er Sheva, 86, 87, 89
Be'er-Yaakov, 119
Beit Hagdudim museum, Avihayil,
    151, 154
Belgium, 50, 71, 72
Belgorod (Bielgorod), 13, 14, 15, 19
Belgorod-Dnestrovski region, 13, 19
Belkin, Israel, 17
Ben-Cohn, Efrat, 120
Ben-Gurion, David, x, 62, 63, 79,
    151, 153, 154, 160
Ben-Zvi, Yitzhak, x, 62, 63, 79,
    152, 154
Benbassa, Esther, 19
Bentwich (Judicial Secretary), 124
Bentwitch, Lizette, 135
Berlin, 43
Bernard, Hyman, 56
Bessarabia, 13
Beyers, Jo, 43
Bialik, Chaim Nachman, 145
Biber, Yehoash, 28
Bielgorod *see* Belgorod
Bilu, 16
Birdwood, Field Marshal Sir
    William, 137, 150
Biron, Colonel, 125
Bishkilim, 119
Black Sea, 43
Blackboy Hill, 34
Blainey, Geoffrey, 10
B'nei Moshe (Children of Moses), 17
Boas, Lieutenant Harold, 36
Boer War, 25, 43, 64, 140
Boers, 43
Boddulin, 148
Bols, Major-General Louis Jean, 95,
    101
Bolshevik Revolution, 71
Boston, 80
Botanic Gardens, Melbourne, 3
Botha, General, 43
Boulder, 142
Bradshaw, Lieutenant, 126
Brandeis, Louis, 104–5, 149
Brenner, Y. H., 125
Brit Hachayal Be-Eretz Israel
    (Soldiers' Organization in
    Israel), 150

Britain *see* Great Britain
British, the, 99, 100, 101, 102–3,
    104, 107, 109, 111, 113, 119,
    141
    see also British Army/British
    forces; Great Britain; Occupied
    Enemy Territory
    Administration (OETA)
British Army/British forces, 37, 51,
    52, 58, 60, 62, 63, 71, 76, 86,
    88, 89, 90, 99, 138
    Jewish battalions in *see* Jewish
    Legion/Jewish battalions
British East Africa, 63, 64
British Empire, 40, 59, 77
    Jews of, 38–9, 60, 141
    see also names of countries
British High Command, 99
British Jewry Book of Honour, The,
    5, 36, 60, 140–1, 142
British Jews/Ango-Jewry, 53, 55,
    58–9, 70–1, 73, 74, 76, 77,
    141
British Navy, 44
British Royal Fusiliers, Jewish
    Battalions of *see* Jewish
    Legion/Jewish battalions
Broadmeadows, 34, 138
Bruce, Lord, 146
Bund, 15, 161

Cairo, 41, 44, 64, 95, 96, 101, 103,
    104, 107, 110
Cambridge University Zionist
    Society, 79
Canada, 79
Cecil, Lord, 88
Ceramic, 35, 41
Cesarini, David, 37
Chanukah, 88
Chauvel, General Henry, 86
Chaytor, Major General E. W. C.,
    92, 93
Churchill, Winston, 105, 113, 115,
    121, 141
Clendinnen, Inga, 6, 7
Cobham: Australian Convalescent
    Home, 50
Cohen, Rabbi Frances, 44

Cohen, Joseph L., 79
Collie, 27, 29, 32, 33, 142
Collie Mail, 29
Colonial Office, 115
Commonwealth Cemetery, Mount
    Scopus, Jerusalem, 3
Commonwealth Census (1901 and
    1902), 30
*Commonwealth of Australia
    Gazette*, 48
Constantinople, 19, 23, 43, 44
Coolgardie, 25, 28, 30
Costello, Colonel-Commandant,
    123, 125
Council of Jewish Affairs, 145, 146,
    149
Council to Combat Anti-Semitism
    in Western Australia, 145
Cousin, Captain T., 154
Crimean War, 43
Cronin, Mr, 3
Crown, Alan, 31, 54
Curzon, Lord, 102, 115
Cyprus, 108

Daiches, Dr Samuel, 75
Damascus, 42, 86, 89
Damieh, 90
Danlow, Rev. Jacob, 37
Dardanelles, 19, 43, 45
De Wet, Christian, 43
Deakin, Alfred, 32
Deedes, Colonel, 123, 124, 125,
    126
Defence Act (1903), 33
Deiran, 87
Derby, Lord, 74
Dizengoff, Meir, 124, 129–30
Djemal Pasha, 79
Dori, Ya'akov, 127
Doron, 17
Drake-Brockman, Senator (formerly
    Lieutenant-Colonel, then
    Brigadier General), 50, 133–4,
    136, 137
Duff, Douglas, 103

Eastern Europe, 103 *see also*
    Eastern European Jews

Eastern European Jews, 7, 9, 10, 15, 16, 29, 32, 58, 103, 104, 148
Egypt, 25, 26, 35, 41, 42, 43, 45, 46, 49, 50, 62, 72, 76, 79, 80, 81, 83, 95, 96, 102, 110, 130
Ein Hai, 128
Eisenberg, Aharon, 17
Elam, Yigal, 79
Elliott, Senator 'Pompey' Harold Edward, 132–3, 134, 136–7, 138, 139
England, Charlotte, 154
England, Ernest Roy, 142
England, Hilda Myrtle see Margolin (née England), Hilda Myrtle
England, Vera, 142, 154
English Zionist Federation, 69
Eretz Israel, 10, 11, 12, 14, 16 17, 21, 25, 29, 31, 42, 51, 53, 54, 62, 80, 81, 107, 108, 120, 121, 129, 131, 132, 140, 143, 149, 150, 151, 153, 156, 157, 158, 161
Es Salt, 90, 92, 94, 95, 134
European Orthodoxy, 9
Evatt, Dr Herbert Vere, 3
Executive Council of Australian Jewry, 5
Executive of the Zionist Federation, 149

Faisal, 94
Falk, Reverend Leib A., 70, 71, 80–1
First Aliyah, 16, 19–26
First Judeans, x, 110–11, 112–13, 114, 118, 119, 127, 128, 130, 152, 153
First World War see Great War
France, 50, 71, 72, 77, 80, 102, 106, 133, 142
Freedman, Reverend David Isaac, 10, 31, 32, 37, 49–50, 54, 58, 60, 145
Freedman, Isaiah, 102
Fremantle, 26, 27, 28, 30, 31
Freulich, Roman, 108
Fuhrman, O. W. C., 3, 4, 152

Gaba Tepa, 45
Gabbari, 42, 43, 62, 76
Gaililee, 20, 82, 86, 112
Gallipoli campaign, x, 4, 8, 38, 41, 42, 43, 44–9, 60, 62, 86, 132, 133, 138, 142, 152
Gammage, Bill, 90, 94
Gaza, 73, 80, 89
German Jews, 54, 146
Germany, 33, 40, 41, 42, 54, 70, 73
Ghorananiye, 90
Gilbert, Martin, 101
Ginsberg, Asher Hirsch, 17
Glasgow, 71
Glukin, W., 143
Godley, Major-General Sir A. J., 46
Great Britain, x, 15, 29, 33, 35, 36, 43–4, 50, 53, 56, 59, 69, 70–1, 72, 73, 74, 102, 106, 111, 115, 116, 121, 122, 134, 141
    see also British, the; British Army/British forces; Occupied Enemy Territory Administration (OETA)
Great Depression, 143, 148
Great Synagogue, Sydney, 44, 70
Great War (First World War), ix, x, 3–4, 5, 8, 23, 29, 33, 36, 41–52, 62, 86–96, 99, 141
Grey, Jeffrey, 33, 34, 47, 48
Griffith, William, 28
Guardian, 78
Gulf War, 8
Gullett, H. S., 86–7, 89, 93, 100–1

Ha'Am, Ahad, 70
Ha'aretz, 130
Ha'asarot, 23
HaCohen, Shimon, 82, 119
Hadera, 20
Haganah, 23, 114, 118, 119, 120, 143, 161
Hai, Rabbi Yehuda, 15
Haida Paseha, 44
Haifa, 109, 151–2, 154
Haluka, 15, 42, 161
Hamel, Battle of, 50
Hamilton, Sir Ian, 45, 49

Hananes, Rabbi Meir Baal, 109
Hankin, Yehoshua, 17
HaShomer, 82, 84, 113–14, 118, 119, 120, 161
Hassan, 22–3
HaTikvah, 110, 150, 161
Haycroft Commission, 121, 122–3, 128, 129, 130, 134
testimony before, 124–6
Hebrew Standard, 5, 54, 55–6, 65, 69, 74–5
Hebrew University of Jerusalem, 84, Plate 8
Hebron, 15, 108
Heliopolis, 41
Helmieth, 80, 81, 83
Hertz, Rabbi Joseph, 60–1, 74, 140
Herut, 151
Herzl, Theodor, 23–4, 145
Hill 60 (Gallipoli campaign), 46
Hoad, Brigadier, 147
Holocaust, 7, 8, 11
Horovitz, Ben-Zion, 153
Hovevei Zion (Lovers of Zion), 16–17, 20, 22
Husseini, Haj al, Grand Mufti of Jerusalem, 122

Imperial Conference (1911), 33
Indian Ocean, 44
Inter-University Council of New York, 79
Isaacs, Sir Isaac, 7, 31
Israel, x, 3, 151–4, 160
Israel Defence Force, 23

Jabotinsky, Vladimir, 42, 43, 49, 51, 60, 62, 63, 69, 70, 71, 73, 74, 76–7, 83, 89, 91, 108, 109, 113, 119, 141, 145, 149
Jacka, Captain, 133, 134
Jaffa, 62, 81, 82, 86, 89, 109, 121, 122, 123, 124, 125, 126, 127, 128, 129, 130, 156
Jaffe, Captain, 112, 123, 124, 125
Jericho, 90, 91
Jerusalem, 3, 15, 43, 45, 78, 84, 86, 87–8, 89, 90, 91, 95, 108, 109, 112, 113, 114, 119, 123,

125, 126, 127
Commonwealth Cemetery, 3
Hebrew University, 84
Menorah Club, 153–4
Jeune, Mr, 123, 124
Jewish Chronicle, 53, 54, 127, 153
Jewish Herald, x–xi, 4, 37–8, 38–9, 40, 54, 56, 57, 59, 78, 88, 111, 130, 138
Jewish Legion/Jewish battalions, x, 43, 49, 51, 53, 54, 55, 58–9, 60, 62–5, 69–85, 86, 89–90, 91–6, 99, 101, 103–4, 106, 107, 108–9, 110, 119, 120, 141, 143, 145, 151, 152, 153, 155, 160
insignia of, Plate 3
38th Battalion British Royal Fusiliers, 63, 70, 76, 77–8, 78–9, 80–1, 89, 90–1, 92, 93, 95, 108, 110, 123
39th Battalion British Royal Fusiliers, x, 52, 61, 63, 79–80, 81, 84, 85, 89, 91–3, 94, 108, 109, 110, 129
40th Battalion British Royal Fusiliers, 82–4, 89, 96, 108, 109, 110, 111, 119, 143
Jewish National Fund (JNF), 149
Jewish Observer, 138
Jewish Standard, The, 44, 77
Jewish State, 151, 152, 153, 154
Jewish Territorial Operation, 32
Jona, Dr Leon, 135
Jordan River, 23, 90, 93, 96, 117, 157
Jordan Valley, 90, 93
Judaism, 9, 14, 29, 31, 109, 145, 147, 157, 159

Kaiajik Aghala, 46
Kalgoorlie, 28, 30
Kalisher, Rabbi Zwi Hirsch, 15
Kantara, 83, 84, 85, 91
Karratta cemetery, Perth, 147
Kefar Giladi, 112
K'far Saba, 128
Khamara, 112
Kimberley, 32

Kinneret, 23
Kishenev pogrom, 32
Kitchener, Field Marshal Lord, 32,
    41, 47, 72
Kol Nidre, 92, 162

Lag B'Omer, 109–10, 162
Langley, George and Edmée,
    99–100
Lask, I. M., 155
Latrun, 91
Lawlers, 28
League of Nations, 115
Leeds, 59, 71
Legacy/Perth Legacy Club, xi, 143,
    159
Lemnos, 44, 45, 46
    Hospital, 142, 143
Levy, Captain, 112
Lloyd George, David, 72, 73,
    106
London, 50, 53, 56, 59, 71, 79,
    140
London Battalion, 20th, 76
London Daily News, 78
London Gazette, 74
Longmore, Captain C., 47–8
Ludd, 94, 95, 113, 123, 130
Lyons, Joseph, 146

Maccabees, 88, 149
McDonald White Paper, 146
McMahon correspondence, 106
Mafruza, 42, 62
Malta, 45
Manchester, 59, 71
Margolin, Lieutenant-Colonel
    Eliazar Lazar
    illustrations of, Plates, 1, 4, 5, 6,
        8, 9
    sources of information for
        biography, xi
    family and early years, 13–14
    and Judaism, 9–10, 14, 145, 147,
        157, 159
    family moves to Palestine, 14,
        15, 16–17
    lives in Palestine, x, 19–25
    goes to Australia, 26

life in Australia, 27–33
in AIF, ix, x, 33, 34–5, 40,
    41–51
encouraged to join Jewish
    battalion by Jabotinsky, 43,
    51, 63, 69, 76–7
transfer to Jewish battalion in
    British Army, 51–2
appointed as lieutenant-colonel of
    39th battalion, 52
service with Jewish Legion in
    39th battalion, x, 61, 79, 80,
    81, 83, 84, 85, 91–6, 108,
    109, 110
relationship with Patterson, 64
and First Judeans, x, 111,
    112–13, 118, 119–20, 121–9
praised in Australian Jewish
    press, 111
and proposed Arab–Jewish
    defence force, 117, 118
and May Day riots, 121–31
departs for Australia, 129–30
attacked in Australian Senate, 7,
    132–9
life after return to Australia, ix,
    140–6
marriage, 142, 146
funeral in Perth, x, 146–9
memorial gathering in Tel Aviv,
    150, Plate 10
sword and medals, 151, 153–4,
    Plate 12
remains taken to Israel and
    honoured, x, 151–3
remains buried in Rehovot
    cemetery, 153, Plates 11 and
    15
and 'Hawaja Nazar', 14, 155–8,
    160
reputation, ix–x, 159–60
exemplifies 'mateship', xi
lack of recognition in Australia,
    3–12, 53, 54, 58, 159
Margolin, Esther (EM's sister), 34
Margolin (née England), Hilda
    Myrtle (EM's wife), 142, 148,
    151, 153, 154, Plates 9, 13,
    14

Margolin, Joseph and Liata Frieda (EM's parents), 13, 14, 15, 16–17, 18
    death of, 24
Maxwell, General, 62–3, 64
May Day riots (1921), 121–31, 143
May Laws (1882), 16
Mediterranean Expeditionary Force, 47
Meinertzhagen, Colonel Richard, 102–3
Melbourne, 8, 10–11, 41, 54, 56
    Botanic Gardens, 3
Mellahah, 92
Menorah Club, Jerusalem, 153–4
Menuha V'Nahalah, 17
Meron, 109
Metulla, 112
Middle East, 102, 111
    campaign, x, 51, 72–3, 78, 80–96, 99, 101, 106, 138
Mifleget Po'alim Sozialistit (Socialist Workers' Party; MOPSI), 122
Mikve Israel agricultural college, 20, 23
Military Service (Convention with Allied States) Act, 71
Mintz, Mattityahu, 62
Moab, 92
Monash, Lieutenant-General Sir John, 3–4, 5, 7, 34, 44–5, 46, 47, 60, 134–5, 136–7, 141, 149
Money, General, 103, 105
Moscow, 17
Montague, Edwin, 70
Montefiore, Moses, 31
Montefiore, Sir Sebag, 74
Mossenson, David, 30, 40
Mount Scopus, 3, 84
Mouquet Farm, 50
Mudros, 45

Naor, Mordechai, 74
National Australia Bank, 142
Nationalization Act (1903), 28
Nazareth, 43
Nazism, 146, 148
Nedlands, 142, 143

Negev desert, 23, 86
Neill, Major, 123, 127
Neveh Shalom, 122, 125
New Encyclopedia of Zionism and Israel, The, 28
New South Wales, 25, 31, 70
New York, 79, 80
New Zealand troops, 45, 99, 100
    see also Anzac Mounted Division; Anzacs
Nova Scotia, 80

Occupied Enemy Territory Administration (OETA), 80, 96, 104, 105, 107, 108, 110, 111, 114
Odessa, 17, 19
Ohel-Shem Hall, Tel Aviv, 152
Orthodoxy, 9
    Anglo-Orthodoxy, 9, 10, 36, 70, 145, 146
    European Orthodoxy, 9
Ottoman Empire, see Turkey/Turks/Ottomans

Pale of Settlement, 13, 15, 162
Palestine
    Jewish migrants from, 9, 29, 30, 42
    EM's family moves to, 14, 15, 16–17
    EM lives in, x, 19–25
    EM revisits while in training, 81–2
    Jewish battalions for service in see Jewish Legion/Jewish battalions
    during First World War, 42, 54, 62, 72, 73, 80–1, 84, 85, 86–96
    EM serves in, 4, 8, 84, 85, 91–6, 108, 109, 110, 111, 112–13, 118, 119–20, 121–9
    situation after Armistice, 99–131
    EM's departure from, 129–30, 140
    EM's popularity in, 143
    letter concerning possiblility of EM returning to, 143–4
    memorial gathering for EM in, 150

establishment of Jewish State in,
    151
return of EM's remains to, 151–3
see also Balfour Declaration;
    Eretz Israel; Yishuv
Palestine Jewish Colonization
    Society (PICA), 144
Palestine Post, 154
Panton, A. H., 147
Paris, 50
    Treaty of (1856), 13
Passchendael, 50
Passover, 109, 110, 112, 119, 162
Patkin, Benzion, 149
Patt, Ya'acov, 151–2
Patterson, Lieutenant-Colonel John,
    49, 51, 63–5, 70, 74, 76, 77,
    92, 93, 94–5, 101, 107
Peace Conference (1919), 104, 106,
    116
Perth, ix, x, 4, 9, 28, 30, 31, 140,
    141, 142, 145, 146–7, 154,
    159
    District Registrar's Office, 142
    Karratta cemetery, 147
Perth Hebrew Congregation, 10, 31,
    37, 49, 58, 145, 146
Perth Legacy Club/Legacy, ix, 143,
    159
Petah Tikva, 16, 20, 128
Phillips, Lieutenant P., 154
Pinsker, Leon, 16
Plymouth, 79
Po'alei Zion Party (Zionist Workers'
    Party), 84
Pochatcheveski, Nechama, 120
Poland, 103–4
Polish Jews, 81
Pope, Lieutenant-Colonel, 46, 50,
    136
Port Said, 26, 27, 30, 130, 140
Protestants, 35

Queensland, 32
Quinn's Post, 46

Rafa, 73, 86, 101
Ramleh, 4, 111
Red Cross Society, xi

Rehovot, x, 4, 17–18, 20, 21, 22,
    23, 24, 34, 80, 81, 91, 96,
    128, 144, 152–3, 154, 155,
    156, 157, 160, Plates 11, 15
    and 16
    Weizmann Institute, 153, Plate 13
Resnik, Chazan David, 153
Returned Soldiers' and Airmen's
    Imperial League of Australia,
    150
Returned Soldiers' League (RSL), xi,
    143, 147, 149, 159
Rishon Le-Zion, 16, 17, 20, 22, 25,
    91, 101, 120, 124, 144
Rochel, Avraham, 119
Rokach,Y., 152
Roman Catholics, 35, 38
Romania, 13
Rosh Pina, 16
Rothschild, Edmund de, Baron, 16,
    17, 20, 21, 22, 24, 25, 74, 82,
    144
Rothschild, James de, Baron, 74,
    82, 143–4
Rothschild, Lionel Walter de, Baron,
    55, 69, 71
Royal Australian Military College,
    Duntroon, 32, 34
Royal Fusiliers, Jewish battalions of
    see Jewish Legion/Jewish
    battalions
Rubinstein, Hilary, 36, 137–8
Russia, 7, 9, 13–15, 17, 19, 20, 34,
    40, 43, 61, 71, 72, 126
Russian Jews, 7, 13, 14, 15, 17, 19,
    25, 30, 58, 59, 71, 75, 77, 78,
    81, 126
Rutland, Suzanne, 36
Ruttenberg, Pinchas, 62, 63

Safed, 15, 108
St Kilda Hebrew Congregation, 37
St Petersburg, 76
Salaman, Dr Redcliffe N., 80, 83,
    84, 91, 92, 94–5, 95–6, 107,
    108, 111, 120, 153
Samuel, Herbert, 114, 115–17, 121,
    122, 126, 127, 128, 130, 131,
    132, 141

Samuels, Colonel Fred, 82, 153
San Remo Conference (1920), 115, 116
Sanders, Liman von, 43
Sapri Camp, 46
Sarafend, 80, 85, 91, 95, 96, 100, 101, 112, 120, 123, 124, 125, 128, 130, 152
Sari Blair, 46
Satariah tribe, 23
Sea of Marmora, 44
Seleucids, 88
Shalita, Rabbi Y. M. Toledano, 150
Shavuot, 110
Shepherd, Naomi, 122
Shoalwater, 154
Shomer, 23
Sinai desert, 80, 86, 91
Sinai Peninsula, 43
Slutzkin, Mrs L., 3
Smilansky, Moshe, 13, 14, 16, 21, 22, 24, 28, 29, 34, 81–2, 83, 140, 144, 152, 153
    'Hawaja Nazar', 14, 155–8, 160
Smolley, Major, 108
Smuts, General, 43
Solomon, Vlaiban Louis, 31
South Africa, 25, 43, 64
South America, 79
Southampton, 79
Souvla Bay, 47
Spielvogel, Nathan Frederick: 'Zion Wakes', 57
Stein, Leonard, 106
Suez Canal, 41, 42, 43, 44, 72, 85
Swaything, Lord, 74
Sydney, 5, 8, 10–11, 27, 28–9, 54
    Great Synagogue, 44, 70
    York Street Synagogue, 15
Sykes, Christopher, 107–8, 115
Sykes-Picot Accord, 72, 106
Syria, 44, 96, 99, 102

Tarsus, 42
Tel Aviv, 62, 81, 109, 122, 123, 124, 125, 126, 127, 128, 129, 130, 150, 154
    Ohel-Shem Hall, 152

Tel-es-Sultan, 92
Tel Hai, 112
Tel-Kabir, 83
Thwaites, Major General Sir William, 103
Tiberias, 15, 108, 157
Times, The, 78, 81
Transjordan, 92, 117
Treaty of Paris (1856), 13
Troy, Abe, 28, 29, 96, 143, 145
Trumpeldor, Yosef, 49, 62, 63, 112, 149
Turkey/Turks/Ottomans, 19, 23, 24, 41, 42, 43, 44, 45, 47, 51, 55, 60, 62, 72, 73, 78, 81, 82, 85, 87, 89, 90, 91, 94, 96, 99, 106
Turkish Army, 62, 87
Turkish Jews, 83, 94

Ukraine, 14, 103
Umn es Shert, 92, 93
United Australia Party, 146
United Buses, 142, 146
United Nations, 151
United States of America, 15, 30, 73, 79–80, 110

Van Paassen, Pierre, 102, 116–17
Victoria, 25, 31

Wady Auja, 90
Wady Hanein, 87
Wailing Wall violence (1928), 103
War Cabinet, 41, 70, 73, 116
War Office, 74, 75, 95, 107
War Pension Act, 59
Warsaw, 17
Watson, Major-General H. D., 110
Watt, E. S., 147, 148
Wedgwood, Josiah, 103
Weimar, SS, 26, 27
Weizmann, Dr Chaim, 70, 71–2, 73, 82, 153, 154
Weizmann Institute, Rehovot, 153, Plate 13
West Indians, 93
Western Australian Council of Jewish Affairs, 145, 146, 149

Western Australian Infantry Regiment, 33, 34
Western Australian Zionist Association, 10, 145, 149
Western Front, x, xi, 4, 8, 37, 38, 40, 43, 50, 59, 60, 78, 89, 132, 133, 152
'White Australia Policy', 7
Wilhelm II, Kaiser, 23
Wilson, President Woodrow, 73, 79
Winter, Denise, 41
Wolfensohn, H., 60

Yadin, Yigael, 153
Yemen, 81
Yishuv, x, 3, 9, 11, 14, 15–18, 19–25, 29, 30, 42, 49, 51, 54, 62, 64–5, 77, 81, 82, 84, 86, 96, 101, 102, 105, 106, 108, 110, 111, 113–14, 116, 118, 119, 120, 122, 126, 143, 145, 155, 156, 157, 159, 160, 162

Yom Kippur (Day of Atonement), 92, 162
York Street Synagogue, Sydney, 15
Yoseph, Charit, 120

Zangwill, Israel, 32
Zarnugah, 23
Zeitrun, 41
Zerubavel, Yael, 4
Zichron Ya'akov, 16
Ziffrin, 119, 152
Zion Mule Corps, 48–9, 51, 62–3, 64, 65, 69, 70, 74, 76, 77, 151, 153, 160
Zionism, 9, 10, 14–15, 16, 17, 19, 23, 30–1, 32, 54–5, 56, 64, 65, 70, 72, 73, 79, 88–9, 102, 104, 106, 107, 110, 111, 115, 116, 117, 121, 129, 135, 155, 156, 157, 160, 162
Zionist Commission, 107–8
Zionist Council, 70
Zionist Organization of America, 93